We would like to dedicate this book to our families for their sacrifices made in allowing us to work on this endeavor. Ed Coulson thanks Linda and Brendan. Yongsheng Wang thanks Ruihua, Freddie, Changzhong, and Suzhen. Clifford Lipscomb wishes to thank his wife Amelia, his mother Angie, and his children Thoreau, Hadassah, Garrison, Araminta, and Barnette.

Editors
N. Edward Coulson
Merage School of Business
University of California, Irvine
Irvine, CA, USA

Clifford A. Lipscomb
Greenfield Advisors
Cartersville, GA, USA

Yongsheng Wang
Washington and Jefferson College
Washington, PA, USA

ISBN 978-1-137-57445-9 ISBN 978-1-137-57446-6 (eBook)
DOI 10.1057/978-1-137-57446-6

Library of Congress Control Number: 2017939876

Printed on acid-free paper

This Palgrave Macmillan imprint is published by Springer Nature
The registered company is Nature America Inc.
The registered company address is: 1 New York Plaza, New York, NY 10004, U.S.A.

N. Edward Coulson · Yongsheng Wang
Clifford A. Lipscomb
Editors

Energy Efficiency and the Future of Real Estate

palgrave
macmillan

Energy Efficiency and the Future of Real Estate

The original version of the book was revised: For detailed information please see Erratum. The erratum to the book is available at https://doi.org/10.1057/978-1-137-57446-6_11

Acknowledgements

We would like to acknowledge the input of Allison Neuburger and Sarah Lawrence. In addition, the editors would like to acknowledge the work of Greenfield Advisors employees Joe Schulman and Patty Eagar for editorial assistance.

Contents

Editors and Contributors

About the Editors

Dr. N. Edward Coulson is Professor of Economics and Public Policy in the Merage School of Business at the University of California, Irvine. He is also co-editor of *Journal of Regional Science* and served as President of the American Real Estate and Urban Economics Association in 2016.

Dr. Yongsheng Wang Associate Professor of Economics, Director of Financial Economics, Washington and Jefferson College. He is also a visiting scholar at the graduate school of public and international affairs at the University of Pittsburgh. His research focuses on energy economics and real estate economics. His past research was funded by LUCE Foundation, Freeman Foundation, Heinz Endowments, and NIST (Department of Commerce).

Dr. Clifford A. Lipscomb Vice Chair and Co-Managing Director, Greenfield Advisors. He is the Chairman of the American Real Estate Society's Practitioner Research Award committee, an Associate Editor of the Journal of Real Estate Literature, and a Visiting Scholar at the Federal Reserve Bank of Atlanta. His research interests include automated valuation models, survey research, and econometrics.

Contributors

Andrea Chegut Massachusetts Institute of Technology, Cambridge, USA

Ryan Colker National Institute of Building Sciences, Washington, DC, USA

N. Edward Coulson University of California, Irvine, CA, USA

Avis Devine Schulich School of Business, York University, Toronto, ON, Canada

David M. Harrison University of Central Florida, Orlando, USA

Rogier Holtermans University of Southern California, Los Angeles, USA

Clifford A. Lipscomb Greenfield Advisors, Cartersville, GA, USA

Junichiro Onishi Xymax Real Estate Institute Corporation, Chiyoda-ku, Tokyo, Japan

Chihiro Shimizu Nihon University, Chiyoda-ku, Tokyo, Japan

Jordan Stanley Department of Economics, Syracuse University, Syracuse, NY, USA

Isabel Tausendschoen University of Graz, Graz, Austria

Yongsheng Wang Department of Economics and Business, Washington and Jefferson College, Washington, PA, USA

Jiro Yoshida The Pennsylvania State University, University Park, State College, PA, USA

Yu Zhou Department of Earth Science and Geography, Vassar College, Poughkeepsie, USA

List of Figures

List of Tables

CHAPTER 1

Introduction

N. Edward Coulson, Clifford A. Lipscomb, Yongsheng Wang and Avis Devine

1.1 Introduction

The built world is a lynchpin to modern society. It impacts personal health, as Americans spent on average 87% of their lives indoors in homes, schools, and workplaces (Klepeis et al. 2001). It impacts economic health,

---

The original version of this chapter was revised: For detailed information please see Erratum. The erratum to this chapter is available at https://doi.org/10.1057/978-1-137-57446-6_11

N.E. Coulson (✉)
University of California, Irvine, CA, USA
e-mail: n.edward.coulson@gmail.com

C.A. Lipscomb
Greenfield Advisors, Cartersville, GA, USA
e-mail: cliff@greenfieldadvisors.com

Y. Wang
Washington and Jefferson College, Washington, PA, USA
e-mail: wysqd01@gmail.com

A. Devine
Schulich School of Business, York University, Toronto, ON, Canada
e-mail: adevine@schulich.yorku.ca

N.E. Coulson et al. (eds.), *Energy Efficiency and the Future of Real Estate*, DOI 10.1057/978-1-137-57446-6_1

as the vast majority of GDP is created in office and industrial buildings, and through sales in shopping and entertainment venues. It impacts environmental health, as buildings consume upwards of 80% of electricity and 40% of total energy consumption (the highest of all use sectors).[1] Since more than 80% of total U.S. energy consumption comes from fossil fuels, buildings are also a leading contributor of greenhouse gas emissions (approximately 40% of total CO_2 emissions).[2] Concurrent management of these three factors (social, economical, and environmental) results in sustainability, and is known as the triple bottom line (Fig. 1.1).

1.2 Energy Efficiency in Commercial Real Estate

Energy efficiency is one way to pursue the goal of sustainability in real estate. Green buildings (energy efficient and otherwise sustainably-constructed and operated buildings) consume less energy than their traditionally-constructed counterparts. An analysis of 7100 Leadership in Energy and Environmental Design (LEED) for New Construction buildings found that 88% of the buildings had improved their energy efficiency by at least 14% (Katz 2012). In an evaluation of existing buildings by the U.S. General Services

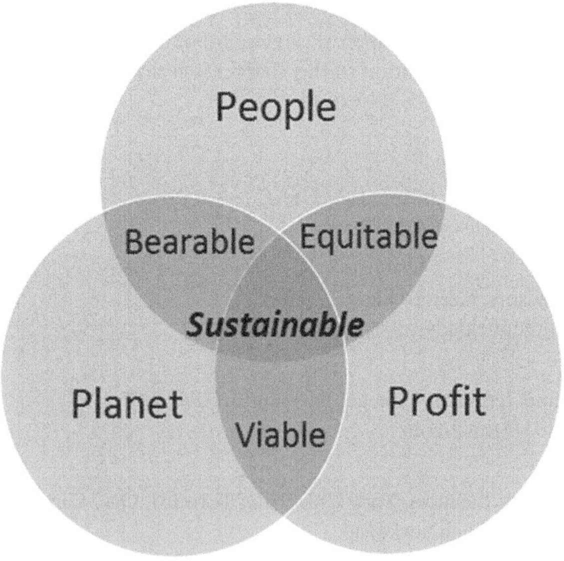

Fig. 1.1 The Venn diagram of the triple bottom line

Administration (the manager of all U.S. federal office space), it was estimated that a building certified under the LEED program at the Gold level consumes 25% less energy and 11% less water. In addition, it produces 34% fewer greenhouse gases, as well as experiences lower maintenance costs and higher occupant satisfaction (U.S. General Services Administration 2011).

In retail uses, energy efficiency impacts both the decision of how to operate space and where to locate space. Not only are energy sources used in the operation of the retail spaces (heating and cooling the space, lighting, etc.), but the same is true of the company's distribution centers. In addition, retailers must incorporate the cost of transporting their goods from their point of creation, through distribution centers, to the retail outlets. These costs are not insignificant, and minimizing them is key to the success of major retailers, such as Wal-Mart (Holmes 2011).

In addition to energy consumption, water and material use management is also important for commercial real estate aiming to be efficient. Fourteen percent of all potable water is used by buildings (Roodman and Lenssen 1995). Efficiency efforts can reduce water use by 15%, but also decrease energy use by 10% and save 11% in operating costs (McGraw-Hill Construction 2011). Buildings use 40% of the raw materials consumed annually worldwide (Roodman and Lenssen 1995). The U.S. Environmental Protection Agency (EPA) estimated that in 2003, 61% (or around 100 million tons) of the U.S. total building-related construction and demolition waste (170 million total tons) was associated with non-residential uses (Clancy 2014). Many green building programs work to ensure that such a waste is decreased and redirected from landfills or recycled.

1.3 Overview of Chapters in This Volume

The chapters of this volume cover the wide range of issues that concern both analysts and practitioners in the green real estate sector. In Chap. 2, Avis Devine surveys the financial performance of energy efficient commercial real estate, through two major themes. First, that certification matters. Energy efficiency is not always easily observable, and interested demand-side parties cannot necessarily be certain of claims made on the supply side. This information asymmetry is resolved by trusted agents who can evaluate and certify such claims—that is, signal energy efficiency to the market. Second, it is critical that, borrowing a phrase from the chapter, a firm can "green in the black." If energy efficiency and certification do not provide a positive net present value, developers will be slow to adopt green technologies to the detriment of the society and the environment. However, Devine emphasizes that there are many ways for energy efficiency to improve the bottom line. Efficient buildings can increase corporate prestige, help with personnel recruitment, and increase demand for space from environmentally-conscious occupants. Devine's survey of the literature indicates that there is broad evidence that the most important observable metrics of revenue generation (rents, values, and occupancy) are improved in the presence of certification.

Chapter 3, by Yongsheng Wang and Jordan Stanley, discusses the ways in which information about green buildings can be codified, and how such codification happens around the world. There are differences across countries in the application of green building standards, but the authors express the hope that these standards will converge to a common set of benchmarks that will aid market participants. As noted above, conveying accurate information to all stakeholders about the eco-friendliness of structures can only aid the market in supplying green buildings.

Given the observed adoption and putative profitability of green building design, the next step is further penetration of energy-efficient design and technology into an increasing stock of both new and existing structures. In Chap. 4, Andrea Chegut, Rogier Holtermans, and Isabel Tausendshoen discuss this topic in light of received theory and knowledge of innovation in the broader economy. Innovation is of course nothing new in real estate—the interplay of costs, design, art, and technology has driven the industry forward since the pyramids. However, innovation can be slow to make a material difference, primarily because so much of the stock of real estate is set in place. In addition, the costs of innovation can often be prohibitive and its payoff uncertain. As the authors point out, this can forestall both adoption and diffusion of this innovation; despite evidence from Chap. 2 on the increased demand for certification, risk for the bottom line is always a factor in the adoption of innovative technologies. The authors outline methods of financing green innovation and adoption that can overcome some of these hurdles.

David Harrison's Chap. 5 notes the political realities attendant on the adoption and use of energy-efficient technologies. Using the heterogeneity of the U.S. as a laboratory, he notes several interesting, but perhaps unsurprising correlations: that states with less expensive sources of "traditional" energy use less environmentally-friendly technologies and that these states are also generally less politically liberal. Indeed, Harrison discusses evidence that the demand for green building discussed in Chap. 2 is much more likely to arise in "blue" states than in more generally conservative "red" states.

Chapter 6, also by Stanley and Wang, presents an econometric analysis of the rental premium attending to LEED certification in a cross section of U.S. cities. The authors attack head-on a major issue in this research area that the observed LEED premium, discussed in Chap. 2, may be the result of other unobserved building characteristics, common to LEED buildings but unrelated to energy efficiency. While some of the studies mentioned in Chap. 2 did try to deal with this issue, Stanley and Wang move forward on this front with the use of propensity score matching to control for such effects. The LEED premium is much reduced when this methodology is used. This is in part attributed to the increased presence of LEED buildings during the study period. This makes sense, both because of competitive pressure on the supply side, but also on the demand side—the most energy-intensive tenants would be the first to sign leases in LEED buildings (because they have the most to gain in terms of reduced expenses), but as time goes on, less intensive users would only be willing to pay the LEED premium if the premium was much reduced.

Then, Chaps. 7 and 8 present findings on green buildings from two prominent Asian economies. Chapter 7 by Jiro Yoshida, Junichiro Onishi, and Chihiro Shimizu discusses the state of green real estate in Japan. After outlining the progress in green building technology and certification in that country, they present a new econometric evidence (like Chap. 6) on the source of the green building premium. Their study is rather unique in that they estimate models of both energy usage and building rents that include the impact of green labels. They find the happy result that buildings that have green labels indeed use less electricity and water. More provocatively, they also find that once this reduction in utility usage is accounted for, there is no statistically discernable impact of the certification itself. This important finding would seem to contradict the need for certification in the first place—that is, the econometric model indicates that buildings that achieve efficiency even without certification achieve higher rents. Thus, information on building performance needs not be asymmetric after all.

Chapter 8 presents a survey of the state of green building in China by Yu Zhou. The Chinese economy has undergone, and continues to undergo tremendous structural shifts, and the roles of market and government forces everywhere in the economy and in particular in the adoption and diffusion of green building technology are still being worked out. Zhou's primary thesis is that such adoption is largely in the hands of the government. Granted, government intervention in green energy has not been absent in the West, but to Zhou, the role of Chinese officials is paramount. This stands in interesting contrast to recent work by

Matthew Kahn and Siqi Zheng (2016) which stresses the importance of Chinese consumer sentiment and demand in creating the milieu necessary for change—whether that change is market- or government driven.

Chapter 9, by Ryan Colker, takes a more engineering-based view of green building performance. In this wide-ranging contribution, Colker discusses both certification and performance of green structures. He emphasizes the ongoing need not only for performance standard and benchmarks that will increase the transparency and comparability of building performance, but also for broader views of energy efficiency that emphasizes the whole life cycle of building. Energy efficiency can be achieved by better integrating the innovations that occur in the construction and operation phases of green building. Colker also emphasizes the concept of resilience—the ability to maintain efficiency in the face of shocks to the building's operation capabilities. Prominent in this view is the ability to innovatively use and (perhaps more importantly) store energy created from passive sources.

Notes

1. See http://www.eia.gov/totalenergy/data/browser/xls.cfm?tbl=T02.01&freq=m and http://www.eia.gov/totalenergy/data/browser/xls.cfm?tbl=T02.01&freq=m.
2. See U.S. Energy Information Administration. Monthly Energy Review June 2015. Available online at: http://www.eia.gov/beta/MER/index.cfm?tbl=T01.03#/?f=A&start=2013&end=2014&charted=1-2-3-5-12.

References

Clancy, Heather. 2014. In California, At Least, The Case for Energy Efficiency is Building. *Forbes*, December 30.

Fuller, Stephen. 2014. *Economic Impact of Commercial Real Estate: 2014 Edition*. Industry Research Report. Herndon, VA: NAIOP Research Foundation.

Holmes, Thomas. 2011. The Diffusion of Wal-Mart and Economies of Density. *Econometrica* 79 (1): 253–302.

Kahn, Matthew E., and Siqi Zheng. 2016. *Blue Skies Over Beijing: Economic Growth and the Environment in China*. Princeton, NJ: Princeton University Press.

Katz, Ashley. 2012. New Analysis: LEED Buildings are in Top 11th Percentile for Energy Performance in the Nation. *USGBC*. November 13. http://www.usgbc.org/articles/new-analysis-leed-buildings-are-top-11th-percentile-energy-performance-nation. Accessed 14 April 2016.

Klepeis, Neil, et al. 2001. The National Human Activity Pattern Survey (NHAPS): A Resource for Assessing Exposure to Environmental Pollutants. *Journal of Exposure Analysis and Environmental Epidemiology* 11: 231–252.
McGraw-Hill Construction. 2011. *Green Outlook 2011: Green Trends Driving Growth*, Industry Forecast. New York: McGraw-Hill Construction.
Roodman, David Malin, and Nicholas Lenssen. 1995. *Worldwatch Paper #124: A Building Revolution: How Ecology and Health Concerns are Transforming Construction.* Washington, DC: Worldwatch Institute.
U.S. General Services Administration. 2011. *Green Building Performance: A Post Occupancy Evaluation of 22 GSA Buildings,* White Paper, Washington, DC: GSA Public Buildings Services.

Authors' Biography

Dr. N. Edward Coulson is Professor of Economics and Public Policy in the Merage School of Business at the University of California, Irvine. He is also co-editor of *Journal of Regional Science* and served as President of the American Real Estate and Urban Economics Association in 2016.

Dr. Clifford A. Lipscomb Vice Chair and Co-Managing Director, Greenfield Advisors. He is the Chairman of the American Real Estate Society's Practitioner Research Award committee, an Associate Editor of the Journal of Real Estate Literature, and a Visiting Scholar at the Federal Reserve Bank of Atlanta. His research interests include automated valuation models, survey research, and econometrics.

Dr. Yongsheng Wang Associate Professor of Economics, Director of Financial Economics, Washington and Jefferson College. He is also a visiting scholar at the graduate school of public and international affairs at the University of Pittsburgh. His research focuses on energy economics and real estate economics. His past research was funded by LUCE Foundation, Freeman Foundation, Heinz Endowments, and NIST (Department of Commerce).

Dr Avis Devine Associate Professor of Real Estate with the Brookfield Centre for Real Estate and Infrastructure in the Schulich School of Business, York University. Prior to her academic career, she was the Assistant Vice President in charge of commercial real estate underwriting and valuation for Dollar Bank, FSB in Pittsburgh, PA. Her research interests include Sustainable and Energy Efficient Real Estate, Commercial Real Estate, Institutions, and Emerging Markets.

CHAPTER 2

Why Energy-Efficient *Commercial* Real Estate Matters

Avis Devine

Commercial real estate plays an important role in pursuit of the triple bottom line (as described in Section 1.1). Development of commercial real estate contributed $528 billion to the 2014 U.S. GDP, creating and supporting 3.9 million jobs and $168 billion in wages and salaries (Fuller 2014). There are nearly six million commercial and industrial buildings in the U.S.[1] These properties are associated with $400 million in annual energy costs and produce 45% of the total U.S. greenhouse gas emissions. Of all commercial buildings, 30% are operated inefficiently; a 10% improvement in energy efficiency would result in $40 billion in collective savings, as well as prevent greenhouse gas emissions equal to 19% of all registered highway vehicles on U.S. roads.[2]

The original version of this chapter was revised: For detailed information please see Erratum. The erratum to this chapter is available at https://doi.org/ 10.1057/978-1-137-57446-6_11

A. Devine (✉)
Schulich School of Business, York University, Toronto, ON, Canada
e-mail: adevine@schulich.yorku.ca

N.E. Coulson et al. (eds.), *Energy Efficiency and the Future of Real Estate*, DOI 10.1057/978-1-137-57446-6_2

2.1 Certification

Many certification programs exist, providing third-party verification of the greening of real estate. However, these programs can be costly, in terms of both money and time. Given this, many owners, operators, and space users ask: why can't I just "green" my building without certifying it? That is, why can't I incorporate the sustainable and energy-efficient building design features and operational practices without seeking costly third-party certification? By skipping the certification process, the product may be brought to market faster and for a decreased expense. This decreased cost and time frame could allow for an increased return. Or, the funds earmarked for certification could instead by utilized to yet further increase the building's efficiency.

The answer is that third-party certification is how an entity communicates a property's energy efficiency to their target audience. It is a signal, allowing for transparent communication of a concept. All forms of certification serve as signals—diplomas, driver's licenses, etc. These are shorthand, widely accepted methods of identifying that someone or something has completed a task or obtained a goal. A driver's license proves to others that the possessor has the capacity to carefully and successfully operate a vehicle. A rental car agency could require that each customer proves their capacity by taking a driving test with an agency employee. However, this would be extremely costly to the agency and the customer. Instead, the agency relies on the signal provided by the customer's possession of a driver's license as proof that they are capable of operating a vehicle. Possessing an energy-efficiency certification on the commercial real estate in question provides the owner, operator, or space user with that signal, or credible evidence, of the property's energy efficiency. This evidence can then be used to inform a target audience, whether it is the government, a prospective tenant or investor, or a company's customers.

However, not all signals are equal. A firm can attempt to signal a property's energy efficiency to the target audience without third-party certification. One approach is benchmarking a subject property's energy use against market data (if available). Another is for a large firm to create an internal certification system. This self-applied seal of approval is awarded to a subset of the firm's properties based on energy efficiency, often as compared to the firm's total portfolio. This method is subject to sample bias, as all of the properties in the sample are owned by the firm. For example, a firm may identify the top 20% of their properties based on energy efficiency. What is missing is data showing the energy efficiency of a firm's properties compared to the energy efficiency of the remaining properties in the market. What if this firm is definitively lagging the market in the basic energy efficiency? In that scenario, the firm's most energy-efficient properties may be average energy users (not efficient) compared to the other similar properties in the market. Additionally, such internal certification systems are subject to puffery (the act of using positive terms to obtain higher prices) or greenwashing/whitewashing. All of these methods are signals of a property's energy efficiency. However, "self-certifications" provide weak signals to the target audience. They are inexpensive (in terms of both time and money) to obtain, while more costly signals, such as the Leadership in Energy and Environmental Design (LEED) certification program, prove stronger. This is why a graduate degree is viewed as a stronger signal of expertise in a field than a bachelor's degree—the added cost of obtaining the graduate degree (and time involved) strengthens the signal.

2.1.1 Evidence: LEED-Certified Apartments

In a study of the relationship between LEED certification and multifamily apartment rental rates in the USA, Bond and Devine (2015) are able to uniquely identify the difference in rental rate premiums between the strong third-party certification signal and the weaker self-applied signals. The authors use unit-level data on market rate, privately constructed multifamily rental properties to examine relative rental rates in 2012. After controlling for a variety of unit and building characteristics, local economic conditions, and an area's propensity to support "green" initiatives, results indicate higher rental rates associated with energy efficient and sustainable properties. Findings show that LEED-certified units earn between 7 and 9% higher rents than comparable non-certified properties.

Of particular interest is the rental rate premium experienced by buildings which self-identify as "green." As multifamily properties are directly marketed to the public, the authors are able to collect data on each unit regarding if it is positioned as being "green" despite not having a third-party certification (LEED or otherwise). A direct comparison is made between LEED-certified units (strong signal), self-identified "green" units (weak signal), and traditional, non-green units (no signal). The findings indicate that while both the strong and weak signals are associated with higher rental rates than the non-green (signal-less) units, the units with the strong signal experience double the rental rate premium of the units with the weak signal. That is, the average rental rate premium of LEED-certified (strong signal) units is 9.1%, while the premium for the weak signal is 4.7%. These findings, which are all highly statistically and economically significant, support the concept that a costly signal is a stronger signal and that energy efficient and sustainable real estate certification programs can be an effective signal for commercial real estate owners, operators, and space users to consider.

2.2 Certification Programs

If a property owner, operator, or space user wishes to effectively communicate the energy efficiency of the property to a target audience, they should invest in a strong signal, such as third-party certification. Once this decision has been made, the next step is selecting a certification program. There are hundreds of energy efficiency and sustainability certification programs for real estate around the world. While many can be eliminated based on geographic limitations and real estate focus (residential versus commercial, etc.), there are still several options from which to choose. Following is a summary of the two largest and best-known certification programs in the world. Information is also provided on a few other well-known energy-efficiency-specific and asset/class-specific programs. For more information on energy-efficient certification programs, see Chap. 3: Energy Efficiency and Green Building Assessment.

2.3 LEED[3]

The LEED is the most widely used energy efficiency and sustainability certification program in the world, certifying over 1.85 million square feet of space every day. The program was piloted by the US Green Building Council (USGBC) in 1998 as a single standard, applicable to any type of real estate. Now, in its fourth complete version, the program offers five rating systems with specialized guidelines for 14 different asset classes and/or real estate phases (planning, design and construction, and operations). Using a points system, properties are certifiable at four levels: Certified (40–49 points); Silver (50–59 points); Gold (60–79 points); and Platinum (80+ points). Certification relies on documentation (not testing) and, with the exception of LEED:O+M, certification is perpetual. LEED:O+M certification is valid for 5 years at a time.

2.4 BREEAM[4]

In 1990, the Building Research Establishment (BRE) established the environmental assessment method (EAM), making BREEAM the world's longest-established building sustainability assessment, rating, and certification program. BREEAM has great market penetration in Europe, capturing in excess of 80% of the market share of green building certification, making the BREEAM brand the well-known leader for that continent. The method is applicable to any format of the built environment, and the certification process involves independent, licensed assessors evaluating procurement, design, construction, and operations against performance benchmarks. These aspects are evaluated using ten categories, with certification awarded on five levels (Pass, Good, Very Good, Excellent, and Outstanding). Approximately 75% of new construction commercial buildings in the UK would meet the BREEAM Pass requirements, while less than 1% of the same group would clear the outstanding certification hurdle.

There are four primary technical standards under which communities, infrastructure, and buildings may seek certification. However, for any building not fitting into one of those four categories, certification may be pursued under the BREEAM Bespoke method. This program allows for buildings to be assessed according to property-specific and appropriate criteria. Of the four technical standards, three are design or construction related and the fourth, In-Use, assesses operations. In-Use certification has a slightly modified rating structure, including an additional category of Acceptable, and In-Use certification must be revalidated annually.

2.5 Green Star[5]

The Green Building Council of Australia (GBCA) launched GreenStarin 2003. Since then, the program remains the dominant green building certification program for the country and Australia's only national, voluntary rating system for buildings and communities. Green Star offers four certification programs: Design and As Built; Interiors; Communities; and Performance. Ratings scale from one to six stars for performance and four to six stars for the other three programs. Buildings earn credit toward certification in the categories of management, indoor environment quality, energy, transport, water, materials, land use and ecology, emissions, and innovation, while communities earn credit in the categories of governance, design, livability, economic prosperity, environment, and innovation.

2.6 Energy Star[6]

In 1992, the US Environmental Protection Agency (EPA) created Energy Star to provide a third-party certification program for energy efficiency in commercial and industrial buildings (in addition to a separate program geared toward homes). While not all property types are eligible for certification, more than 20 categories of properties are now included in the program. Through an online tool, the program rates the energy efficiency of a property on a scale of 1–100, and properties rating 75 or higher are eligible to apply for Energy Star certification, subject to third-party verification. Recertification must be sought annually. The Energy Star program is incorporated into several other green building certification programs, including LEED and Green Globes, and is an item of consideration in the ranking of green building lists by Travelocity, CoStar, Honest Buildings, AAA Tour Book, and several others.

2.7 Greening in the Black (Energy Efficiency Must Make Financial Sense)

While the social and environmental benefits of energy-efficiency measures are clear, a company will be unable or unwilling to pursue them without it making sense to their firm. There are a variety of forces driving the growth of the green building market, and Fig. 2.1 highlights the seven most commonly cited reasons (McGraw-Hill Construction 2011). Many of these reasons translate to supply and demand features, including direct observation of the increased demand for green buildings, the observation of the increased prominence of green building projects, and the benefits to the health of those using the space. All of these categories reflect the push from the market for more green buildings. Additionally, there are several benefits to the owners and operators of green buildings, including increased cost savings and property values, and decreased vacancy rates. Lastly, the list notes the role of policy, as it incentivizes and requires green building. The former policy provides a financial benefit to the developer and/or owner.

- Strong Market Demand
- High cost savings for business and tax payers
- Public health gains from green buldings
- Steady gains in the percentage of large, non-residential commercial or institutional projects that are green
- Federal, state, and municipal mandates and policies
- Increased property values
- Lower rental vacancy rates for LEED-certified buildings

Fig. 2.1 The list of the seven most commonly cited reasons for green building market growth (McGraw-Hill Construction 2011)

These observations of increasing demand and supply of green buildings are accurate. In 2005, only 2% of non-residential building starts were green buildings—a number that increased to 44% by 2012 and is expected to surpass 50% of the new non-residential structures market in 2016 (McCook 2013). Total green non-residential construction is estimated to exceed total in excess of $120 billion, representing a notable economic opportunity to firms that elect to pursue green building (McGraw-Hill Construction 2011).

In addition to new construction, opportunities exist to enhance the efficiency of existing buildings. The market for green retrofits is estimated to be near $1 trillion between 2015 and 2023 (Clancy 2014). Firms that have completed such retrofits report decreased operating expenses (down 9% in 1 year and down 13% over 5 years) and increased expected asset values (McGraw-Hill Construction 2011).

2.8 Corporate Image Benefits

Direct financial benefits from efficiency are not the only economic benefit of sustainable and energy-efficient commercial real estate. There is also the importance of the firm's association with energy efficiency and sustainable investment. Decisions to invest in green commercial real estate may be done to please a variety of stakeholders, including the tenants, customers, management, and investors.

Through association with third-party-certified green real estate, companies can communicate their commitment to energy efficiency to their stakeholders. Research reveals government organizations and mining and construction companies are more likely to rent green office space (Eichholtz et al. 2016). The government users are unsurprising—governments utilize a variety of techniques to encourage environmentally sensitive real estate use. This can be accomplished through government policies that impact private construction, offering incentives for green building, or requiring that properties meet certain energy-efficiency thresholds in order to pass inspection.

However, governments can also encourage environmentally sensitive real estate through their own investment activities. By mandating government entities may operate only in buildings that are environmentally certified, government can encourage the adoption of energy-efficient buildings. The mining and construction industry result is interesting and dovetails with another finding: the industry with the fourth highest percent of green space utilization is crude petroleum and gas. That is, the firms that profit from fossil fuels and their higher use are heavy users of real estate that specifically uses *fewer* fossil fuels. The fact that mining and petroleum firms heavily utilize energy-efficient space highlights the use of green space as a signal of corporate environmental responsibility to their stakeholders, because it is otherwise in direct contrast to these firms' income sources.

2.8.1 Evidence: Fortune 200 Firms Utilize LEED

A 2015 USGBC survey of one-quarter of the Fortune 200 companies indicates that leading companies value the importance of green building certification, both for its associated financial benefits and for its role in stakeholder relations (Long 2015). Of the firms surveyed, 93% use LEED programs and 82% intend to use the program in the next three year's construction and retrofit projects. Of those that use the LEED program, 70% do so to save money through energy efficiency and 60% believe it positively impacts their return on investment. With respect to corporate image and green buildings, four out of five of these firms believe that using this certification program is an important and effective way of communicating their sustainability efforts to their stakeholders.

2.9 Appeasing Customers

Also of particular interest to firms is communicating their commitment to environmental sustainability with their customers. Much research in the marketing and consumer behavior fields has been dedicated to understanding the environmentally motivated consumer, and how economic, demographic, and personal value measures impact their purchase decisions (Schlegelmilch et al. 1996; Shrum et al. 1995; Mazar and Zhong 2010). There is evidence of a relationship between product demand growth and environmentally products (Chen 2001; Crane 2001). Consumers consider not only prices and quality but also their personal values and beliefs (Caruana 2007; Irwin and Baron 2001), and they express this through consumption of environmentally sensitive products (Anderson and Cunningham 1972; Kinnear et al. 1974).

The literature has substantiated the relationship between environmental certification and consumer decisions, and between environmentally certified commercial real estate and its operation (see Sect. 2.11 for more information). However, this raises the question of a tenant's willingness or ability to pay higher rents in a building simply because it is environmentally certified. While decreased energy costs may be passed along to the tenant (or may be retained by the owner), there is no evidence that the energy savings completely offset the rental rate premiums. Therefore, the tenants truly are paying a rent premium for situation in a green building. How is that premium being justified in the tenant's business plan? Is there evidence that consumers' incorporation of environmental certifications into their purchasing decisions results in a business benefit to the space user of the green building? Fig. 2.2 describes this set of relationships.

Devine and Chang (Working Paper 2016) examine the benefits of sustainable and energy-efficient-certified buildings to the retail businesses that operate within them. By utilizing data on retail bank branch deposits, the authors find that LEED-certified bank branches have a higher probability of above average deposit growth than non-certified branches, and experience above average deposit growth. In an event study analysis, these findings persist both during 1 year prior to certification (based on the announcement of the LEED certification being pursued) and for 1 or 2 years after the event. Energy star-certified branches are also associated with above-average deposit growth, but the magnitude of the results is nominal, and the results are not as statistically strong.

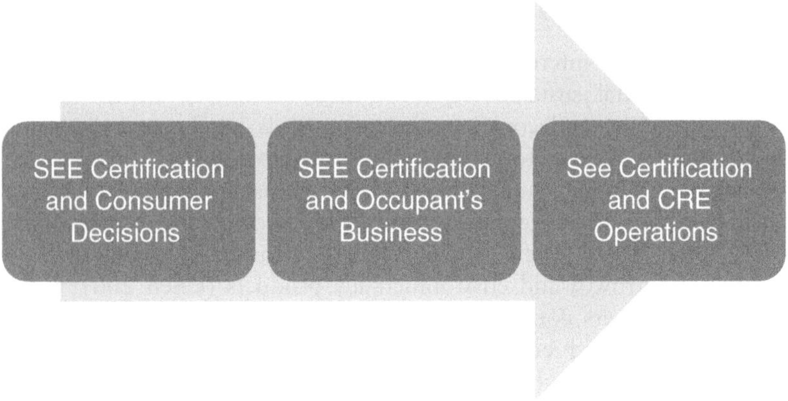

Fig. 2.2 A description of the relationship between consumers, businesses, and real estate owners as it relates to a willingness and ability to support rental rate premiums in environmentally-certified real estate (Chang and Devine 2016)

There has also been work on one specific aspect of energy efficiency and its impact on retail sales: daylighting. By introducing skylights into retail outlets that are traditionally lit through artificial means, the business garners a two-fold benefit: increased retail sales and decreased lighting-related utility costs. A study was completed on 73 retail chain store outlets in California in which 24 stores became daylight illuminated, while the others continued to operate under artificial light. There was a 40% increase in gross sales of the day lit store after the skylight installation, and the energy savings associated with the daylight ranged from $0.24 to $0.66 per square foot (Heschong Mahone Group 1999).

2.10 Talent Productivity, Attraction, and Retention

For an average company, more than 90% of its operating costs are tied to human resources, with only 9 and 1% linked to rent and utility expenses, respectively (Terrapin Bright Green, LLC 2014). Because of this, changes in the built environment that increase worker productivity and happiness can lead to substantial financial implications for a firm. Research has found that LEED-certified buildings experience worker productivity increases associated with: daylight (18%); better lighting (23%); better ventilation (11%); and individual temperature control (3%) (World Green Building Council 2013).

As the millennial generation begins to advance in the workforce, attracting and retaining their skilled talent become more important. Studies find that this generation wants evidence that their employer is environmentally compliant. A survey of office workers aged 18–25 and 26–35 found that 96 and 98%, respectively, want to work in a greener office. Additionally, survey responses revealed desire for resource efficiency in many categories, as highlighted in Fig. 2.3 (Puybaraud 2010). While environmentally sensitive corporate values do not outrank the importance of job-specific details in most cases, situating in a green building and operating their space in an energy-efficient manner may provide a company with the marginal benefit needed to capture the attention of a prospective employee.

Finally, employee turnover can cost a company between 1- and 2-year salaries in total, so finding ways to retain good employees is critical (Fitz-enz 1997). The Colliers International 2012 Office Tenant Survey found that 95% of office tenants were interested in occupying a green building. This was up from 75% of respondents in 2010 (Green Building Council Australia 2013). Employees benefit from the improved efficiency and healthfulness of the green building, and they too benefit from the corporate image—they can say that they work in an environmentally sensitive space.

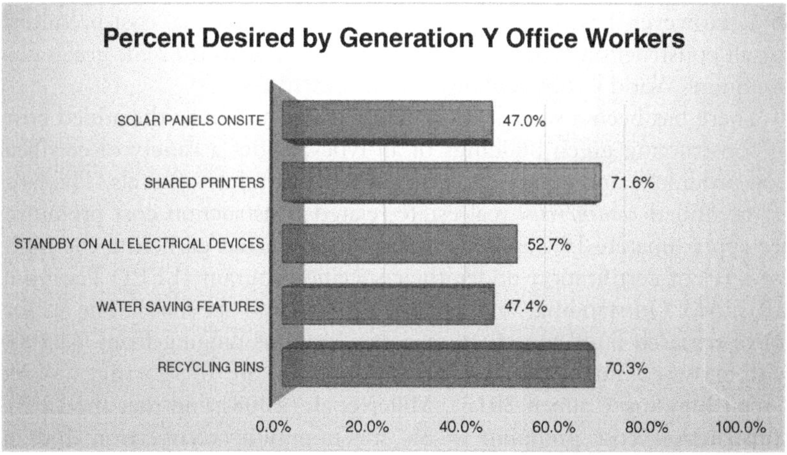

Fig. 2.3 The summary of the percent of Generation Y office workers that specified their desire for the indicated energy-efficiency features in their work environment (Puybaraud 2010)

2.11 Research Findings

While the benefits to society, the space users, and the environment are clear, a real estate owner or developer will be unlikely or unwilling to pursue them without it being financially viable. Much research has been completed addressing this point at various stages of the real estate process. The following section will examine research findings regarding the financial implications to commercial real estate investors across the different stages of the real estate lifecycle, from development and construction, through operation and disposition.

2.12 Construction

The financial concern regarding sustainable or energy-efficient commercial real estate construction is simple: If there is a marginal financial benefit to operating environmentally sensitive space, does that benefit exceed any marginal cost to construct a building to those specifications? The answer to this question is yes, because now, it is possible to construct a sustainable and/or energy-efficient building with little to no additional cost. This answer comes as a surprise to many; based on a compilation of design-stage cost estimates and surveys, the perceived cost premium for green real estate construction (all construction types) is between 0.9 and 29%. However, based on factual cost analyses, the actual cost premiums for all construction types scale from 0.4% savings to a 12.5% green cost premium (World Green Building Council 2013).

There has been a substantial amount of research into the added costs of constructing green buildings of all types, under a variety of certification programs, and obtaining certification at a variety of levels. The largest identified *commercial* real estate-related construction cost premiums are approximately 10% and all earned for properties garnering the highest level of certification under their specific program (LEED Platinum, BREEAM Outstanding, and Green Star five and six stars). The majority of research finds construction cost premiums ranging from 0 to 8%, with most commercial real estate findings in the 0–3% range (World Green Building Council 2013). Miller et al. (2008) find that the LEED construction cost premium is 3% for minimum certification and an additional 2.5% for Silver certification, and Kats (2010) examines 150 green-certified buildings across 11 countries and finds green buildings cost approximately 2% more to construct than their traditionally constructed counterparts.

Two recent works address the question of construction cost differences and BREEAM certification. Chegut et al. (2015, Working Paper) found the cost to construct a BREEAM-certified office building in the UK to be effectively the same as the cost associated with the traditional construction techniques, but did find design fees higher relative to the traditional construction. Other research into the added capital cost to certify an office building under the BREEAM program found no added costs for a Pass or Good rating and less than 1% added cost for Very Good and Excellent ratings (Abdul 2013). This nominal added cost is estimated to be paid back through utility cost savings within 2–5 years. Also of note in this study was the comparison of added costs over the progressing versions of the BREEAM program. For instance, to achieve an Excellent rating under the 2004 BREEAM rating scheme, added costs ranged from 0.1 to 5.7%. This range decreased to 0.8–1.71% by the 2011 iteration of the rating scheme. This provides evidence that as time passes, the construction cost premium decreases.

A similar gradual reduction in the construction cost premium associated with LEED certification over a 10-year period is described in the World Green Building Council's report (2013). This decrease in cost may be due to a few key factors. First, as building codes become more stringent and environmentally sensitive buildings become more popular, the technology required for such energy-efficient improvements becomes commercially available to the masses and decreases in price. Second, one way to prevent unnecessary added costs during building construction is to incorporate the green features from the beginning of the design process. This prevents costly modifications and value engineering mid-process.

2.13 Evidence: LEED-Certified PNC Bank Branch Construction

PNC Bank has been constructing Energy Star and LEED-certified bank branches for over 5 years and has been very open about the associated benefits experienced through construction, operation, and employee satisfaction and productivity. Since launching this construction program and streamlining it, PNC has constructed over 250 green bank branches and is now focused on constructing net zero branches (buildings which create as much energy as they use on an annual basis). The firm estimates their LEED-certified branches cost $100,000 less to construct and are built 1 month faster than comparable traditionally constructed branches. In addition to these construction-related benefits, these branches use one-third less energy and water, divert 80% of their waste from landfills, and experience 50% higher employee satisfaction (USGBC 2010).

2.14 Rental Rate, Occupancy Rate, and Asset Value

This is the area in which the majority of related research has been completed. Numerous studies have examined the relationship between sustainable and energy-efficient building certification and rental rates, occupancy rates, and asset values, with most finding premiums for some certification schemes. The concept behind these premiums relates back to the corporate benefits experienced by tenants of green buildings. Tenants are willing to pay a premium rental rate for space in buildings which provide the green features they seek, and the impact of many tenants desiring such space leads to higher occupancy rates as well. These two facts, assuming that operation costs are constant, will lead to greater net operating income and, therefore, higher asset value (assuming capitalization rates are held constant).

Early findings by Nelson (2007) and Miller et al. (2008) examine CoStar data on office buildings in the US and find higher occupancy and rental rates and evidence of sales' price premiums, respectively. This research was further developed in the coming years through several bodies of work. Eichholtz et al. (2010) use actual rent data (corrected for occupancy levels) and nearest neighbor matching to compare LEED and Energy Star-certified buildings to traditionally constructed buildings. Findings indicate that Energy Star-certified buildings rent for approximately 3% more per square foot. This translates into a 7% higher effective rent and, based on then-prevailing capitalization rates of 6%, an added $5.5–$5.7 million in value (a 19% premium) for the energy-efficient office buildings. The authors updated this research 3 years later, verifying that the premiums still exist, despite the volatility of the real estate market and the added supply of green buildings (Eichholtz et al. 2013). Similar findings are corroborated in Wiley et al. (2010) and Fuerst and McAllister (2011a, b).

A variety of additional dynamics have been added to this type of analysis as well. Fuerst and McAllister (2011a, b) show that dual-certified office buildings experience added rent and asset value premiums, and Holtermans and Kok (2017) indicate that while green rents may be associated with a premium, green rent growth is not. Two European analyses also add unique information to the field. First, the analysis of Dutch office space showed that poor-energy-efficiency buildings (rated D or lower) rent at 6.5% below the market rental rates experienced by more energy-efficient buildings (rated A, B, or C) (Kok and Jennen 2012). Second, Chegut et al.'s (2014) study of BREEAM-certified office buildings in London indicates that, while the certified buildings do experience the previously highlighted benefits, the marginal benefit decreases as the green building supply increases. Finally, Devine and Kok (2015) verify the rental and occupancy rate premium findings, but also find that environmentally labeled buildings pay out less in rent concessions. Average rent concessions for their Canadian subsample were 11% for traditionally constructed buildings and 7% for green-certified buildings, respectively. This indicates a greater rent capture rate for green buildings.

All of this taken together indicates that there is a rental rate, occupancy rate, and asset value premium associated with energy efficient and sustainably certified buildings. Limitations to this analysis include the body of research's overwhelming focus on office buildings and on the US market. Multifamily rental rate premiums have also been found (Bond and Devine 2015) and are described in the Evidence: LEED-Certified Apartments section above. However, data limitations have made it difficult to examine evidence for similar findings in other commercial real estate asset classes. Additionally, many of these studies find that the premiums associated with Energy Star-certified properties are smaller than those associated with LEED-certified properties. Lastly, there is evidence that these premiums may shrink as more of the market becomes green certified. As this happens (i.e., as "green" becomes the market standard), results may shift from market rate premiums for green buildings to discounts for non-green buildings (a "brown" discount).

2.15 Operations

At the root of the green building concept lies the goal to decrease resource usage and greenhouse gas emissions. Because of this, the direct benefit of energy-efficient commercial real estate is a decreased level of energy use. Several studies have approached this key issue, beginning with a report on California LEED-certified commercial buildings (Kats 2003). This study found that the LEED-certified buildings were up to 35% more energy efficient than their traditionally constructed counterparts. The higher the certification level achieved (Certified, Silver, and Gold were examined), the greater the energy efficiency experienced.

In 2009, a set of analyses emerged using the same database, the Commercial Building Energy Consumption Survey. The first study (Newsham et al. 2009) compared 100 LEED-certified buildings to similar traditionally constructed buildings and found that the LEED buildings used between 18 and 39% less energy per square foot. However, they also found that approximately one-third of LEED buildings used more energy than their comparable buildings, likely due to the high-tech nature of the green buildings. The second study (Scofield 2009) questioned the former study's findings, as it did not account for both site and source energy.[7] After incorporating that into the analysis, and measuring area-weighted energy use intensities (which captures the characteristic energy-use differences between large and small buildings), Scofield found no difference in the amount of energy consumed by LEED and traditionally constructed buildings. The author recently completed a similar study of New York City LEED-certified office buildings examining the impact of different levels of LEED certification and found that while LEED Gold buildings used 20% less energy, LEED Silver and Certified buildings actually used more energy (Scofield 2013).

Focusing on retail space, Kahn and Kok (2014) examined all Wal-Mart stores in California and finds that newer stores (with more advanced energy-efficient technology) utilize significantly less electricity than comparable older stores. They also find no difference in energy usage associated with whether a retail space is rented or owned. This provides an interesting offset to Kahn et al.'s (2014) findings that higher quality, newer commercial buildings (studying office, flex, industrial, and retail buildings in California) use more energy. The authors indicate that these more advanced buildings allow for more discrete ambient comfort control (setting the temperature by area rather than for a full floor), but that meeting such demands requires more electricity to operate the associated advanced equipment.

Other studies further develop these findings. Kats (2010) extended his original study to 150 green buildings across 11 countries and found that these buildings experience a one-third reduction in energy use. Additionally, these buildings are associated with a nearly 40% decrease in water consumption. A study of New Zealand of environmentally labeled buildings found energy savings of one-third to one-half as compared to traditionally constructed buildings (Fullbrook et al. 2006). Finally, Devine and Kok's (2015) examination of US and Canadian office buildings found a positive relationship between BOMA BESt certification (a Canadian green certification program evaluating operations) and improved energy efficiency and that LEED core and shell-certified buildings in the USA use notably less power than both non-certified properties and those certified under other LEED programs and the Energy Star program.

2.16 Indirect Operational Benefits

While power usage may be the first aspect of operations to come to mind when considering energy-efficient buildings, it is not the only way environmentally sensitive building operations can impact commercial real estate. Devine and Kok (2015) examined the broader operational benefits of environmentally labeled office buildings in the USA and Canada. Findings show that green buildings have more satisfied tenants and that tenants in green buildings have a higher probability of re-leasing their space. These two results are related (as happy tenants would want to stay in their space) and point to a less-obvious operational benefit of green buildings: stickier tenants mean decreased "re-tenanting" costs. When a tenant vacates their space, the building must cover costs related to "resetting" the space to make it rentable again, marketing the space, and leasing the space. This includes many expenses related to brokerage fees, legal fees, and likely below-market rents at the beginning of the new lease, in the form of rent concessions offered to entice the new tenant. In addition, it means no income associated with that space during its interim vacancy. All of this taken together can be a substantial cost, and one which is decreased in green buildings, because the tenants turnover less frequently and have relatively lower concessions.

2.17 Existing Buildings

New construction represents only 2% of the US building stock, and 86% of building construction expenditures is associated with renovation of existing buildings. In 2008, the American Society of Heating, Refrigerating, and Air-conditioning Engineers (ASHRAE) estimated that 150 billion square feet of existing buildings—half the US building stock—will need to be renovated (Holness 2008). Taken together, it is clear that the place to make the greatest impact in energy-efficiency improvements is in the modification of the existing building stock.

Given the relative newness of environmental certification programs tailored to existing buildings, and the greater difficulty in measuring both the financial commitment to and financial output from making an existing building more energy efficient, there has been limited research on this topic. Holtermans and Kok (2017) evaluate the 30 largest markets in the USA and find that environmentally certified office space has increased from 5.7% in 2005 to nearly 40% in 2014. Regression results indicate that US office buildings certified under the LEED Existing Buildings Operations and Management (EB:OM) program do not experience statistically significant effective rental rate premiums, but do sell at higher prices.

In 2008, the Leonardo Academy completed survey analysis of 23 LEED EB:OM property owners and managers (Leonardo Academy Inc. 2009). Findings indicate implementation and certification cost between $0.02 and $5.01 per square foot, with an average of $1.58 per square foot. The cost was not correlated with the level of certification achieved (instead, it is believed that the level of certification achieved is more heavily impacted by the pre-renovation condition of the building). The survey results also indicated that of the 14 prerequisites for LEED Existing Buildings certification, all but four were consistently rated as low cost or no cost to implement. Finally, the authors compared the operating costs of LEED existing building-certified properties to industry standards and found that the total expenses per square foot were lower. While this provides a limited amount of evidence in support of the certification program, the evidence is compelling and the logic behind needed improvements to the existing built world is intuitive. This is an area that needs to be a priority for building owners and operators in the future.

2.18 REITs and Other Real Estate Holding Companies

If energy efficiency in commercial real estate impacts the profitability of a property, then it may not only impact direct property owners, but also those that own property indirectly through (REITs) real estate investment trusts and other real estate holding companies. There is extensive research into the impact of corporate social responsibility (CSR) policies on firm performance. Margolis et al. (2009, Working Paper) provide a meta-analysis of the research completed on this topic between 1972 and 2007, finding a non-significant relationship between CSR and firm performance in the majority of cases (59%). There is a positive correlation between the two in approximately one-quarter of the analyses and very few findings that support a negative correction (2%). Given the recently changing attitudes of society regarding the environment, this analysis may not tell the full story. A more recent study finds that firms which voluntarily adopt sustainability policies achieve above average stock market returns and stronger accounting metrics (Eccles et al. 2014).

REIT managers have taken notice of the CSR benefits to firm performance and are identifying how to best incorporate CSR into a property-holding firm model. Pivo (2008) surveyed REIT managers and found that while most firms identified their sustainability efforts as exceeding compliance levels, they were primarily concerned with the impact of environmentally sensitive real estate decisions on the firm's financial outcomes. This desire to pursue green real estate for risk and return-related reasons, more than social and moral ones, highlights the importance of energy-efficient commercial real estate providing a financial benefit in order to be widely adopted (see the Greening in the Black section of this chapter). A study by Eichholtz et al. (2014, Working Paper) examines the question of who (based on CEO characteristics) is investing in environmentally labeled commercial real estate. Findings indicate that Democrat-affiliated CEOs are more likely to invest in Energy Star-certified properties, while LEED certification is sought more frequently by Republican-leaning CEOs. The existing literature finds Democrat CEOs more socially minded (Hong and Kostovetsky 2012), while Republican CEOs are more concerned with mitigating risk (Hutton et al. 2014), which provides interesting parallels to the Eichholtz et al. (2014, Working Paper) findings. Additionally, the authors find that more experienced managers are more likely to invest in environmentally labeled real estate.

There are only a few papers that have evaluated the financial impact of sustainability and energy efficiency on REIT performance. The earliest findings were provided by Eichholtz et al. (2012) in a study of US REIT investments. By analyzing REITs based on their portfolio greenness (a measure of the percent of the portfolio that is certified under LEED or Energy Star), the authors determined that environmentally sensitive portfolios experienced superior operating performance and lower systemic risk. Green REITs had higher returns on assets, higher returns on equity, and superior ratios of funds from operations to total revenue. There was no evidence of abnormal return, indicating that this information is already priced into the stock prices, but these REITs had lower market betas. A similar study of Singaporean REITs yielded mixed results (Ho et al. 2013), and a third study found green initiatives in US REITs associated with higher firm value, greater return on assets, and superior stock performance (Sah et al. 2012). Most recently, Fuerst (2015, Working Paper) completed an analysis of the relationship between a REIT's Global Real Estate Sustainability Benchmark (GRESB) score and its operating performance. Results indicate that a higher GRESB score is associated with superior operational performance and decreased risk exposure and volatility. Perhaps, most importantly, this research identified tremendous room for financial improvement in the REITs of North America, Europe, and Asia, given greater efforts to comprehensively invest in sustainable and energy-efficient commercial real estate.

In addition to evidence regarding benefits of environmentally certified commercial real estate and firm performance, there are also two papers which examine debt benefits. The first examines US REITs and finds that those invested in green buildings receive lower spread on their commercial real estate mortgages (35–36 basis points lower than average), as well as lower spreads associated with their bond issuances and trades of their debt on the secondary market (Eichholtz et al. 2015, Working Paper). The second paper examines the default risk associated with CMBS mortgages and finds that mortgages on properties situated near fixed transit stations (a measure of walkability), those with higher Walk Scores, and those certified under the Energy Star program are all associated with below average default risk (An and Pivo 2015, Working Paper). The findings regarding superior operating performance, lower systemic risk, superior cost of capital, and decreased default risk all support findings similar to those described at the property level: sustainable and energy-efficient buildings are associated with decreased variance.

2.19 Evidence: GRESB

A 2011 article outlined a global survey tool for real property portfolios which would measure the environmental performance of listed property companies and private property funds (Bauer et al. 2011). Once scored, these real estate firms may be compared and evaluated, both cross sectionally and over time, allowing transparency and consistent measurement of real estate firms' sustainability and energy efficiency. This survey is known as the Global Real Estate Sustainability Benchmark, or GRESB, and since its origination in 2009, has grown to include benchmarking on over 200 member firms.

The organization's goal is to provide real estate investors and owners with the insight into environmental, social, and governance issues needed to manage and monitor commercial real estate sustainability performance at a portfolio level. Participation in the GRESB survey has become a "best practices" tool for leading real estate firms worldwide, allowing firms to evaluate themselves both against their track record and against their competitors. One of the key benefits of GRESB is that the survey results allow for worldwide comparison of private equity funds, pension funds, and both public and private real estate companies. Encouraging this transparency and benchmarking not only encourages firms to improve their own performance, but also helps advance developments in sustainable and energy-efficient real estate. As of 2015, the GRESB survey received responses from over 700 firms (170 listed, 537 private) across six continents, representing 61,000 total assets valued at $2.3 trillion.[8]

2.20 Conclusion: Mitigating Risk and Increasing Return

This chapter began by explaining why commercial real estate is key in the shaping of society and in the health of the planet. Through the pursuit of the triple bottom line (Fig. 1.1), owners, occupants, and users of commercial real estate can help protect the environment and future generations while also capturing financial benefits. Pursuit of environmentally sensitive commercial real estate can take many forms, including sustainable and/or energy-efficient design, construction, and operations. Certification programs, such as LEED, Energy Star, BREEAM, Green Star, and hundreds of others, provide third-party evidence of those actions, signaling the environmentally sensitive nature of a building's design or operations to outside observers.

Such certifications are associated with a variety of benefits. First, there are the corporate benefits. Firms associated with environmentally certified buildings may experience corporate image benefits. By affiliating with third-party-certified green real estate, companies communicate their commitment to the environment to their stakeholders. As customers of all types, both business-to-business and business-to-consumer, begin to demand greater environmental sensitivity from the companies they support, third-party verification of green initiatives becomes imperative. Additionally, corporate image benefits do not help relations with only external parties, but with internal parties as well. Employees are now valuing an environmentally sensitive employer and workplace in their job decisions. In addition to employee's desire to work in a green building, green buildings are associated with more productive workers and with greater employee retention. Given the large cost associated with employee turnover, retaining good talent is key in a firm's success, particularly after having attracted and maximized the productivity of a high-quality employee in conjunction with a green building investment.

Second, there are the real estate-related benefits. Despite the benefits to society and the environment, a commercial real estate owner or investor is unlikely to pursue energy-efficiency strategies unless it also makes financial sense in the ownership and operation of the property. Given this, extensive research has been conducted to examine the relationship between energy efficiency and commercial real estate construction and operations.

The long-held question regarding energy-efficient real estate construction is how much more it costs to build as compared to a traditionally constructed building. Findings indicate that while the perceived added cost is substantial, the actual cost is nominal and shrinking. As energy-efficient technology becomes widely commercially available, its price begins to fall. Additionally, when plans to pursue energy efficiency are incorporated from the beginning of the design stage, there are no added construction costs, with the only remaining additional costs being related to design fees. Evidence from the industry supports this, and also suggests accelerated construction schedules.

Once construction is complete, buildings have other opportunities to capitalize on energy efficiency, both in the income and in the expense side of operations. Benefits associated with building income are captured in rental rates, occupancy rates, and their impact on asset value. The majority of research on environmentally certified buildings to date has been completed in this field, examining the impacts of energy efficiency on income. Given the aforementioned business benefits to a corporation occupying the environmentally certified space, it is reasonable to expect a tenant to pay a premium to situate within an environmentally certified building. Research findings support this hypothesis, with extensive work across many countries providing evidence of both rental rate and occupancy rate premiums for energy-efficient buildings, and decreased rent concessions paid to tenants of environmentally certified buildings. Related research finds that while green buildings have rental and occupancy rate premiums, those rates do not increase at an above-market pace, and that as the supply of green buildings grows the marginal benefit of certification decreases. Results also show that green buildings have higher asset values, a natural finding given higher rental and occupancy rates and little reason to expect higher operating expenses or greater risk.

In fact, the natural assumption is to expect decreased natural resources use in environmentally certified commercial real estate. This is often true, with research finding energy and water savings associated with energy-efficient buildings. However, many environmentally certified buildings are "smart" buildings, using advanced technology to operate the building as efficiently as possible. This advancement is associated with lower operating variance and, therefore, risk. But this notable level of technology is also associated with higher levels of energy use. Other indirect operational benefits that lead to decreased operating variance include more satisfied tenants and a higher propensity of tenants to re-lease their space.

We also consider questions of energy efficiency in existing (not just newly constructed) buildings, and to how and if these benefits filter through from individual building operations to corporate owners, particularly in listed real estate companies. Evidence indicates the importance of understanding the unique aspects of both these categories as well, and that impacts for all types of operations and ownership scenarios are associated with cost savings, increased income levels, and decreased risk levels, all of which may translate to greater financial returns.

Throughout this chapter, we have discussed ways in which energy-efficient commercial real estate can improve returns to both property owners and the space users. We have also touched on ways green buildings decrease risk exposure, particularly through decreasing the variability to operating costs. While the majority of this commercial real estate research has been completed on office buildings due to the availability of data, a few studies branch out into multifamily, retail, industrial, and flex buildings as well. Taken together, this young literature tells a compelling story about the importance of energy-efficient buildings in shaping the health of future societies and the environment, truly supporting the goal of sustainability: to meet the needs of today without sacrificing the well-being of tomorrow.

Notes

1. Energy Information Administration. "A Look at the U.S. Commercial Building Stock: Results from EIA's 2012 Commercial Buildings Energy Consumption Survey (CBECS)." Available online at: https://www.eia.gov/consumption/commercial/reports/2012/buildstock/.
2. https://www.energystar.gov/buildings/about-us/facts-and-stats.
3. Information taken from www.usgbc.org/leed unless otherwise noted.
4. Information taken from http://www.breeam.com unless otherwise noted.
5. Information taken from http://www.gbca.org.au unless otherwise noted.
6. Information taken from http://www.energystar.gov unless otherwise noted.

7. Source energy is the energy used in creating and transmitting the power to the building.
8. Information taken from https://www.gresb.com/results2015/introduction.

References

Abdul, Yetunde. 2013. *Delivering Sustainable Buildings: Savings and Payback.* Presentation Deck, BREEAM.

An, Xudong, and Gary Pivo. 2015. Default Risk of Securitized Commercial Mortgages: Do Sustainability Property Features Matter? Working Paper.

Anderson, W. Thomas, and William Cunningham. 1972. The Socially Conscious Consumer. *Journal of Marketing* 36 (2): 23–31.

Bauer, Rob, Piet Eichholtz, Nils Kok, and John Quigley. 2011. How Green is Your Property Portfolio? The Global Real Estate Sustainability Benchmark. *Rotman International Journal of Pension Management* 4 (1): 33–34.

Bond, S., and A. Devine. 2015. Certification Matters: Is Green Talk Cheap Talk? *Journal of Real Estate Finance and Economics* 52 (2): 117–140.

Caruana, Robert. 2007. A Sociological Perspective of Consumption Morality. *Journal of Consumer Behavior* 6: 287–304.

Chang, Qingqing, and Avis Devine. 2016. The Financial Benefits to Occupants of Environmentally-Certified Buildings. Working Paper.

Chegut, Andrea, Piet Eichholtz, and Nils Kok. 2014. Supply, Demand and the Value of Green Buildings. *Urban Studies* 51 (1): 22–43.

Chegut, Andrea, Piet Eichholtz, and Nils Kok. 2015. The Price of Innovation: An Analysis of the Marginal Cost of Green Buildings. Working Paper #05–15, Center for Real Estate, M.I.T.

Chen, Chialin. 2001. Design for the Environment: A Quality-Based Model for Green Product Development. *Management Science* 47: 250–263.

Clancy, Heather. 2014. In California, At Least, The Case for Energy Efficiency is Building. *Forbes*, December 30.

Crane, Andrew. 2001. Unpacking the Ethical Product. *Journal of Business Ethics* 30: 361–373.

Devine, Avis, and Nils Kok. 2015. Green Certification and Bulding Performance: Implications for Tangibles and Intangibles. *Journal of Portfolio Management* 41 (6): 151–163.

Eccles, Robert, Ioannis Ioannou, and George Serafeim. 2014. The Impact of Corporate Sustainability on Organizational Processes and Performance. *Management Science* 60 (11): 2835–2857.

Eichholtz, Piet, Nils Kok, and Erkan Yonder. 2012. Portfolio Greenness and the Financial Performance of REITs. *Journal of International Money and Finance* 31: 1911–1929.

Eichholtz, Piet, Nils Kok, and Erkan Yonder. 2014. CEO Political Preferences and the Sustainability of REITs. Working Paper.

Eichholtz, Piet, Nils Kok, and John Quigley. 2010. Doing Well by Doing Good? Green Office Buildings. *American Economic Review* 100 (5): 2492–2509.

Eichholtz, Piet, Nils Kok, and John Quigley. 2013. The Economics of Green Building. *The Review of Economics and Statistics* 95 (1): 50–63.

Eichholtz, Piet, Nils Kok, and John Quigley. 2016. Ecological Responsiveness and Corporate Real Estate. *Business and Society* 55 (3): 330–360.

Eichholtz, Piet, Rogier Holtermans, Nils Kok, and Erkan Yonder. 2015. Environmental Performance and the Cost of Capital: Evidence from Commercial Mortgages and REIT Bonds. Working Paper.

Fitz-enz, Jac. 1997. It's Costly to Lose Good Employees. *Workforce* 76 (8): 32.

Fuerst, Franz. 2015. The Financial Rewards of Sustainability: A Global Performance Study of Real Estate Investment Trusts. Working Paper.

Fuerst, Franz, and Pat McAllister. 2011a. Eco-Labeling in Commercial Office Markets: Do Leed and Energy Star Offices Obtain Multiple Premiums? *Ecological Economics* 70 (6): 1220–1230.

Fuerst, Franz, and Patrick McAllister. 2011b. Green Noise or Green Value? Measuring the Effects of Environmental Certification on Office Values. *Real Estate Economics* 39 (1): 45–69.

Fullbrook, Dave, Q. Jackson, and Graeme Finlay. 2006. *Value Case for Sustainable Building in New Zealand.* Government Report, Wellington: Ministry for the Environment.

Fuller, Stephen. 2014. *Economic Impact of Commercial Real Estate: 2014 Edition.* Industry Research Report. Herndon, VA: NAIOP Research Foundation.

Green Building Council Australia. 2013. *Evolution: A Year in Sustainable Building.* Industry Report, Sydney: Wingrove Design.

Heschong Mahone Group. 1999. *Skylighting and Retail Sales: An Investigation into the Relationship Between Daylighting and Human Performance.* Condensed Report, San Francisco: Pacific Gas and Electric Company.

Ho, Kim Hin, Satyanarain Rengarajan, and Ying Han Lum. 2013. "Green" Buildings and Real Estate Investment Trust's (REIT) Performance. *Journal of Property Investment and Finance* 31 (6): 545–574.

Holness, Gordon. 2008. Improving Energy Efficiency in Existing Buildings. *ASHRAE Journal* 1: 12.

Holtermans, Rogier, and Nils Kok, 2017. On the Value of Environmental Certification in the Commercial Real Estate Market. *Real Estate Economics* Accepted Author Manuscript. https://doi.org/10.1111/1540-6229.12223.

Hong, Harrison, and Leonard Kostovetsky. 2012. Red and Blue Investing: Values and Finance. *Journal of Financial Economics* 103: 1–19.

Hutton, Irena, Danling Jiang, and Alok Kumar. 2014. Corporate Policies of Republican Managers. *Journal of Financial and Quantitative Analysis* 49 (5–6): 1279–1310.

Irwin, Julie, and Jonathan Baron. 2001. Response Mode Effects and Moral Values. *Organizational Behavior and Human Decision Processes* 84: 177–197.

Kahn, Matthew, and Nils Kok. 2014. Big-Box Retailers and Urban Carbon Emissions: The Case of Wal-Mart. NBER Working Paper Series. February. http://www.nber.org/papers/w19912.pdf. Accessed 30 May 2016.

Kahn, Matthew, Nils Kok, and John Quigley. 2014. Carbon Emissions from the Commercial Building Sector: The Role of Climate, Quality, and Incentives. *Journal of Public Economics*, 113 (February): 1–12.

Kats, Greg. 2003. *The Costs and Financial Benefits of Green Buildings: A Report to California's Sustainable Building Task Force*. Government Report.

Kats, Greg. 2010. *Greening Our Built World: Costs, Benefits, and Strategies*. Washington, DC: Island Press.

Kinnear, Thomas, James Raylor, and Sadrudin Ahmed. 1974. Ecologically Concerned Consumers: Who Are They? *Journal of Marketing* 38 (2): 20–24.

Kok, Nils, and Maarten Jennen. 2012. The Impact of Energy Labels and Accessibility on Office Rents. *Energy Policy* 46: 489–497.

Leonardo Academy Inc. 2009. *The Economics of LEED for Existing Buildings for Individual Buildings: 2008 Edition*. White Paper, Madison, WI: Leonardo Academy.

Long, Marisa. 2015. New Survey Shows Top Companies Prioritize Global Green Building Rating System LEED. *USGBC*. April 7. http://www.usgbc.org/articles/new-survey-shows-top-companies-prioritize-global-green-building-rating-system-leed. Accessed 16 April 2016.

Margolis, Joshua, Hillary Anger Elfenbein, and James Walsh. 2009. Does it Pay to be Good...and Does it Matter? A Meta-Analysis of the Relationship Between Corporate Social and Financial Performance. Working Paper.

Mazar, Nina, and Chen-Bo Zhong. 2010. Do Green Products Make Us Better People? *Psychological Science* 21 (4): 494–498.

McCook, Kevin. 2013. *U.S. Construction Outlook*. Presentation. Las Vegas, NV: McGraw-Hill Construction.

McGraw-Hill Construction. 2011. *Green Outlook 2011: Green Trends Driving Growth*. Industry Forecast. New York, NY: McGraw-Hill Construction.

Miller, Norm, Jay Spivey, and Andy Florence. 2008. Does Green Pay Off? *Journal of Real Estate Portfolio Management* 14 (4): 385–400.

Nelson, Andrew. 2007. *The Greening of U.S. Investment Real Estate—Market Fundamentals, Prospects and Opportunities*. Research Report No. 57, RREEF.

Newsham, Guy, Sandra Mancini, and Benjamin Birt. 2009. Do LEED-Certified Buildings Save Energy? Yes, but.... *Energy and Buildings* 41 (8): 897–905.

Pivo, Gary. 2008. Exploring Responsible Property Investing: A Survey of American Executives. *Corporate Social Responsibility and Environmental Management* 15 (4): 235–248.

Puybaraud, Marie. 2010. *Generation Y and the Workplace.* Annual Report, London: Johnson Controls.

Sah, Vivek, Norman Miller, and Biplab Ghosh. 2012. Are Green REITs Valued More? *Journal of Real Estate Portfolio Management* 19 (2): 169–177.

Schlegelmilch, Bodo, Greg Bohlen, and Adamantios Diamantopoulos. 1996. The Link Between Green Purchasing Decisions and Measures of Environmental Consciousness. *European Journal of Marketing* 30 (5): 35–55.

Scofield, John. 2009. Do Leed-Certified Buildings Save Energy? Not Really. *Energy and Buildings* 41 (12): 1386–1390.

Scofield, John. 2013. Efficacy of Leed-Certification in Reducing Energy Consumption and Greenhouse Gas Emission for Large New York City Office Buildings. *Energy and Buildings* 67: 517–524.

Shrum, L.J., John McCarty, and Tina Lowrey. 1995. Buyer Characteristics of the Green Consumer and Their Implications for Advertising Strategy. *Journal of Advertising* 24 (2): 71–82.

Terrapin Bright Green, LLC. 2014. *The Economics of Biophilia: Why Designing with Nature in Mind Makes Financial Sense.* New York: Terrapin Bright Green.

USGBC. 2010. *USGBC Case Study: LEED Volume Program, PNC Financial Services Group, Inc.* www.usgbc.org/sites/default/files/CaseStudy_Volume_PNC.pdf. *Accessed 19 April 2016.*

Wiley, Jonathan, Justin Benefield, and Ken Johnson. 2010. Green Design and the Market for Commercial Office Space. *Journal of Real Estate Finance and Economics* 41: 228–243.

World Green Building Council. 2013. *The Business Case for Green Building.* Industry Report, World Green Building Council.

Author Biography

Dr Avis Devine Associate Professor of Real Estate with the Brookfield Centre for Real Estate and Infrastructure in the Schulich School of Business, York University. Prior to her academic career, she was the Assistant Vice President in charge of commercial real estate underwriting and valuation for Dollar Bank, FSB in Pittsburgh, PA. Her research interests include Sustainable and Energy Efficient Real Estate, Commercial Real Estate, Institutions, and Emerging Markets.

CHAPTER 3

Energy Efficiency and Green Building Assessment

Jordan Stanley and Yongsheng Wang

3.1 Introduction

Skyscrapers used to be the pride of the changing landscapes of our urban cities. They were the pinnacle of modern engineering and innovation. Over time, people gradually realized the undeniable impacts those giant structures have on the natural environment and our way of life. The high demand on energy and other resources to maintain their operation put a burden on both skyscrapers' users and owners. Under the mission of combating climate change and increasing economic efficiency, governments and various agencies (profit and non-profit) across the globe proposed their own versions of standards to access the environmental and operational

J. Stanley (✉)
Department of Economics, Syracuse University, Syracuse, NY, USA
e-mail: jstanley@syr.edu

Y. Wang
Department of Economics and Business, Washington and Jefferson College, Washington, PA, USA
e-mail: wysqd01@gmail.com

N.E. Coulson et al. (eds.), *Energy Efficiency and the Future of Real Estate*, DOI 10.1057/978-1-137-57446-6_3

efficiencies of commercial and residential structures. This chapter examines these assessment procedures in order to compare their differences and effectiveness in promoting green building practices in different countries.

3.2 Development of Green Real Estate Movement

While certain simple green building practices have existed for centuries, the modern green building movement originated in the second half of the twentieth century. The environmental movement moved to the forefront during the oil embargo of the 1970s, forcing government officials to be more energy efficient, as well as convincing the U.S. population to be more conscious of their energy consumption. Even after the energy crisis receded, energy efficiency continued to be researched and pursued.[1] In the United States, the 1990s were a time of great expansion in the green building movement. Architecture groups began to more heavily consider energy and environmental consequences. In 1989, the American Institute of Architects (AIA) formed the Committee on the Environment. Likewise, environmental and energy organizations developed programs for building, design, and operation. The ENERGY STAR program was jointly initiated in 1992 by the U.S. Department of Energy (DOE) and the U.S. Environmental Protection Agency (EPA) . The first local green building program was started in Austin, Texas, in 1992.[2]

A monumental year for the green building movement was 1993. From a visibility perspective, the "Greening of the White House" initiative played an essential role in promoting green building. The Clinton administration set out to be a model for green building practices and showcased both the environmental and cost-saving benefits of energy efficiency. In addition, in 1993, the U.S. Green Building Council (USGBC) was formed.[3] Green building councils are immensely important in promoting green building and now exist in many countries around the world. The USGBC launched the pilot version of its green building assessment program in 1998. Dubbed the Leadership in Energy and Environmental Design (LEED) program, it has grown into a domestic and international pillar in green building certification and proliferation.

Green building assessment programs like LEED have been instrumental in vastly expanding the green building movement.[4] The first green building assessment system was developed in the late 1980s. The United Kingdom-based Building Research Establishment (BRE) group officially released their Environmental Assessment Methodology (BREEAM) in 1990. The BRE group was originally a government organization but was privatized in 1997. BREEAM was the world's first green building assessment method and remains an enormous international system in both size and influence. While BREEAM can presently be found in 73 countries, it is most popular in Europe, where it boasts an 80% green building market share.[5] Buildings can earn credits in ten different assessment categories: energy, health and well-being, innovation, land use, materials, management, pollution, transport, waste, and water. After inspection is performed by licensed, third-party assessors, credits are awarded and totalled to determine a final performance rating. Over 2 million commercial and residential buildings are registered with BREEAM, accounting for over 500,000 certificates. BREEAM is also extending into the U.S. market in 2016.[6]

One major contribution of BREEAM was setting the template for future green building assessment systems. The development of such systems has increased green building practices in numerous countries. For other nations, additional programs can achieve different goals and help serve interests not included in BREEAM. Just as BREEAM has expanded over time, other assessment systems have expanded within and across other countries. Participants in LEED alone currently represent 160 countries and territories around the world.

The trajectory of LEED is emblematic of the green building movement as a whole. LEED is the most successful offshoot of BREEAM. Since its inception, LEED has flourished by evolving the program itself over time, as well as expanding its reach both globally and domestically. LEED has become an internationally recognized signal of green building and energy efficiency. LEED is available in over 150 countries and territories with 72,000 projects and counting.[7] As of 2015, the top ten LEED countries outside the U.S. were Canada, China, India, Brazil, Republic of Korea, Germany, Taiwan, United Arab Emirates, Turkey, and Sweden. These ten nations are a diverse group economically, as well as socially. Such a sample is just one example of the universality of green building.

Domestically, LEED began around the start of the twenty-first century primarily as a tool for new construction projects. The first few years of the program saw slow but steady growth in project registrations. Participation increased quickly when the program revised its rating system and expanded to include other kinds of buildings. Between 2000 and 2006, about 5000 projects registered for LEED certification; by the end of 2008, the total number of registered projects had risen to 18,400. Certifications between 2007 and 2008 were double the total number of certifications from 2000 through 2006. In terms of the green building movement, the number of credentialed LEED professionals went from 40,000 at the end of 2007 to 75,000 by the end of 2008.[8] Even as the real estate market has fluctuated since 2008, LEED has continued its steady growth. Logically following the spike in registrations, LEED certifications increased sharply from 2009 onward.[9]

LEED can be applied to new construction or existing buildings and has subsystems for Building Design and Construction, Interior Design and Construction, Building Operation and Management, Neighborhood Development, and Homes. Most LEED projects are commercial properties, but participation is increasing for residential (mostly multi-family properties), government, and education buildings.

As shown in Fig. 3.1, about 40% of LEED participation in the United States (based on 2014 data) was for office space. As of May 2016, an average of 1.85 million square feet is certified LEED each day with almost 80,000 registered commercial projects, 32,500 of which are officially certified. Furthermore, LEED participants include over 230,000 total home units (101,000 certified), nearly 6000 education buildings (about 5400 certified), and about 3000 LEED-certified state and local government projects.[10]

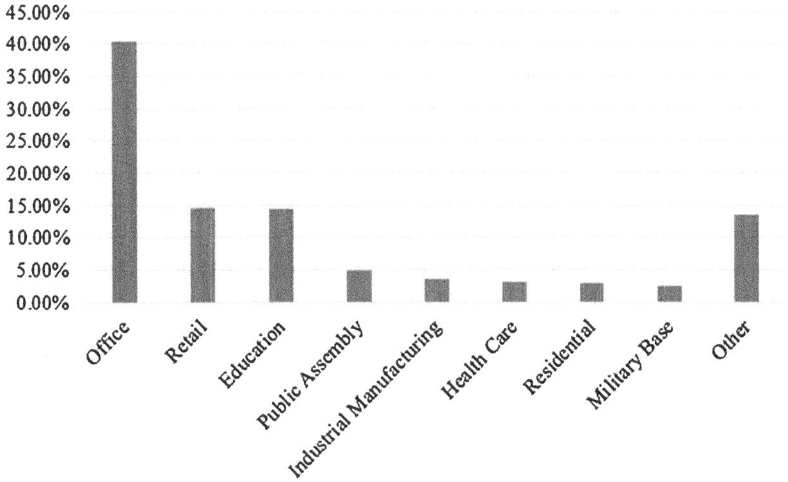

Fig. 3.1 Space types in all LEED buildings

The LEED process includes multiple stages; registering for LEED is the first step. Building owners and operators can weigh the costs and benefits of earning certification to determine if LEED is right for them. After a building registers in the program, a certification application is submitted for the project and a certification review fee is due. Then, the LEED application is reviewed by the Green Building Certification Institute.[11] To attain certification, projects must earn enough credits to pass the required threshold. Credits cover objectives regarding building design, environmental footprint, energy usage, and community impacts. Buildings earn credits in these different categories and are awarded certification at a particular level depending on the points earned.

Many opportunities for credits exist and cover assorted aspects of sustainable building. Categories include location and transportation, sustainable sites, water efficiency, energy and atmosphere, materials and resources, indoor environmental quality, and innovation. Some credits such as construction activity pollution prevention, water use reduction, and storage and collection of recyclables are required. The project managers can then decide how they will earn the additional necessary points for a given certification level. Examples of such credits include renewable energy production (three points), access to quality transport (five points), and light pollution reduction (one point). Beyond the basic certification, buildings can become LEED Silver, Gold, or Platinum. Currently, 40–49 points is the basic certification, 50–59 points is Silver, 60–79 points is Gold, and 80 and above is Platinum. Figure 3.2 shows LEED 2014 participation by level. Note that Gold is the most popular level, with a major drop occurring beyond that level as fewer buildings opt to certify at the Platinum level.

Assessment systems like LEED and BREEAM have helped push the green building movement forward. They induce participation by providing information and direction as well as objective and accepted standards. These promote green building practices as both a means (energy efficiency) and an end (certification). Having a clear signal-like certification introduces the concept to those unaware of the program. Dissemination of information regarding the benefits of energy efficiency and the visibility of certification signals have helped increase the popularity of green building. Shared elements across programs allow consistency in messaging, as well as proper pursuance of the common goal.

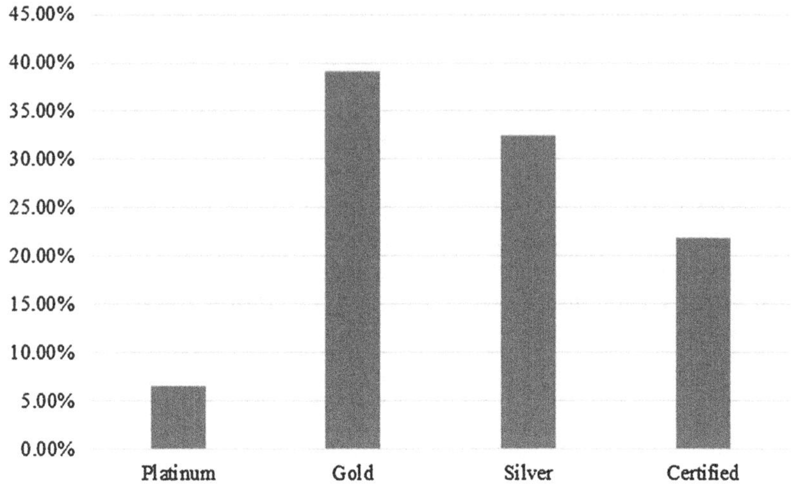

Fig. 3.2 List of LEED buildings of different levels in all LEED buildings. *Data Source* USGBC, 2014

3.3 Other Green Building Standards in the World

Many green building assessment programs share key characteristics; however, each program is also unique in its own right. Participation in green building assessment is typically voluntary, even if the program is run by the government. One notable exception is the Pearl Building Rating System (PBRS) in the United Arab Emirates. The PBRS is part of the Estidama sustainability program run by the Abu Dhabi Urban Planning Council. Estidama is the first such system in the Middle East, and was conceived by the late Sheikh Zayed bin Sultan Al Nahyan. The focus lies on "four pillars of sustainability"—environmental, energy, social, and cultural.

The PBRS is a key tool in developing communities along these pillars. An executive order in 2010 required all new buildings to meet the Pearl level 1 requirements. The PBRS requires development projects across all building types (e.g., warehouses, hospitals, hotels, and laboratories) to meet this minimum Pearl rating. The mission of the PBRS is to "promote the development of sustainable buildings and improve quality of life."[12] Specifically, the PBRS advocates water, energy, waste minimization, sustainable and recycled materials and products, and locally developed materials.

Participation is voluntary in other government-based initiatives such as Australia's National Australian Built Environmental Rating System (NABERS), Green Mark in Singapore, and Green Building Evaluation Label (GBEL) in China. GBEL was developed in 2006 and is run by the Ministry of Construction. It has a three-star rating system, hence its alternative name "China Three Star". GBEL overlaps with LEED, and the two systems serve as complementary drivers of green building in China. As of 2015, nearly, 6000 projects are certified or registered to one or both these programs. GBEL participation skyrocketed from ten projects in 2008 to over 1000 in 2014. Government policy in China requires all large (over 215,000 sq ft) construction areas to apply for GBEL. The government also encourages green building by offering cash incentives and subsidies for projects which attain above the minimum, one star GBEL certification. The expectation is that by 2020, all government-funded property developments and 30% of all new constructions in China will meet GBEL standards.[13]

NABERS, in existence for over a decade, is run at the national level by the New South Wales Office of Environment and Heritage (OEH). NABERS uses a star system of one to six stars to signify a building's sustainability performance. The star rating is calculated from performance measures such as utility bills, and it accounts for building characteristics such as size, hours of use, and energy sources. NABERS is available for offices, shopping centers, hotels, data centers, other commercial buildings, and homes.

Singapore's Building & Construction Authority (BCA) started Green Mark in 2005. It strives to promote sustainable real estate as well as increase awareness of environmental issues pertinent to building design and develop. Green Mark can be acquired by new or existing buildings, including residential homes, schools, healthcare facilities, parks, and businesses. Interested participants submit an application form to the BCA, after which an assessment team will meet with the building's project team. An assessment of the building is performed. If the building passes the assessment, the building receives the appropriate level of certification. The certification levels are "Certified", "Gold", "Gold Plus", and "Platinum". Assessment criteria involve energy efficiency, water efficiency, environmental protection, indoor environmental quality, and green features and innovation. In order to maintain its Green Mark, a building is reassessed every 3 years.[14]

3.4 Green Building Assessment Systems

Independent and objective assessment is an essential component of many green building assessment systems. The credibility of a standard is crucial to induce participation as well as properly signal high performance. The ENERGY STAR system, run by the United States Environmental Protection Agency and Department of Energy, began in 1992 as a domestic program but has since become an international standard. ENERGY STAR can be applied to products, homes, or buildings. Participation is voluntary, and certification is subject to third party review. Products and homes are subject to specific benchmarks and requirements; however, buildings are rated relative to peer performance.[15]

The government will typically be involved in green building assessment programs either directly or indirectly. Some assessments are done by the government, while many employ independent reviewers. Government support can be helpful in extending the reach of a green building assessment program while also rallying public interest in sustainable real estate. For example, there may be tax incentives for LEED participation. Furthermore, government buildings can participate in sustainable building practices themselves. As noted earlier, the Clinton administration's efforts to make the White House a model of green building helped increase public knowledge of the movement.

Clear, objective standards are important to legitimize and perpetuate a given assessment system—especially if there is no explicit government backing. While they may be indirectly supported by the government, many programs are actually run by non-profit or private organizations. These can be industry-driven initiatives with involvement from both the private and public sectors. For example, green building can be promoted by a country's green building council. Green building councils are comprised of individuals from the private and public sectors that have some interest in promoting sustainable real estate. The World Green Building Council (World GBC)—a coalition of national GBCs—was founded in 2002 and currently consists of GBCs from more than 100 countries.[16]

Green building councils are important in promoting green building, and they may oversee green building assessment. Green building councils run green building assessment programs such as BEAM Plus in Hong

Kong, Japan's Comprehensive Assessment System for Built Environment Efficiency (CASBEE), and Green Star Programs in Australia and South Africa. BEAM Plus started as an offshoot of BREEAM in 1996. BEAM can be applied to new buildings (e.g., demolition, design, and construction) as well as existing properties (e.g., major renovations and additions). BEAM also covers an array of building types including commercial, residential, and industrial. Categories for assessment are site, materials, energy use, indoor environmental quality, materials, water use, and innovations and additions. After passing a final assessment, buildings earn certification at one of four levels: Bronze, Silver, Gold, and Platinum.

CASBEE was developed in 2001 by a research committee consisting of representatives from academia, industry, and government. This same committee established the Japan Sustainable Building Consortium (JSBC) that operates under the Ministry of Land, Infrastructure, Transport and Tourism. Though run by the Japan Green Building Council, CASBEE is supported by both national and local governments. All stages of the design process are assessed, and certification is available for entities beyond single buildings. The program has expanded over time and currently includes certification options for new construction, existing buildings, renovations, market promotion, commercial interiors, heat islands, urban development, cities, and homes. The first international CASBEE earned certification in China in 2014.[17]

Green Star South Africa is based on the Australian system. The Green Star systems emphasize independent and objective measurement. Ratings can be given for existing buildings' energy performance, offices, interiors, retail space, multi-unit residential homes, public and education buildings, retail centers, and others. Green Star South Africa's objectives are to "Establish a common language and standard of measurement for green buildings; promote integrated, whole-building design; raise awareness of the benefits of green building; recognize environmental leadership; and reduce the environmental impact of development."[18]

LEED is run by the USGBC, which was founded in 1993 by Rick Fredizzi, David Gottfried, and Mike Italiano. The USGBC has a mission centered on promoting sustainable building practices. In addition to running the LEED program, the USGBC (and other green building councils) are active social advocates for sustainability. Green building councils can work with representatives from the government, business sector, educational institutions, and local communities. For example, the USGBC participated in the White House's national conference on resilient building codes in May 2016.[19]

Major assessment systems need not be run by GBCs. Another worldwide standard is BOMA 360 run by Building Owners and Managers Association (BOMA), a non-profit organization. BOMA 360 differs from other assessment systems such as LEED that BOMA is based on a building's peers, determining whether a building is outperforming its competition in all major areas of building management and operation. A key aspect of this is the notion of "industry best practices" in six areas not solely limited to green building. These areas are Building Operation and Management; Safety, Security and Risk; Training; Energy; Environmental Sustainability; and Tenant Relations. BOMA 360 has participants in over 100 global markets.[20]

Run in part by BOMA Canada, Green Globes is a green building standard in both Canada and the United States. Green Globes was developed by ECD Energy and Environmental Canada Ltd. in 2000, and it is supported by Canada's Department of National Defense and Public Works and Government Services (PWGSC).[21] In the U.S., Green Globes was initiated in 2004 and is run by the Green Building Initiative as part of the American National Standards Institute (ANSI). Green Globes differs from other assessment systems in that participation is through self-assessment.[22]

3.5 Differences Across Green Building Standards

Differences among programs may be subtle or stark, but present the opportunity for coexistence among assessment systems. Building owners have the choice to be assessed relatively or absolutely. Standards such as ENERGY STAR (for buildings), BOMA 360, and NABERS are based on peers (relative standards), while others such as LEED and BREEAM are acquired through earning enough credits or points to meet a consistent threshold (absolute standards). The certification process can vary as well—building owners may find the self-assessment of Green Globes more suitable for their preferences than a stricter standard such as LEED. Relating to this idea, the body that is performing the certification also presents a choice for building owners. LEED is popular in China, and building owners can opt for the government standard (GBEL), the non-government standard (LEED), or even both if they so choose. The Building and Construction Authority in Singapore offers Green Mark, while a different green labeling is offered by the Singapore GBC. As with any product, assessment systems will differ in price based on the requirements for certification. Higher levels of certification will be costlier to attain than lower rating level, but can offer greater benefits.

In a less quantitative manner, systems can also differ in their stated purpose—some focus specifically on performance, while some programs offer certification options for both design and performance. BOMA 360 is a broader building performance standard that extends beyond sustainable building practices, while LEED specializes in green building practices with certification options for design, construction, and performance. The flexibility of assessment systems aids in meeting energy-efficiency goals. A wide range of options within a system and among systems allows interested parties to improve energy efficiency in the manner which best suits them. Components of the credit library may be more attractive to certain projects—water efficiency improvements could be of greater use in particular geographic areas compared to others. Assessment systems can cover all stages of building design and operation. For example, the options for LEED certification options exist for both new and existing buildings. The multitude of assessment systems means that parties can opt for a standard or certification that best fits with their own interests.

If green building assessment systems differ in purpose, they need not be substitutes. Passivhaus, originating in Germany in the 1990s, is globally used for both residential and commercial properties. Passivhaus focuses on heating and cooling buildings naturally, and addressing fuel poverty is one of its primary missions. The overall goal of Passivhaus is quite simple—high-energy performance through heating and cooling efficiency.[23] This is not in conflict with other, broader sustainability standards. The complementarity of standards can be more explicit—ENERGY STAR is used as a benchmark for BOMA 360. Investment in sustainable building design and performance can be applied to multiple green building certifications. Being LEED does not preclude a building from also being BOMA 360 or ENERGY STAR.

The key to the coexistence of these green building assessment systems is the voluntary nature of most of these programs. Buildings make the choices to do green building certification, to what extent to become certified, and which certification(s) to attain. Each building can determine what is best for their interests and behave accordingly. Green building assessment systems are essential in providing information, direction, and clearly-defined standards to help building owners make such decisions. This includes the development and upholding of standards of excellence in sustainable real estate. Beyond architecture, LEED has been a force in other areas such as forest conservation and the development of green products such as low-flush toilets and low-emitting paints.[24] Adherence to green building standards has also been linked to increased worker productivity due to improved work environment.[25]

3.6 Conclusion

The perseverance of the green building movement is tied to green building assessment standards. The ability to stay relevant and continue to improve energy efficiency and sustainability are essential. Education is one way for assessment systems to remain relevant. Public promotion of green building is directly and indirectly initiated by green building assessment systems. The public can enter buildings and see green certification labels, governments work with green building councils in developing policy, and program representatives work with industry to develop plans for certification. Education also can come at the individual level as training and accreditation are often offered by the various programs. Companies may have their employees become accredited green building professionals. Any interested individual can take courses or training in green building assessment. This furthers the spread of knowledge and increases the influence that green building programs can have in other spheres in society.

It is crucial for green building assessment programs to evolve in order to maintain relevance and effectiveness. Old standards will likely become obsolete, and changes in markets or technology can occur rapidly. Green building programs work to develop updates—adding different types of real estate, including new opportunities for certification credits, or tightening standards. Striking a balance between attracting participation while keeping standards high enough to actually be environmentally beneficial can be difficult. Standards that are too tough or costly may deter participation, while weaker thresholds may make little difference in developing truly sustainable buildings.

Evolutions will often be based on feedback from both public and private sectors. The collaborative setup of many green building assessment systems fits nicely with this idea. Having a system based on collaborative efforts, among all aspects of society makes it easier to make appropriate adjustments in an efficient manner. For example, criticism of the previous versions of LEED was that LEED over-rewarded minor actions, created improper incentives, and failed to factor in lifetime effects; LEED v4 was developed with these points in mind.[26] Each LEED update alters the previous edition by amending items such as available earnable credits, value of credits, certification requirements, and certification thresholds. Technology improvements, higher expectations for being "green" in both private and public sectors, and other developments led the USGBC to "raise the bar in a way that challenges the building industry to reach higher than ever before".[27]

Notes

1. The Marble Institute."Green Building". http://www.marble-institute.com/default/assets/File/consumers/historystoneingreenbuilding.pdf.
2. The U.S. Environmental Protection Agency. (2016). Basic Information: Green Building, February 20. Retrieved from https://archive.epa.gov/greenbuilding/web/html/about.html (U.S. Environmental Protection Agency 2016).
3. U.S. Green Building Council. (2016a). About. http://www.usgbc.org/about. Accessed 2 Feb 2016.
4. Additional information can be found in Vierra, Stephanie. (2016). Green Building Standards and Certification Systems. https://www.wbdg.org/resources/gbs.php. Accessed 12 July 2016.
5. Building Research Establishment. (2016). BREEAM. https://www.bre.co.uk/page.jsp?id=829. Accessed 2 Feb 2016.
6. Roberts, Tristan. (2016). BREEAM USA Jolts Existing Buildings Market, June 10. Retrieved from https://www.buildinggreen.com/newsbrief/breeam-usa-jolts-existing-buildings-market (Roberts 2016).
7. U.S. Green Building Council. 2016b. LEED. http://www.usgbc.org/leed. Accessed 2 Feb 2016.
8. Shutters, Cecilia and Robb Tufts. (2016). LEED by the numbers: 16 years of growth, May 27. Retrieved from http://www.usgbc.org/articles/leed-numbers-16-years-steady-growth (Shutters and Tufts 2016).
9. Arny, Michael and Mary Reames. Leonardo Academy. Retrieved from http://fmlink.com/articles/leed-registration-and-certification-trends/.
10. U.S. Green Building Council. (2016c). USGBC Statistics, June 1. Retrieved from http://www.usgbc.org/articles/usgbc-statistics (U.S. Green Building Council 2016).

11. U.S. Green Building Council. (2016d). Guide to LEED certification: Commercial. Retrieved from http://www.usgbc.org/cert-guide/commercial.
12. Abu Dhabi Urban Planning Council. Estidama—Pearl Rating System. Retrieved from http://estidama.upc.gov.ae/pearl-rating-system-v10.aspx (Abu Dhabi Urban Planning Council 2016).
13. Bisagni, Alessandro. (2015). LEED and GBEL: Hand in Hand in Promoting Green Building in China. Green Building Information Gateway, August 13. Retrieved from http://insight.gbig.org/leed-and-gbel-hand-in-hand-in-promoting-green-building-in-china/ (Bisagni 2015).
14. Singapore Government Building and Construction Authority. (2016). BCA Green Mark Criteria. https://bca.gov.sg/GreenMark/green_mark_criteria.html. Accessed 2 Feb 2016
15. ENERGY STAR. (2016). About ENERGY STAR. https://www.energystar.gov/about. Accessed 2 Feb 2016.
16. World Green Building Council. About Us. Retrieved from http://www.worldgbc.org/index.php?cID=220.
17. Japan Sustainable Building Consortium (JSBC) and Institute for Building Environment and Energy Conservation (IBEC). (2016). CASBEE. http://www.ibec.or.jp/CASBEE/english/. Accessed 2 Feb 2016.
18. Green Building Council South Africa. Green Star SA Rating System. Retrieved from https://www.gbcsa.org.za/green-star-sa-rating-system/ (Green Building Council South Africa 2016).
19. Long, Marissa. (2016). U.S. Green Building Council Media, May 11. Retrieved from http://www.usgbc.org/articles/usgbc-joins-national-leaders-white-house-during-building-safety-month-commits-continue-focu (Long 2016).
20. Building Owners and Managers Association International. (2016). Awards & Recognition. http://www.boma.org/awards/360-program/pages/default.aspx. Accessed 2 Feb 2016.
21. Green Globes. (2016). About Green Globes. http://www.greenglobes.com/about.asp. Accessed 19 Feb 2016
22. Fuller, Felicia. (2016). A Comparison of LEED and Green Globes. Green Building Research Institute, January 28. https://www.gbrionline.org/a-comparison-of-leedand-greenglobes/. Accessed 2 Feb 2016.
23. Passivhaus. (2016). The Passivhaus Standard. http://www.passivhaus.org.uk/standard.jsp?id=122. Accessed 19 Feb 2016.
24. Schnaars, Christopher and Hannah Morgan. (2013). In U.S. building industry, is it too easy to be green? USA TODAY, June 2013. Retrieved from http://www.usatoday.com/story/news/nation/2012/10/24/green-building-leed-certification/1650517/ (Schnaars and Morgan 2013).

25. New South Wales Office of Environment and Heritage. Benefits of NABERS. Retrieved from https://nabers.gov.au/public/webpages/ContentStandard.aspx?module=10&template=3&include=Benefits.htm&side=CommitmentAgrTertiary.htm (New South Wales Office of Environment and Heritage 2016).
26. Schnaars, Christopher and Hannah Morgan. (2013). In U.S. building industry, is it too easy to be green? USA TODAY, June 2013. Retrieved from http://www.usatoday.com/story/news/nation/2012/10/24/green-building-leed-certification/1650517/.
27. Long, Marissa. (2014). USGBC Announces Extension of LEED 2009. U.S. Green Building Council Media, October 29. Retrieved from http://www.usgbc.org/articles/usgbc-announces-extension-leed-2009 (Long 2014).

References

Abu Dhabi Urban Planning Council. 2016. Estidama—Pearl Rating System. http://estidama.upc.gov.ae/pearl-rating-system-v10.aspx. Accessed 19 Feb 2016.

Arny, Michael and Mary Reames. LEED Registration and Certification Trends. Leonardo Academy. Retrieved from http://fmlink.com/articles/leed-registration-and-certification-trends/.

Bisagni, Alessandro. 2015. LEED and GBEL: Hand in Hand in Promoting Green Building in China. Green Building Information Gateway, August 13. http://insight.gbig.org/leed-and-gbel-hand-in-hand-in-promoting-green-building-in-china/. Accessed 2 Feb 2016.

Building Owners and Managers Association International. 2016. Awards & Recognition. http://www.boma.org/awards/360-program/pages/default.aspx. Accessed 2 Feb 2016.

Building Research Establishment. 2016. BREEAM. https://www.bre.co.uk/page.jsp?id=829. Accessed 2 Feb 2016.

ENERGY STAR. 2016. About ENERGY STAR. https://www.energystar.gov/about. Accessed 2 Feb 2016.

Fuller, Felicia. 2016. A Comparison of LEED and Green Globes. Green Building Research Institute, January 28. https://www.gbrionline.org/a-comparison-of-leedand-greenglobes/. Accessed 2 Feb 2016.

Green Globes. 2016. About Green Globes. http://www.greenglobes.com/about.asp. Accessed 19 Feb 2016.

Green Building Council South Africa. 2016. Green Star SA Rating System. https://www.gbcsa.org.za/green-star-sa-rating-system/. Accessed 2 Feb 2016.

Hong Kong Green Building Council. 2016. About US. https://www.hkgbc.org.hk/eng/Abouthkgc. Accessed 2 Feb 2016.

Japan Sustainable Building Consortium (JSBC) and Institute for Building Environment and Energy Conservation (IBEC). 2016. CASBEE. http://www.ibec.or.jp/CASBEE/english/. Accessed 2 Feb 2016.

Long, Marissa. 2016. U.S. Green Building Council Media, May 11. Retrieved from http://www.usgbc.org/articles/usgbc-joins-national-leaders-white-house-during-building-safety-month-commits-continue-focu.

Long, Marissa. 2014. USGBC Announces Extension of LEED 2009. U.S. Green Building Council Media, October 29. Retrieved from http://www.usgbc.org/articles/usgbc-announces-extension-leed-2009.

New South Wales Office of Environment & Heritage. 2016. An Introduction to NABERS. https://www.nabers.gov.au/public/WebPages/ContentStandard.aspx?module=10&temple=3&include=Intro.htm&side=EventTertiary.htm. Accessed 2 Feb 2016.

Passivhaus. 2016. The Passivhaus Standard. http://www.passivhaus.org.uk/standard.jsp?id=122. Accessed 19 Feb 2016.

Roberts, Tristan. 2016. BREEAM USA Jolts Existing Buildings Market, June 10. Retrieved from https://www.buildinggreen.com/newsbrief/breeam-usa-jolts-existing-buildings-market.

Schnaars, Christopher and Hannah Morgan. 2013. In U.S. Building Industry, is it too Easy to be Green? USA TODAY, June 2013. Retrieved from http://www.usatoday.com/story/news/nation/2012/10/24/green-building-leed-certification/1650517/.

Shutters, Cecilia and Robb Tufts. 2016. LEED by the Numbers: 16 years of Growth, May 27. Retrieved from http://www.usgbc.org/articles/leed-numbers-16-years-steady-growth.

Singapore Government Building and Construction Authority. 2016. BCA Green Mark Criteria. https://bca.gov.sg/GreenMark/green_mark_criteria.html. Accessed 2 Feb 2016.

The Marble Institute. Green Building. Retrieved http://www.marble-institute.com/default/assets/File/consumers/historystoneingreenbuilding.pdf.

U.S. Green Building Council. 2016a. About. http://www.usgbc.org/about. Accessed 2 Feb 2016.

U.S. Green Building Council. 2016b. LEED. http://www.usgbc.org/leed. Accessed 2 Feb 2016.

U.S. Green Building Council. 2016c. USGBC Statistics, June 1. Retrieved from http://www.usgbc.org/articles/usgbc-statistics.
U.S. Green Building Council. 2016d. Guide to LEED certification: Commercial. Retrieved from http://www.usgbc.org/cert-guide/commercial.
U.S. Environmental Protection Agency. 2016. Basic Information: Green Building, February 20. https://archive.epa.gov/greenbuilding/web/html/about.html. Accessed 15 March 2016.
Vierra, Stephanie. 2016. Green Building Standards and Certification Systems. https://www.wbdg.org/resources/gbs.php. Accessed 12 July 2016.

Authors' Biography

Mr. Jordan Stanley Ph.D. Candidate in Economics, Department of Economics, Syracuse University. His research focuses on environmental economics. He is a graduate of Washington and Jefferson College.

Dr. Yongsheng Wang Associate Professor of Economics, Director of Financial Economics, Washington and Jefferson College. He is also a visiting scholar at the graduate school of public and international affairs at the University of Pittsburgh. His research focuses on energy economics and real estate economics. His past research was funded by LUCE Foundation, Freeman Foundation, Heinz Endowments, and NIST (Department of Commerce).

CHAPTER 4

Innovation in the Built Environment: Energy Efficiency and Commercial Real Estate

Andrea Chegut, Rogier Holtermans and Isabel Tausendschoen

New ideas are not only the enemy of old ones; they also appear often in an extremely unacceptable form.
—Carl Gustav Jung.

4.1 Introduction

Innovation is the economic and commercial development of invention. Distinct from invention, innovation is an economic process: the commercial delivery of a new product, process, or organizational system to

The original version of this chapter was revised: For detailed information please see Erratum. The erratum to this chapter is available at https://doi.org/10.1057/978-1-137-57446-6_11

A. Chegut (✉)
Massachusetts Institute of Technology, Cambridge, USA
e-mail: achegut@mit.edu

R. Holtermans
University of Southern California, Los Angeles, USA
e-mail: rogierho@price.usc.edu

I. Tausendschoen
University of Graz, Graz, Austria
e-mail: isabel.tausendschoen@edu.uni-graz.at

N.E. Coulson et al. (eds.), *Energy Efficiency and the Future of Real Estate*, DOI 10.1057/978-1-137-57446-6_4

the market place. Innovation is also thought to be a source of profit—specifically economic profit—that rewards the innovator for taking up the uncertainty or, in some cases, quantifiably high risk for bringing something new into the market place.[1]

Innovation is not a term commonly brought to use in the context of the built environment, where capital has a long lifespan, and the capacity to make changes after construction is limited. However, this may be due to factors linked to the one-off and context based information set experienced by developers, contractors and designers at the time of development. Innovation concepts are more traditionally applied to working capital—such as equipment—and processes that enhance the efficiency of their use. Yet, like in other physical capital contexts, there are competitive forces driving market actors in the built environment to differentiate and innovate to attract tenants as well as to seek out efficiencies in their development and operational practices. Thus, when the real estate community applies innovation concepts to the built environment, there is an opportunity to understand the lifecycle and impact of new building products, processes, and organizational systems on real estate markets. In this way, the study of innovation contributes to real estate performance analysis by tangibly identifying the economic outcomes of change. In addition, an innovation lens helps the building community expand the building products and processes that support economic growth, contribute to expanding investor portfolios, and disrupt current market practices to move towards a more technological focus.

In reality, innovation has always existed for the built environment, but it is difficult to observe empirically. For example, real estate product innovations, such as skyscrapers, have gradually taken up market share from the multi-story "walk-up" building in the high-rise building domain, and the big-box shopping mall in the suburbs absorbed for some time shopping demand from the "mom-n-pop" retailers. These market shifts are long-run changes, as they can happen over a 10-year period or greater. In this way, innovation has been disrupting the building community for some time. Yet, there is no archive of building products or processes' technological progress from "niche" to "mainstream," or any measures of how this technological change impacts investment in the real estate market. This lack of information on technological change within the built environment is problematic, as it inhibits innovation and the commercial diffusion of those innovations that could move the real estate market towards better standards.

Moreover, the lack of information justifies uncertainty when it comes to innovation. Hence, the slow adoption by investors of new products or processes in an environment, where comparable experiences with innovation are difficult to observe. Slow uptake could be due to effort in searching for innovations; fear of irreversibility when developing the innovative building product; risk in changing the architectural, construction, or engineering process in developing the building; survivorship potential; fear of unknown physical, functional, and economic obsolescence; prospects of market share; or lack of observation of financial incentives—costs (revenues)—of (from) innovation. In summary, the building community knows very little about the path of adoption that any real estate innovation makes in the built environment.

One such series of interventions and innovations that have been developed for the built environment is observable in the rise of energy-efficient and sustainable buildings—so-called "green" buildings. The innovation in building products stems from inefficiency in the use of building resources. Commercial and residential buildings are responsible for 10% of U.S. greenhouse gas emissions, 38% of energy consumption, 13.6% of potable water, as well as 170 million tons of building waste.[2]

The U.S. office market provides a good example of the diffusion of green building innovation. Moreover, there has been a demonstrable precedent for documenting how a change in design and the implementation of services and technology can be used to systematically transform the performance of buildings. For example, technologically, it is feasible to develop commercial buildings that produce net-zero carbon emissions—a type of building that produces or saves as much energy as it consumes—yet, net-zero buildings are currently observed as the frontier of green real estate development. Substantial research and development in the built environment has been developed to produce at least 3,000 such buildings around the world.[3] At the frontier of this technology are precedents that document how buildings can move from being net consumers of energy to actually net producers of energy. However, the interdisciplinary transformation of the building industry has taken more than 40 years to move from fundamental research to scalable and commercially diffusible real estate products held in institutional real estate portfolios at a scale beyond the current potential Class A real estate portfolio.[4]

At the end of 2005, only 1.2% of U.S. office buildings were certified green; this share has increased to 12.4% at the end of 2016. In terms of square footage, these buildings represent almost 40% of the commercial office market in the U.S. (Holtermans et al. 2017). McGraw-Hill projects that 50% of newly developed space will be green.[5] Initiatives, such as Leadership in Energy and Environmental Design (LEED) and Energy Star, aim to lessen building energy consumption.[6] In San Francisco and Chicago, green office space has a market share of more than 60%. However, in most markets, there is limited new or redeveloped space added to the inventory of existing space that will abate energy consumption and carbon emissions. Non-residential construction represents on average 4.3% of U.S. gross domestic product.[7] The Bureau of Labor Statistics also reported 487,709 green construction jobs, equaling 9.8% of total construction employment in 2011.[8] These figures represent tangible changes in the design, construction, and human capital necessary to generate technological progress and economic growth for and from the built environment.

The goal of this chapter is to understand how the built environment can learn about this innovation process from the creation, innovation, and market uptake of green buildings. Green building products have moved from bespoke one-off trophy buildings to necessities within institutional investor's portfolios as standards have been introduced into the planning, development, and financing of green buildings. In this way, the real estate sector can learn about the pathway of innovation through the rise of developing institutional green buildings for the real estate sector. Not unlike standard capital innovations, these changes come about through the process of innovation—research and development, invention, innovation and commercial diffusion. However, this dynamic process has been a long time in the making: starting with design and system interventions several decades ago to making a single building green and concluding with the mass diffusion of certifiable green buildings.

The remainder of this chapter outlines the innovation process for the green building sector. In Sect. 4.2, we develop an introductory context of innovation fundamentals for the real estate market. In Sect. 4.3, we link the process of innovation to the development of green buildings. In Sect. 4.4, we document how the green building industry is overcoming obstacles to commercial diffusion through capital, technology, and standardization. Finally, in Sect. 4.5, we summarize our findings with some recommendations for open innovation in the built environment.

4.2 Innovation Fundamentals for Real Estate

The path of innovation is important for understanding the adoption of new technologies and the method that has been developed to bring new products and processes to the market efficiently. The stage of innovation—research and development, invention, innovation, and diffusion—is an important consideration in understanding costs, human capital requirements, value changes, and market incentives. Moreover, these distinctions may vary over new product, process and organizational innovation types, and the extent of innovation—incremental, modular, architectural, and radical (Abernathy and Clark 1985; Henderson and Clark 1990; Slaughter 1993, 1998).[9] Like manufacturing products or other forms of physical capital, buildings undergo a cycle of invention, innovation, technical change, and standardization. Combining these factors impacts the uptake, scale, and standardization of a new product or process in the economy.

4.2.1 Stage of Innovation in Real Estate

When we consider the stage of innovation, it is important to consider the human, physical, and financial capital necessary in developing new and innovative products. Human capital is distinct across the four stages of innovation, and even within each stage, it can be quite complex to meet the needs to survey and identify new methods, tools, and processes. Physical capital–like buildings–is able to agglomerate in distinct phases to meet the necessary equipment and human capital challenges to innovate and in turn financial capital clusters agglomerate around distinct sectors and locations to meet the different stages in the innovative process. When applying process innovation to the built environment, there are numerous examples, one example is to think simply about a process innovation in construction. Figure 4.1 highlights examples of process innovations in construction with the use of robotics, but identifies various process innovations across different stages in the innovation process.

Within the context of research and development, the basic research is executed by universities and laboratories, and financed by government and foundation grants to explore areas that are unknown. One such example of basic research that is at the frontier is robotic self-assemblage of structures. The image illustrates micro-bots that self-create new structures through magnetic fields.[10] In addition, research and development is generally done by scientists and engineers who are working to explore the boundaries of fundamental research.

In the next phase, basic research that is deemed feasible moves towards the invention stage through prototypes. In 2015, the industry moved 3D printing robots for on-site wall construction from basic research into patentable technologies. At this stage, invention is being rapidly prototyped by engineers who are applying fundamental research to realize potentially patentable applications in the field. In some areas, robotic construction is

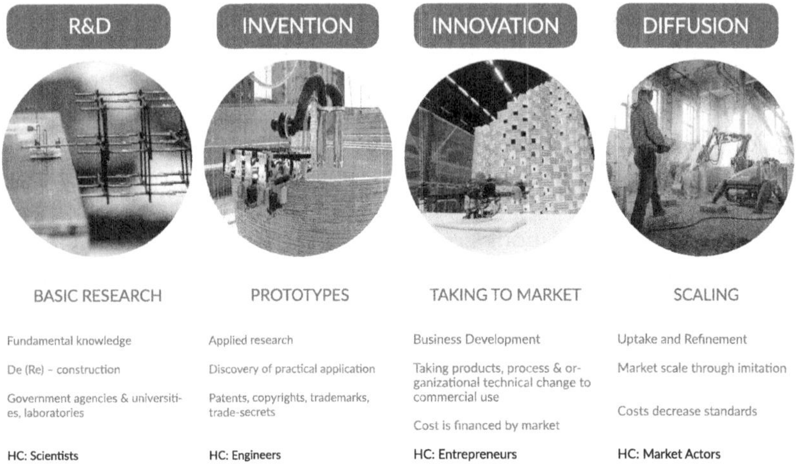

Fig. 4.1 Stages of Innovation Application: Process Innovations in Construction with Robotics.
Notes: This figure depicts the four stages of innovation applied to robotics. R&D, invention, innovation, and diffusion are phases that almost all innovations go through. Research and Development corresponds to basic research, invention to developing prototypes, innovation to market deployment, and diffusion to scaling in the market place. Human Capital (HC) corresponds to the actors within the innovation ecosystem that develop the technology at each stage

already moving towards commercial laying of bricks for housing development. In this context, firms are attempting to apply patented applications to commercially viable developments. Technologies are advanced enough for contractors to remotely control demolition robots, which are being commercially scaled across leading construction companies. When multiple firms are able to commercially diffuse a technology, this enables market uptake, potentially economies of scale, and maybe decreasing marginal costs for each new adopter of the technology. In this example, each innovation stage takes on distinct processes of human capital, financing costs, development, market deployment, and commercial diffusion.

4.2.2 *Type of Innovation in Real Estate*

Real estate can also have three pillars of innovation—process, product, and organizational innovation—that generates technological change. Process innovations in developing a building stem from changes in architecture practice, construction, development, and planning. These changes enable different types of structures to be built. For example, building information modeling (BIM) attempts to link architecture, construction, development, and planning together in a unified framework to create a 3D modeling platform that delivers live planning of delivering the building.

In addition, there are new commercial real estate products that either comprise new development or are giving new economic, physical, or functional purpose to buildings. Examples of these products range from fiber-lit buildings and data centers meeting the exponential digital demand of data bytes, to supertall skyscrapers serving the burgeoning market for mixed-use development and billionaire capital. There has been and always will be a new building product developing on the horizon.

Moreover, there is the organizational innovation in information collection—data. Prior to the National Council of Real Estate Investment Fiduciaries (NCREIF) and the rise of CoStar and Real Capital Analytics (RCA), large-scale databases beyond the local registrar were limited. Data organizational innovations have expanded with the extension of data sources from NCREIF, CoStar, and RCA to new sources, such as Compstak, Reonomy, SHoP Envelope, etc., allowing for further exploration of market fundamentals, drivers, and disruptions. Since 2008, there has been the development of numerous data sources in the real estate and urban technology domains. The Urban Technology database at the Massachusetts Institute of Technology Real Estate Innovation Lab documents more than 1600 new technology companies servicing data or generating new platforms for technologically advancing the built environment.

4.2.3 *Extent of Innovation in Real Estate*

Fundamentally, there can be different types of innovations, and innovation theory has documented the extent of the physical and human capital change. Incremental, modular, architectural, and radical innovation are concepts used to describe the extent of innovation, which impact if and how firms are able to move across the stages of innovation for a given product, process, or organizational innovation (Abernathy and Clark 1985; Henderson and Clark 1990). Henderson and Clark (1990) document that it is not only incremental changes in production that changes a product, but also a reconfiguration of a product can lead to disruption of the existing status quo. Thus, the move from seemingly progressive changes that come in the form of incremental improvements in the building development process or modular additions to building products are seemingly harmless to one factor alone. However, it is the arrival of architectural innovations that reconfigure existing products or buildings in this case to new uses that are the most unanticipated, debated, and uncertain for other market participants. This is mainly because the core concepts that compose a product or process are reinforced, but at the same time, the way they are connected can be reconfigured in numerous ways and across many agents to make a new product or process. This linkage can lead to new permutations or new processes that may not be adopted by competitors immediately. Figure 4.2 highlights the dynamics across the stages of innovation and linkages of core concepts.

Slaughter (1998) fundamentally extended these concepts on the extent of innovation to the construction industry, but she also added an additional concept—a systems innovation. This conceptual addition allowed her to identify the assembly of a complex new product or process. In a system innovation in construction, incremental, modular, and architectural changes are being made to alter the product or process. This combination of innovations can generate a new system dynamic that cannot be easily absorbed or adopted in the marketplace. In this way, system innovations in construction can lead to dramatically different approaches to constructing buildings.

These simple concepts of stage, type, and extent of innovation can aid real estate in understanding the following: where a product or process is in its development; the human, physical and financial capital needed to produce, alter, or organize the innovation, and the extent of specialized human and physical capital required to innovate. In this way, investors and other market participants can begin to plan for innovation, track its performance, and assess how innovation moves from niche to mainstream.

4.3 Linking Innovation to Green Buildings

Green buildings are at a very distinct and important stage of their uptake and diffusion in real estate markets across the globe. Over some 40 years of research and development, invention, and innovation and

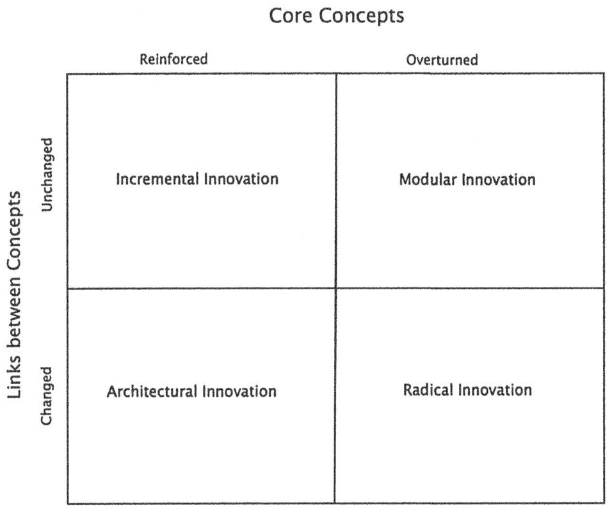

Fig. 4.2 This figure outlines the four types of innovation that can be applied to the built environment. Incremental, modular, architectural, and radical innovation types play a distinct role in how other market participants can take up building innovations

now commercial diffusion, the commercial real estate product has moved from niche to a mainstream building product.

Research and Development started in the 1970s with architects, environmentalists, and ecologists focusing efforts on energy-efficiency to combat energy shortages stemming from the OPEC oil shortages. Design intervention continued when the American Institute of Architects (AIA) formed the Committee on Energy, which focused on both passive design elements and technological solutions. Research continued on the subject through the 1970s, 1980s, and 1990s and resulted in more inventions, including solar panels, pre-fabricated modular construction of efficient wall systems, water reclamation systems, smart grid technology, day-lighting strategies, and more fuel-efficient transportation

(Murphy 2016). This led to the development of some buildings by early, first-moving developers, but due to the regulatory standards of buildings, the implementation of new technologies and design interventions not understood by building codes was a significant challenge.

The arrival of standards was critical for starting the innovation and scale process in commercial real estate. In 1990, the Building Research Establishment (BRE) published BREEAM (Building Research Establishment Environmental Assessment Method) for assessing, rating, and certifying the sustainability of buildings for the United Kingdom (Chegut et al. 2014). In the U.S., there were energy-efficiency provisions in the National Affordable Housing Act of 1990 and the Energy Policy Act of 1992 that further pushed these initiatives. In 1993, the U.S. Green Building Council (USGBC) was formed and began to put in place a rigorous framework for energy-efficient design and development. It was not until 2000, when the LEED rating system was introduced publicly. LEED is one of many standards around the globe that enable a standard approach to energy-efficiency and sustainability (see Chegut and Kok, 2011 for a review). Later, government standards were enabled in cities, such as Boston, San Francisco, Miami, and Kansas City, which began to amend building codes to include the USGBC's rating standard of LEED certification. Adoption increased, and governments around the world also moved to take initiatives towards standardization, such as Energy Performance Certificates (EPC) in the European Union.

The present day standards towards commercial diffusion at the institutional investment scale are commonplace. However, early on in the built environment, very simple aspects of the standard innovation process gave mixed signals to the market on where green buildings were in the innovation process. Today, in an open innovation platform, what commonly occurs with equipment is that the type of innovation is mixed (Tirole 1988). What is on the one hand a process innovation in design, architecture, or construction for generating a building can be simultaneously thought of as a product innovation for the real estate sector itself. As a result, there was some misunderstanding on what the commercially viable outcomes were for green buildings in the marketplace. Second, the lack of a clear distinction between a process or product innovation can potentially be explained by the extent of innovation, where green building innovation corresponds to a fundamental reconfiguration of architectural and engineering design alongside engineering system interventions that aim to decrease the use of natural resources—waste, water, energy, and materials—to construct and occupy buildings. This means that distinct coordination efforts must occur on behalf of building designers, developers, and owners, which can be complex in a system that has numerous actors. Third, without standards, there was no governing board that enabled a system of innovations or a platform to feasibly execute and diffuse what is an acceptable standard for green buildings. In this way, without recognizing the system, and to some extent standardizing it, the industry could not lower costs to enable commercial diffusion for the building sector.

4.3.1 A System Innovation for Real Estate

Green buildings themselves are a combination of incremental, modular, and architectural innovations—a so-called system innovation. Energy-efficiency has already been documented as requiring changes in the design methods (Mapp et al. 2011), contracting (Fisher and Bradshaw 2010), and materials used in the construction process (Tatari et al. 2011). Modular innovations, such as triple-glazed windows, building monitoring systems, and embodied carbon-free insulation, may have changed the material and labor processes in construction over the last decade. Moreover, even more sophisticated architectural innovations, such as photovoltaic roof coverage or window panes, may require reconfiguration of a building's system infrastructure, and in turn change material and labor needs.

Currently, research on a suite of design and system interventions across all dimensions of green buildings is limited, and this may be because the buildings themselves are a complex system reconfiguration. As a result, there is no comprehensive database of design and system interventions for green buildings. Various agencies and manufacturers of systems detail some suite of interventions, but they are limited to guides on energy-efficiency interventions (see the USGBC, EPA, and Department of Energy for some guidance).[11] Moreover, there are numerous special consultants that are engaged to try to design a system for a building itself. A literature review conducted by Murphy (2016) documents 44 distinct design and system interventions that are used to reconfigure a building or modify its construction to enable green building outcomes. These interventions were obtained from many different sources and ideals on green buildings that are inclusive of waste, water, and materials.

4.3.2 Linking Green Building Innovation to Economic Outcomes

Like in other economic sectors, the cost of switching towards cleaner production in the built environment is important for innovation, technology diffusion, and general technical change in the building sector. The realized cost for switching to cleaner production capital and technologies is unclear, but it is predicted that the switch to cleaner production is positive yet, and less costly in the long run than maintaining dirty technology (Acemoglu et al. 2012). Buildings are a dirty factor in production, representing 30% of global carbon emissions and 40% of raw materials and energy consumption (Kahn et al. 2014; Glaeser and Kahn 2010). According to a report by the U.S. Department of Energy, 40% of the total energy costs can be attributed to the building sector, which is about $400 billion each year. If the energy use in the built environment is reduced by 20%, about $80 billion annually could be saved, and the commercial building sector would account for $40 billion.[12] However, these mostly externalized costs do not necessarily lead to clear and transparent economic incentives that translate back to making changes in the design, development, and construction of buildings.

When we put the commercial building development process into context, the average commercial building cycle is 4–10 years. Construction is a temporary alliance of diverse actors, involving architects, engineers, regulators, owners, occupants, builders, suppliers, and financiers who all to a large degree contribute to the overall energy and resource consumption of buildings (Slaughter 1998). Should society desire to meet the energy consumption abatement goals laid out in the Paris Climate Agreement by 2030, there are just a few building cycles left to shift quality and decrease energy consumption in the built environment to help meet these goals.[13,14]

These design and system interventions are anecdotally linked to higher costs for developing and constructing green buildings. Prior research is limited to a handful of case studies Kats (2003), Langdon (2004) and Crawford et al. (2009) compare LEED-certified buildings with their peers and document an average cost premium of 0 to 3%. In Europe, the BRE Center for Sustainable Construction and Cyril Sweett (2005) estimate the incremental construction costs for a single BREEAM certified building at between 0.4 and 7.0%. Atkinson (2010) looks at three individual building sites that seek BREEAM Excellent,

Outstanding and Zero Carbon status in new construction. Results suggest that moving towards an Outstanding and Zero Carbon BREEAM 2008 certification costs 15.4 and 37.4% more, respectively. However, these case studies only cover a grand total of 135 certified and non-certified buildings around the world. In an empirical study, Chegut et al. (2016) document that a sample of almost 200 certified green buildings relative to a control sample of 400 non-certified buildings do not economically or statistically cost more than a conventional body of similar buildings.

Following this evidence, we can then assess the marginal benefits reported in the literature as reflected by rental and value premiums for green commercial buildings (Eichholtz et al. 2010, 2013; Miller et al. 2008; Fuerst and McAllister 2011a; Kok and Jennen 2012; Chegut et al. 2014). Table 4.1 summarizes studies that link the environmental performance of buildings to economic outcomes by study, country, transaction type, and findings. The studies show significant variation, where transaction price premiums range from 13 to 30% and rental cash flow premiums from 6.5 to 21.5%. Less is known about the determinants of the green premium found in this literature. Some argue that the source of the premium lies in capitalizing on savings in operational expenditures from the use of green buildings (Eichholtz et al. 2013), while others suggest a market disequilibrium, where a mismatch between limited green building supply and high tenant and investor demand is a possible factor driving green premiums (Chegut et al. 2014).

To date, there has been no study that has been able to follow the design and system interventions of green buildings to their stabilized adoption in the market place. However, Deng and Wu (2014) document the incremental value for a multi-family developer in the Singapore residential market, where the market premium of Green Mark-certified real estate trades for only 4% more in the pre-sale stage of development versus 10% for investors in the secondary market. This is an important gap in understanding green buildings as an innovation for the built environment. Clearly, linking the design and engineering interventions to their development and stabilized real estate market outcomes requires linking buildings across multiple agents in the building process, as well as capturing data that can provide a platform for measuring such insights.

Table 4.1 Studies on the value of energy-efficiency in the commercial real estate market

Study	*Country*	*Transaction type*	*Energy-efficiency measurement*	*Findings*	*Notes*
Kok and Jennen (2012)	The Netherlands	Rental	Energy Performance Certificates	+6.5% label category A-C compared to D-G	The rental premium for energy-efficient office space is mainly driven by offices with an EPC label of B or C
Fuerst and McAllister (2011b)	U.K.	Rental and capital values	Energy Performance Certificates	No relation	No significant effect of energy-efficiency on the rental and capital values based on a small sample of appraised values
Chegut et al. (2014)	U.K.	Sales and rental	BREEAM certification	+17% in price, +21.5% in rent for green certification	The marginal effect of BREEAM certification decreases with an increasing green building supply
Eichholtz et al. (2010)	U.S.	Sales and rental	Energy Star and LEED certification	+16.5% in price, +7.9% in rent for green certification	The rent is corrected for the occupancy level. The value of a green building is \$5.5–\$5.7 million more
Wiley et al. (2010)	U.S.	Sales and rental	Energy Star and LEED certification	+13–55% in price, +7–17% in rent for green certification	Offices with an Energy Star label rent for 7.3–8.6% more and sell for \$30 per sq. ft. more A LEED label commands a rental premium of 15.2–17.3% and transact for \$130 per sq. ft. more

(continued)

Table 4.1 (continued)

Study	*Country*	*Transaction type*	*Energy-efficiency measurement*	*Findings*	*Notes*
Fuerst and McAllister (2011a)	U.S.	Sales and rental	Energy Star and LEED certification	+30% in price, +5% in rent for green certification	Premium for LEED varies with the level of certification, and platinum-rated buildings receive the highest premium
Eichholtz et al. (2013)	U.S.	Sales and rental	Energy Star and LEED certification	+13.3% in price, +7.6% in rent for green certification	The vintage of an Energy Star label has a mitigating impact on the observed premium

4.3.3 *Limits to Commercially Diffusing Green Buildings*

Certified green office buildings represent 12.4% of the commercial building stock in the U.S., which represents 38.3% of the market in terms of square footage (Holtermans et al. 2017). Given that the literature suggests that there are sufficient value benefits for re-selling green buildings and that there are limited costs in developing these buildings, there must still be some market failures that limit the massive market uptake of green buildings.

First, there are significant split incentives across stakeholders in the development process. Overall, there is a clear disconnect between who receives the rewards for reconfiguring the buildings towards green building standards and who bears the costs. This may be one reason why the signal to invest in green building construction is not making its way back to the real estate development sector. In this way, the returns to energy-efficiency are spread across the real estate development lifecycle, where the asset managers at the end of the lifecycle are able to capitalize on the design and system interventions made at the beginning of a building's creation. Known more commonly as a split incentive problem and generally spoken of in the housing literature. The majority of real estate experiences a more extreme form of split incentives, where the disconnect is not just potentially between tenants and landlords, but between building developers (architects, planners, engineers, and developers) and building asset holders (public, private, and institutional real estate investors).

Second, the information transmission mechanism that signals to investors that this type of real estate product is sufficiently standard is lacking in the commercial real estate sector. Notably, commercial real estate markets need sufficient information to push institutional capital towards developing an asset class. The potential profit signaling mechanism that the economic literature on energy-efficiency suggests is slowed when a product remains idiosyncratic across institutional portfolios rather than systematic. Investors do not experience large-scale portfolios of certified buildings as suggested in these studies, but substantially smaller pools of them. Thus, the experience of one developer or investor may significantly vary from one another. However, this has been decreasing over time.

Finally, there may be sufficient need to subsidize early investment capital in design and system interventions for first time adopters or developers of green buildings until they have sufficiently learned how to "reconfigure" technologies to implement green buildings. However, this may also mean that there is not a sufficient amount of human capital or new technologies to supply green buildings. Slaughter (1998) documents that building development or redevelopment is a complex one-off process of a singularly-combined group of stakeholders, which makes scaling the transfer of skills across multiple building projects very complex in non-multifamily development. Importantly, commercial diffusion of innovation necessitates either a revenue or scale model of production. The complexity of commercial buildings combined with existing density of the built environment limits the scaling strategy (Acemoglu et al. 2012). In this way, learning across multiple building developments is slow. In addition, transferring human capital, technologies, and skills across organizations at the time of real estate development is limited in a framework that lacks standardization. The high degree of complexity combined with the lack of routine in commercial real estate development makes that these distinctions have significant impacts on the speed and diffusion of energy-efficient technologies that support a greener built environment.

4.4 Overcoming Diffusion Obstacles Through Capital and Standardization

The enormous potential investments in energy-efficiency projects would not only reduce the energy consumption but would also create new investment opportunities, new jobs, drive economic growth, and reduce greenhouse gas emissions (Kim et al. 2012). The commercial sector would present an important investment opportunity as it accounts for 65% of the total end-use-efficiency potential in the US. Unfortunately, certain barriers hamper the realization of these large investment opportunities. Structural and outreach problems must be addressed to stimulate investments in energy-efficiency, and one of the biggest challenges is thought to be the lack of attractive financing (Freehling 2011). However, this is not always the case as there is significant research that identifies that financing and capital are available, but there is a gap in uptake around these financing schemes as standards and regulations do not push second movers to take up these investments. In addition, there may be some issues with commercial diffusion due to the adoption and uptake of design and engineering interventions.

4.4.1 *Distributing Capital*

When conducting energy-efficiency projects, many stakeholders are involved, e.g., end-users, investors, project developers, engineers, construction companies, and utilities. The various stakeholder interests, the application of new technologies, and changing regulatory structures induce a considerable degree of complexity. The major issues of energy-efficiency projects are the following: financing the energy-efficiency improvements with little or no up-front cost to the end-user; balancing the timing mismatch between the longer lifecycle of energy-efficiency measures and the probably shorter occupancy of the property; aligning the split incentives and time horizons between the property owner and the tenant; and overcoming financial restrictions stemming from existing mortgages (Kim et al. 2012).

Innovative energy-efficiency models could overcome these issues. Possible financing sources in the commercial real estate sector are traditional bank loans, internal funding, loans backed by bonds, lease financing options, PACE financing, on-bill utility funding, ESCO/ESPC funding models, ESA financing, and MESA models. However, it is often anecdotally noted that there is not sufficient demand for the funds as investors do not seek out the assistance that is being offered by programs, subsidies, and credits.

The Energy Service Company (ESCO) model represents a successful third-party financing model that has emerged over the last several years. The Energy Savings Performance Contract (ESPC) model has dominated the ESCO energy-efficiency market. In such a structure, the ESCO is engaged in the development and implementation of the energy-efficiency measures as well as the arrangement of the financing structure of comprehensive performance-based projects. The ESCO might also monitor the energy savings' performance and provide upgrade services. The energy-efficiency improvements are owned by the customer, which might be financed using a combination of debt, leasing options, subsidies, or grants. In an ESPC model, the ESCO might guarantee certain energy savings. Usually, the energy savings are split between the ESCO and the customer during the duration of the ESPC. After the contract terminates (usually between 5 and 20 years), the savings of the customer should exceed the sum of the payments, including payments to the ESCO and financing payments (Vine 2005).

A variant of the ESCO structure is the Energy Services Agreement (ESA). In such a structure, a project developer arranges the development and installation of the energy-efficiency measures by an ESCO and coordinates the capital investments. The project developer is the owner, operator, and maintainer of the energy-efficiency implementations for the duration of the ESA. The host customer pays for the energy saved as a service and buys the equipment at the expiration of the ESA. In short, the ESA is similar to an operating lease in that it eliminates the burden from building owners to raise debt or make capital expenditures.

A similar financing mechanism is the Managed Energy Service Agreement (MESA), where a project developer owns the energy-efficiency measures and serves as an intermediary between the customer and the utility. The project developer is the single point of contact for the customer and pays a single amount for all utility expenses.

Property Assessed Clean Energy (PACE) programs are a special form of state and local financing. In this program, local governments establish an energy financing district and are, therefore, able to finance energy-efficiency measures, usually through the issuance of bonds. The repayments occur through an evaluation of the property tax bills of buildings owners who participated in a PACE program and are secured by a lien. In case of a sale or transfer, the lien remains on the property and is deferred to the next property owner.

Another financing mechanism is on-bill financing/on-bill repayment. In this structure, utility or third-party capital is used to pay for energy-efficiency measures. The central feature of this financing model is that the repayment of the cost is bundled into the customer's monthly utility bill. Further features which are mostly common to the varying programs is that the up-front costs as well as the interest rates are very low (Palmer et al. 2012).

4.4.2 *Diffusing Technology and Standards*

Physical capital innovation stems from augmenting the existing quality of a product or process, which requires an 'effort cost' incurred by the innovator who brings the product to market (Aghion and Durlauf 2005). Technology improves over time through these efforts. In turn, the quality of the product in the previous period forms the basis of learning, development, and cost for the current period (Baltagi and Griffin

1988). Over time, standards are born as organizations or 'committees' propose a market mechanism towards a process of 'standardization' (Farrell and Saloner 1985). In this way, there is a continued tension between technological progress and standards for the production of goods and services.

Developing new technologies that can push the built environment towards higher and higher standards of energy-efficiency and sustainability is never ending. The Green Building Information Gateway (GBIG) is a non-profit platform that continues to identify and support efforts that push the envelope in design and engineering interventions. Murphy (2016) identified from a review of the highest certified LEED Platinum buildings (score 80 and higher on a scale from 0 to 100) in institutional investor portfolios that there is a limited uptake of interventions outside of energy-efficiency and not to other areas of green building technology, such as waste, water, or materials interventions. Given this lack of systematic adoption across all types of interventions, it appears that "green" in many cases still means energy-efficient rather than a comprehensive scalable green strategy that can adopt a system approach. Lam and Olsen (2014) identified that innovating in the design process as well as a culture of innovation are missing in diffusing commercially viable green building design interventions. There is a significant time and discipline separation between design and system interventions and construction, but these factors are not coordinated or discussed between the different agents in the development, construction, and asset markets (Lutzenhiser 1994; Xue et al. 2014).

Lam and Olsen (2014) identify several technologies to incorporate in a buildings' design: triple-glazed windows, low emissivity, window frames, exterior shades, radiant panel systems, structurally integrated radian slab systems, and geothermal systems. Importantly, these technologies are rarely applied, and it is unclear whether they are cost prohibitive or lacking in general knowledge across the design phase of a building.

However, they also point out that innovating in the design process is another facet missing in developing high-performance buildings. There are coordination failures in linking designers, contractors, and engineers to create spaces that are high performing and desirable, but also the link to economic outcomes is missing. Moreover, the human capital as well as assembly of each highly skilled team to build consistently at this level requires effort or cost. Building development or redevelopment is a complex one-off process of a singularly combined group of stakeholders

(Slaughter 1998). In this way, learning across multiple building developments is slow. In addition, transferring human capital, technologies, and skills across organizations at the time of real estate development is limited in such a framework lacking standardization.

Consequently, a significant obstacle in the scalable deployment of green buildings in the built environment is measurement and standardization. Progressive standards that are able to link design and engineering interventions to social and economic outcomes are the continued market failure of the built environment. In many instances, the baseline assessment of what building energy use is in the first place is unknown. Let alone allowing for consumer and regulatory demands to demand disclosure and improvements. However, regulatory policies are nudging decision makers to get the measurement implemented so energy consumption can get efficient. This is an important stage in overcoming the technology challenges. Moreover, it is an important moment to be able to link rewards for invention, such as citations and licensing fees on patents, back to the designers and engineers that transform the buildings to be more sustainable (Popp 2002; Popp et al. 2013).

However, more challenging still is limited acknowledgement from national policies and standards. Energy building codes are popping up across cities throughout the US and Europe, where developers that previously considered green buildings too far afield are now rethinking it as a baseline technology. This is an important shift in the domestic and international push towards a less costly built environment. However, the rise and development of large-scale private sector labels have motivated progress more so in the commercial and institutional real estate sector similar to that of the health and safety standards of the twentieth century. With the rise of programs, such as BRE, LEED, Energy Star, and Green Star, the built environment has seen progress in normalizing what was once a niche idea by designers to important economic tools to enable efficient management of real estate.

4.5 Green Buildings as an Innovation Platform for the Built Environment

There is much to learn from the innovation cycle of green buildings. The innovation process for green buildings is well underway. Over the last 40 years, green buildings have moved from a niche to a mainstay of the building industry. Green buildings were developed to meet a genuine need to make the built environment more efficient, but this, such as many other innovations, turned into a complex systemic innovation that has transformed the building sector for generations to come. However, these buildings have demonstrated that there is an economically significant payback to investors and society for switching to cleaner production techniques for the built environment.

Although there remain significant obstacles to adopting any innovation in the built environment, the transformation that buildings have undergone to become more environmentally friendly is substantial, with economically significant outcomes for the industry. Going forward, the real estate sector will need to address areas that have a significant impact on the uptake of green buildings.

Namely, the gap is in the economical and social incentives faced by the developers of the design and engineering interventions and the asset owners that realize the financial gains of the building. This divide is important as it points to a significant gap in human capital, inter-disciplinary coordination, and time to diffusing technologies. Architects and engineers generate the fundamental changes in design and creation of new technologies that enable buildings to move towards lower energy consumption. The construction sector and the developer are empowered with the task of implementing these innovations. Thus, the immediate distinction of four stakeholders that are required to implement the innovation makes the diffusion of the product challenging.

In addition, the incentives to innovate from a financial perspective are not necessarily linked back to the innovators themselves, which inhibit the research and development sector which designs the buildings and technologies that enable green buildings. Research has documented that energy-efficiency and sustainability receive significant rental and transaction price premiums in the institutional commercial real estate sector. Thus, it seems that there is a signal from the capital market that energy-efficiency is a positive capital budgeting decision. However, the diffusion of green buildings remains limited. This may point to value drivers not returning to the building innovators, but to the last movers in the supply chain of building development. There has been limited research to document widespread premiums in design or systems that reduce energy consumption. Ultimately, innovators respond to incentives in energy-efficiency.

Finally, there is limited ability to achieve returns to scale from energy-efficiency. Buildings are a bundle of complex compilations of design and engineering interventions. These interventions are generally not made and scaled across more than five to ten buildings at a time, which make the uptake, scale, and diffusion of buildings a difficult process. The development and deployment of standards have enabled the built environment to make a significant progress in assisting in the commercial diffusion of green buildings. However, more work needs to be done to link design and engineering interventions back to their economic and social outcomes.

Combined, these obstacles can have significant impacts on the speed and diffusion of energy-efficient technologies that support a greener built environment, as well as the reduction of carbon emissions from the built environment. In the long run, this could be economically and environmentally more costly for society to not resolve these issues for green buildings. However, there is another reason why this is problematic in the long run: many innovative building products, processes, and technologies face a similar change. Thus, the built environment as a whole may be lagging in technological progress, because, as an industry, it struggles to find meaningful solutions to advance innovation for the betterment of the built environment.

Notes

1. Schumpeter (1942) established profit incentives from innovation. However, the theory was expanded by Tirole (1988) and laid out distinctively by Aghion and Griffith (2005).
2. Retrieved from: US Green Building Council, web source: http://www.usgbc.org/articles/green-building-facts.
3. Net Zero Energy Coalition cites at least 3399 multi-family buildings, but there is limited knowledge on the absolute number of office, retail or hotel structures.
4. The earliest papers on energy-efficiency in the built environment started in the 1970s with the global oil shortages, which led to significant research in understanding the energy consumption of the built environment.
5. McGraw Hill Construction. 2013. World Green Building Trends.
6. Retrieved from: Green Building Information Gateway, web source: http://www.gbig.org/places/935.

7. Retrieved from: http://www.bea.gov/industry/gdpbyind_data.htm. Representing mean figures over the 2003–2013 period.
8. http://www.bls.gov/news.release/pdf/ggqcew.pdf, accessed June 25, 2014. McGraw-Hill indicates a higher number of green jobs as of 2011, approximately 611,000. However, this includes designers, engineers and architects. http://www.carpetrecovery.org/pdf/annual_conference/2012_conference_pdfs/Presentations/USGreenMarketTrends.pdf, accessed June 14, 2013.
9. They vary even further by the extent of innovation—incremental, modular, architectural and radical. These distinctions have proven significant for who can capture value within an innovation system (Henderson and Clark 1990). This can be important for real estate such as in the example of data centers, indoor vertical food farms, micro-units, etc.
10. https://www.engadget.com/2014/04/17/SRI-microbots/, accessed March 21, 2015.
11. USGBC: http://www.usgbc.org/education-at-usgbc, August 21, 2016; Energy Performance Administration: https://www.epa.gov/energy, August 21, 2016; and the Department of Energy: http://energy.gov/science-innovation.
12. http://www.Energy.gov, accessed August 21, 2016.
13. https://ec.europa.eu/clima/policies/international/negotiations/paris/index_en.htm, accessed August 21, 2016.
14. Retrieved from: Selkowitz, S. (2014)."Technology and Design Comments on White Papers." 2014 MITEI Associate Member Symposium. May 12, 2014. (Selkowitz 2014)

References

Abernathy, William, and Kim Clark. 1985. Innovation: Mapping the Winds of Creative Destruction. *Research Policy* 14 (1): 3–22.

Acemoglu, Daron, Philippe Aghion, Leonardo Bursztyn, and David Hemous. 2012. The Environment and Directed Technical Change. *American Economic Review* 102 (1): 131–166.

Aghion, Philippe, and Rachel Griffith. 2005. Competition and Growth: Reconciling Theory and Evidence. *Zeuthen Lectures*. Cambridge: MIT Press.

Aghion, Philippe, and Steven Durlauf (eds.). 2005. *Handbook of Economic Growth*, 1. Amsterdam: Elsevier.

Atkinson, Jon. 2010. Capital Cost Sustainable Offices. Discussion paper, Halcrow Yolles, Southwest of England Regional Development Agency, Davis Langdon LLP and Cyril Sweett.

Baltagi, Badi, and James Griffin. 1988. A General Index of Technical Change. *The Journal of Political Economy* 96 (1): 20–41.

BRE Center for Sustainable Construction and Cyril Sweett. 2005. Putting a Price on Sustainability. BRE, United Kingdom.

Chegut, Andrea, and Nils Kok. 2011. A Global Perspective on "Green" Value in Commercial Property. in *Sustainable Investment in Real Estate*, ed. By P. McNamara, chap. 2, pp. 21–30. PEI, Sycamore Street London EC1Y 0SG United Kingdom.

Chegut, Andrea, Piet Eichholtz, and Nils Kok. 2014. Supply, Demand and the Value of Green Buildings. *Urban Studies* 51 (1): 22–43.

Chegut, Andrea, Piet Eichholtz, and Nils Kok. 2016. The Price of Innovation: The Marginal Cost of Green Buildings. Working Paper MIT Center for Real Estate, No. 5.

Crawford, Jennifer, Melanie Dubin, Susan Kaplan, Penny Knops, Richard Leigh, Lisa Fay Matthiessen, Jeff Rios, Michael Rudin, Alexis Sparko, and Russel Unger. 2009. Cost of Green in NYC. Discussion paper, Urban Green and U.S. Green Building Council, http://blog.urbangreencouncil.org/wp-content/uploads/2012/03/Cost_Study_Full_Download.pdf?_ga=2.125974029.1479647362.1504023358-1379112811.1504023358.

Deng, Yongheng, and Jing Wu. 2014. Economic Returns to Residential Green Building Investment: The Developers' Perspective. *Regional Science and Urban Economics* 47: 35–44.

Eichholtz, Piet, Nils Kok, and John Quigley. 2010. Doing Well by Doing Good: Green Office Buildings. *American Economic Review* 100 (5): 2492–2509.

Eichholtz, Piet, Nils Kok, and John Quigley. 2013. The Economics of Green Building. *Review of Economics and Statistics* 95 (1): 50–63.

Farrell, Joseph, and Garth Saloner. 1985. Standardization, Compatibility, and Innovation. *The RAND Journal of Economics* 16 (1): 70–83.

Fisher, Lynn, and Will Bradshaw. 2010. Green Building and the Organization of Development. *46th Annual AREUEA Conference Paper.*

Freehling, Joel, 2011. Energy Efficiency Finance 101: Understanding the Marketplace. *American Council for an Energy-Efficient Economy.*

Fuerst, Franz, and Patrick McAllister. 2011a. Green Noise or Green Value? Measuring the Effects of Environmental Certification on Office Values. *Real Estate Economics* 39 (1): 45–69.

Fuerst, Franz, and Patrick McAllister. 2011b. The Impact of Energy Performance Certificates on the Rental and Capital Values of Commercial Property Assets. Energy Policy 39 (10): 6608–6614.

Glaeser, Edward, and Matthew Kahn. 2010. The Greenness of Cities: Carbon Dioxide Emissions and Urban Development. *Journal of Urban Economics* 67 (3): 404–418.

Henderson, Rebecca, and Kim Clark. 1990. Architectural Innovation: The Reconfiguration of Existing Product Technologies and the Failure of Established Firms. *Administrative Science Quarterly* 35 (1): 9–30.

Holtermans, Rogier, Nils Kok, and Dave Pogue. 2017. *National Green Building Adoption Index*. CBRE. http://www.cbre.com/rgrc.

Kahn, Matthew, Nils Kok, and John Quigley. 2014. Carbon Emissions from the Commercial Building Sector: The Role of Climate, Quality, and Incentives. *Journal of Public Economics* 113: 1–12.

Kats, Greg. 2003. The Costs and Financial Benefits of Green Buildings. Discussion paper, A Report To California's Sustainable Building Task Force, http://evanmills.lbl.gov/pubs/pdf/green_buildings.pdf.

Kim, Charlotte, Robert O'Connor, Kendall Bodden, Sara Hochman, Wendra Liang, Sheridan Pauker, and Scott Zimmermann. 2012. *Innovations and Opportunities in Energy Efficiency Finance*. Palo Alto: Wilson Sonsini Goodrich & Rosati. Retrieved from http://www.wsgr.com/publications/PDFSearch/WSGR-EE-Finance-White-Paper.pdf.

Kok, Nils, and Maarten Jennen. 2012. The Impact of Energy Labels and Accessibility on Office Rents. *Energy Policy* 46: 489–497.

Lam, Linda, and Erik Olsen. 2014. Technology, Design, Culture: Interconnected Ingredients for Moving Beyond Best Practice in Commercial Buildings. *MIT Energy Initiative—Associate Member Symposium*.

Langdon, Davis. 2004. Costing Green: A Comprehensive Cost Database and Budgeting Methodology. Lisa Fay Matthiesen and Peter Morris. July.

Lutzenhiser, Loren. 1994. Innovation and Organizational Networks Barriers to Energy Efficiency in the US Housing Industry. *Energy Policy* 22 (10): 867–876.

Mapp, Chad, Mary Ellen Nobe, and Brian Dunbar. 2011. The Cost of LEED—An Analysis of the Construction Costs of LEED and Non-LEED Banks. *Journal of Sustainable Real Estate* 3 (1): 254–273.

Miller, Norm, Jay Spivey, and Andrew Florance. 2008. Does Green Pay Off? *Journal of Real Estate Portfolio Management* 14 (4): 385–400.

Murphy, Kevin. 2016. Sustainable and Energy-Efficient Development Interventions and their Application toward Net-Zero or Net-Positive Energy and Water Building Development. *Massachusetts Institute of Technology*.

Palmer, Karen, Margaret Walls, and Todd Gerarden. 2012. Borrowing to Save Energy: An Assessment of Energy-Efficiency Financing Programs. *Resources for the Future Report*.

Popp, David. 2002. Induced Innovation and Energy Prices. *The American Economic Review* 92 (1): 160–180.

Popp, David, Nidhi Santen, Karen Fisher-Vanden, and Mort Webster. 2013. Technology Variation vs. R&D Uncertainty: What Matters Most for Energy Patent Success? *Resource and Energy Economics* 35 (4): 505–533.

Schumpeter, Joseph. 1942. *Creative Destruction. Capitalism, Socialism and Democracy, 825.*

Selkowitz, S. 2014. Technology and Design Comments on White Papers. 2014 MITEI Associate Member Symposium, May 12.

Slaughter, Sarah. 1993. Builders as Sources of Construction Innovation. *Journal of Construction Engineering and Management* 119 (3): 532–549.

Slaughter, Sarah. 1998. Models of Construction Innovation. *Journal of Construction Engineering and Management* 124 (3): 226–231.

Tatari, Omer, and Murat Kucukvar. 2011. Cost Premium Prediction of Certified Green Buildings: A Neural Network Approach. *Building and Environment* 46 (5): 1081–1086.

Tirole, Jean. 1988. The Theory of Industrial Organization. MIT Press, Cambridge

Vine, Edward. 2005. An International Survey of the Energy Service Company (ESCO) Industry. *Energy Policy* 33 (5): 691–704.

Wiley, Jonathan A., Justin D. Benefield, and Ken H. Johnson. 2010. Green Design and the Market for Commercial Office Space. *Journal of Real Estate Finance and Economics* 41 (2): 228–243.

Xue, Peng, C.M. Mak, and H.D. Cheung. 2014. The Effects of Daylighting and Human Behavior on Luminous Comfort in Residential Buildings: A Questionnaire Survey. *Building and Environment* 81: 51–59.

Authors' Biography

Dr. Andrea Chegut is a Research Scientist and Director of the MIT Real Estate Innovation Lab, which is an inter-disciplinary research group that identifies the frontier in built environment products, processes and technologies and their economic impact. Andrea is also a Co-Founder and the Head of Research for DesignX, an entrepreneurial accelerator for new student and faculty ventures from MIT's School of Architecture and Planning that focuses on design, cities and the built environment.

Dr. Rogier Holtermans is a Postdoctoral Research Associate at the USC Lusk Center for Real Estate. Rogier's research interests include the financial implications of information asymmetry and sustainability in real estate markets. Specific research topics include: the value of environmental certification in commercial real estate, the economic effects of owner distance, and the added value of commercial real estate brokerage.

Isabel Tausendschon, MSc. is a PhD Candidate at the University of Graz, Austria. Her research focuses on the impact of innovation districts, incubators and accelerator real estate space activities on small and medium enterprise firm performance. Isabel holds a Bachelor's degree in Business Administration and a Master's degree in Finance from Maastricht University. Before starting her PhD she worked as a risk manager in Vienna, Austria.

CHAPTER 5

The Political Economy of Energy Efficiency

David M. Harrison

5.1 Introduction: The Political Economy of Energy Efficiency

The past two decades have witnessed unprecedented attention paid to issues involving sustainability and energy-efficient design within the real estate industry. From the proliferation of eco-friendly building certification programs, to innovations in building design and construction techniques, "Green" real estate initiatives have emerged from a minor topic of concern primarily to policy wonks and industry visionaries to assume a position of relevance within the broader commercial development industry. This emergence has also been accompanied by both an expanding political awareness and consciousness of the potential long-run implications of environmental development and housing policy decisions and a concomitant rise in both academic and industry-driven research into the potential costs, benefits, and viability of an expanding array of policy initiatives. While general agreement abounds that increased environmental

The original version of this chapter was revised: For detailed information please see Erratum. The erratum to this chapter is available at https://doi.org/10.1057/978-1-137-57446-6_11

D.M. Harrison (✉)
University of Central Florida, Orlando, USA
e-mail: david.harrison2@ucf.edu

N.E. Coulson et al. (eds.), *Energy Efficiency and the Future of Real Estate*, DOI 10.1057/978-1-137-57446-6_5

quality and awareness are laudable goals, considerably more disagreement exists with respect to the appropriate manner in which to arrive at these desired outcomes. This chapter introduces the reader to some of the key environmental policy issues and debates confronting the real estate development industry today in the United States. We first provide broad-based evidence on the economic impact of political orientation on energy policy outcomes, and then examine broader challenges to real estate markets arising from these divergent worldviews.

5.1.1 A Politically Divided Nation

The American political landscape today is deeply divided along rigid ideological lines. Such differences of opinion are not new; however, what is unique about the modern political reality is the virtually even support of the two major political parties. To illustrate, consider that the Republican and Democratic Party nominees each won twice in the first four contested Presidential elections in the U.S. since the turn of the twenty-first century. Further evidencing this even divide, across each of these four elections, is that the losing party candidate won at least 20 different states (and/or the District of Columbia) (Table 5.1).

While these numbers in the aggregate would suggest an evenly divided country, they mask a further political reality related to the geographic clustering of ideologically like-minded voters. Of note, using the traditional red state/blue state dichotomy to separate and identify Republican/conservative leaning jurisdictions from Democratic/liberal-progressive regions, respectively, very few true swing ("purple") states are found at the national level. More specifically, across these

Table 5.1 Results of U.S. presidential election results since 2000

Year—Winner	*Republican nominee*	*States won (vote %)*	*Democratic nominee*	*States won (vote %)*
2012—Barack Obama	Mitt Romney	24 (47.2)	Barack Obama	27 (51.1)
2008—Barack Obama	John McCain	22 (45.7)	Barack Obama	29 (52.9)
2004—George W. Bush	George W. Bush	31 (50.7)	John Kerry	20 (48.3)
2000—George W. Bush	George W. Bush	30 (47.9)	Al Gore	21 (48.4)

Source U.S. Federal Election Commission

aforementioned four elections, only five states (Colorado, Florida, Nevada, Ohio, and Virginia) cast a plurality of their popular votes for the national winner every time, while 41 states cast a plurality of their popular votes for the same political party each cycle. Nineteen states, including large portions of New England and the Northeast, the Upper Mid-west, and the West Coast, went Democratic in all four elections. Twenty-two states, including most of the South, the Farm Belt, and the Mountain West, consistently voted for Republican candidates each election cycle. As will be outlined in more detail below, these strong and robust patterns of geographic clustering in political ideology evidence stark divisions which may manifest themselves in tangible policy differences of significant importance to real estate professionals (Table 5.2).

5.2 Political Orientation and Energy Market Outcomes

One key area where political orientation informs key policy outcomes of interest to real estate market participants is energy. While both sides vociferously argue for and defend their desired policies, these debates often lack a broad recognition of the trade-offs and potential unintended consequences of governmental mandates, regulation, and intervention, or conversely, the lack thereof. For example, consider the following case of renewable energy production.

5.2.1 Renewable Energy Production

In recent elections, Democratic and liberal/progressive candidates have tended to emphasize and prioritize policy initiatives designed to foster increased production and reliance upon renewable energy sources such as solar, hydro, wind, geothermal, and/or biomass. Touting the perceived environmental superiority of these energy sources over more traditional fossil fuels, many political candidates, particularly those in politically progressive jurisdictions, have called for a "green energy revolution" to reimagine the way we power American enterprise. Given that residential and commercial buildings account for an estimated 30–40% of both energy consumption and carbon dioxide emissions (e.g., Choi 2009; Goering 2009; Egging 2013; Estiri 2016), such a transformation would materially alter the nature of the real estate profession as we know it today. As shown in Tables 5.3 and 5.4, the early evidence suggests that political ideology is beginning to have meaningful impacts along this dimension.

Table 5.2 State-by-state political orientation and presidential election results since 2000 (# of times state was carried by each party's nominee)

State	*Political orientation*	*State*	*Political orientation*
Alabama	Red—($R = 4$; $D = 0$)	Montana	Red—($R = 4$; $D = 0$)
Alaska	Red—($R = 4$; $D = 0$)	Nebraska	Red—($R = 4$; $D = 0$)
Arizona	Red—($R = 4$; $D = 0$)	Nevada	Purple—($R = 2$; $D = 2$)
Arkansas	Red—($R = 4$; $D = 0$)	New Hampshire	Purple—($R = 1$; $D = 3$)
California	Blue—($R = 0$; $D = 4$)	New Jersey	Blue—($R = 0$; $D = 4$)
Colorado	Purple—($R = 2$; $D = 2$)	New Mexico	Purple—($R = 1$; $D = 3$)
Connecticut	Blue—($R = 0$; $D = 4$)	New York	Blue—($R = 0$; $D = 4$)
Delaware	Blue—($R = 0$; $D = 4$)	North Carolina	Purple—($R = 3$; $D = 1$)
District of Columbia	Blue—($R = 0$; $D = 4$)	North Dakota	Red—($R = 4$; $D = 0$)
Florida	Purple—($R = 2$; $D = 2$)	Ohio	Purple—($R = 2$; $D = 2$)
Georgia	Red—($R = 4$; $D = 0$)	Oklahoma	Red—($R = 4$; $D = 0$)
Hawaii	Blue—($R = 0$; $D = 4$)	Oregon	Blue—($R = 0$; $D = 4$)
Idaho	Red—($R = 4$; $D = 0$)	Pennsylvania	Blue—($R = 0$; $D = 4$)
Illinois	Blue—($R = 0$; $D = 4$)	Rhode Island	Blue—($R = 0$; $D = 4$)
Indiana	Purple—($R = 3$; $D = 1$)	South Carolina	Red—($R = 4$; $D = 0$)
Iowa	Purple—($R = 1$; $D = 3$)	South Dakota	Red—($R = 4$; $D = 0$)
Kansas	Red—($R = 4$; $D = 0$)	Tennessee	Red—($R = 4$; $D = 0$)
Kentucky	Red—($R = 4$; $D = 0$)	Texas	Red—($R = 4$; $D = 0$)
Louisiana	Red—($R = 4$; $D = 0$)	Utah	Red—($R = 4$; $D = 0$)
Maine	Blue—($R = 0$; $D = 4$)	Vermont	Blue—($R = 0$; $D = 4$)
Maryland	Blue—($R = 0$; $D = 4$)	Virginia	Purple—($R = 2$; $D = 2$)
Massachusetts	Blue—($R = 0$; $D = 4$)	Washington	Blue—($R = 0$; $D = 4$)
Michigan	Blue—($R = 0$; $D = 4$)	West Virginia	Red—($R = 4$; $D = 0$)
Minnesota	Blue—($R = 0$; $D = 4$)	Wisconsin	Blue—($R = 0$; $D = 4$)
Mississippi	Red—($R = 4$; $D = 0$)	Wyoming	Red—($R = 4$; $D = 0$)
Missouri	Red—($R = 4$; $D = 0$)	U.S. Total	Purple—($R = 2$; $D = 2$)

Source U.S. Federal Election Commission

Table 5.3 presents the share of each state's total energy production attributable to renewable sources. In addition, Table 5.4 highlights both those states with the highest and lowest renewable energy production

Table 5.3 Renewable energy as % of total energy production (by state)

State	*% Renewable*	*State*	*% Renewable*
Alabama	16.1	Montana	10.8
Alaska	0.8	Nebraska	61.1
Arizona	15.5	Nevada	94.7
Arkansas	12.0	New Hampshire	30.2
California	24.4	New Jersey	5.9
Colorado	3.1	New Mexico	1.4
Connecticut	13.0	New York	44.8
Delaware	100.0	North Carolina	25.7
District of Columbia	100.0	North Dakota	8.1
Florida	41.0	Ohio	9.2
Georgia	36.4	Oklahoma	3.0
Hawaii	100.0	Oregon	99.8
Idaho	100.0	Pennsylvania	4.4
Illinois	11.5	Rhode Island	100.0
Indiana	15.8	South Carolina	16.0
Iowa	91.7	South Dakota	93.9
Kansas	11.2	Tennessee	35.2
Kentucky	2.4	Texas	2.6
Louisiana	1.5	Utah	1.5
Maine	100.0	Vermont	32.1
Maryland	17.1	Virginia	10.5
Massachusetts	42.7	Washington	92.3
Michigan	25.0	West Virginia	1.0
Minnesota	66.5	Wisconsin	57.5
Mississippi	11.7	Wyoming	0.3
Missouri	42.3	U.S. Average	36.1

Source U.S. Energy Information Administration (EIA)

shares and their corresponding political ideology leanings. Examining the results across these two tables, we find that renewable sources account for more than one-third (36.1%) of total U.S. energy production, with significantly larger shares across many sections of the United States. Interestingly, when these production shares are segmented along ideological lines, we find that "Blue" states are characterized by significantly higher renewable energy production shares. More specifically, across those 19 states that have voted Democratic in the past four election cycles, renewable energy accounts for more than half (54.6%) of their production. On the other hand, similar production shares for those "Red" states which have voted Republican across these same four

Table 5.4 Political orientation and renewable energy production Leaders and Laggards

Leaders			*Laggards*		
State	*Percent*	*Orientation*	*State*	*Percent*	*Orientation*
Delaware	100.0	Blue	Colorado	3.1	Purple
District of Columbia	100.0	Blue	Oklahoma	3.0	Red
Hawaii	100.0	Blue	Texas	2.6	Red
Idaho	100.0	Red	Kentucky	2.4	Red
Maine	100.0	Blue	Utah	1.5	Red
Rhode Island	100.0	Blue	Louisiana	1.5	Red
Oregon	99.8	Blue	New Mexico	1.4	Purple
Nevada	94.7	Purple	West Virginia	1.0	Red
South Dakota	93.9	Red	Alaska	0.8	Red
Washington	92.3	Blue	Wyoming	0.3	Red
Blue state average	54.6				
Purple state average	32.3		Blue state edge		32.6%
Red state average	22.0				

Difference of Proportions Test
t = 3.10
(Prob. = 0.0036)

elections are only 22%—a production gap of over 30 percentage points. These differences are both statistically significant (at the 99% confidence level in a difference of proportion test) and economically meaningful. Further evidencing this political divide, of the ten states with the highest proportion of renewable energy production, only two (Idaho and South Dakota) exhibit conservative political ideologies, while conversely, on the lagging end of the scale, no "Blue" state appears on the list. Clearly, the evidence suggests that political ideology is highly correlated with energy policy and production.

5.2.2 *Energy Costs for Consumers*

On the other hand, as most independent and rational policy observers correctly note, policy decisions typically involve costly trade-offs. One such trade-off frequently cited by conservative politicians and green energy opponents is the potential for employment loss related to higher costs engendered by alternative energy sources. Given the

Table 5.5 Residential electric costs per kilowatt hour (by state)

State	*¢/kWh*	*State*	*¢/kWh*
Alabama	12.08	Montana	11.60
Alaska	21.42	Nebraska	12.11
Arizona	12.70	Nevada	10.72
Arkansas	10.28	New Hampshire	18.00
California	18.49	New Jersey	16.15
Colorado	12.43	New Mexico	12.51
Connecticut	19.78	New York	17.95
Delaware	12.99	North Carolina	11.19
District of Columbia	12.30	North Dakota	11.26
Florida	11.18	Ohio	12.25
Georgia	12.29	Oklahoma	9.99
Hawaii	28.04	Oregon	10.79
Idaho	10.81	Pennsylvania	13.76
Illinois	12.06	Rhode Island	17.11
Indiana	11.27	South Carolina	12.58
Iowa	14.07	South Dakota	12.19
Kansas	13.06	Tennessee	10.45
Kentucky	10.28	Texas	10.86
Louisiana	9.06	Utah	11.72
Maine	15.87	Vermont	17.29
Maryland	14.05	Virginia	11.71
Massachusetts	18.19	Washington	9.60
Michigan	15.39	West Virginia	11.19
Minnesota	13.20	Wisconsin	14.55
Mississippi	10.21	Wyoming	11.88
Missouri	12.28	U.S. Average	12.68

Source U.S. Energy Information Administration (EIA), July 2016

marked differences in renewable energy production across state political ideology, an obvious next question is whether such production differences are associated with average energy costs within those jurisdictions. Tables 5.5 and 5.6 are designed to shed light on this question.

Table 5.5 presents the average cost of residential electricity per kilowatt hour (kWh) by state, while Table 5.6 highlights both those states with the most and least affordable residential electricity and their corresponding political ideology leanings. Examining the results across these two tables, we note that residential electric rates in the U.S., as of July 2016, averaged 12.68 cents per kWh. Rates across the continental U.S. ranged from 9.06 cents per kWh in Louisiana to more than double that

Table 5.6 Political orientation and state energy prices Leaders versus Laggards

Leaders			*Laggards*		
State	*¢/kWh*	*Orientation*	*State*	*¢/kWh*	*Orientation*
Louisiana	9.06	Red	New Jersey	16.15	Blue
Washington	9.60	Blue	Rhode Island	17.11	Blue
Oklahoma	9.99	Red	Vermont	17.29	Blue
Mississippi	10.21	Red	New York	17.95	Blue
Arkansas	10.28	Red	New Hampshire	18.00	Purple
Kentucky	10.28	Red	Massachusetts	18.19	Blue
Tennessee	10.45	Red	California	18.49	Blue
Nevada	10.72	Purple	Connecticut	19.78	Blue
Oregon	10.79	Blue	Alaska	21.42	Red
Idaho	10.81	Red	Hawaii	28.04	Blue
Blue state average	15.66				
Purple state average	12.53		Blue state surcharge		32.4%
Red state average	11.83				

Difference of Means Test
t = 3.73
(Prob. = 0.0006)

level, 19.78 cents per kWh, in Connecticut. Not surprisingly, rates in both Alaska (21.42 cents/kWh) and Hawaii (28.04 cents/kWh) exceed those of any of their continental peers. Once again, comparing energy market outcomes segmented along ideological lines, we find that "Blue" states are characterized by significantly higher residential electricity rates than their "Red" state peers. More specifically, across those 19 "Blue" states that have voted Democratic in the past four election cycles, average residential electricity rates averaged 15.66 cents/kWh. Comparable Republican or "Red" state residential electricity rates averaged only 11.83 cents/kWh—a statistically significant (at the 99% confidence level) cost/price premium of over 30% for "Blue" state consumers.

As with production rates, further evidence of the impact of political ideology and policy on electric rates may be gleaned from examining states which are high- and low-cost providers of energy.

Throughout much of the U.S. today, electric utilities continue to operate as regulated monopolies or face oligopolistic competition for the provision of their goods. As such, consumer costs provide an instructive lens through which to view the economic costs of many policy initiatives within this industry. Not surprisingly, in a near complete reversal from the analysis of political ideology and renewable energy production shown earlier, those ten states leading the way on cost efficiency with the lowest reported average residential electricity cost per kilowatt hour include seven "Red" states and only two "Blue" states (with the toss-up or "Purple" state of Nevada rounding out the list). Conversely, the list of the ten high cost providers is populated with eight "Blue" states, the "Purple" toss-up state of Nevada, and only the aforementioned special case of Alaska representing a high cost "Red" state residential energy provider. Once again, the evidence clearly supports the notion that political ideology is highly correlated with energy market outcomes, and a combined reading of the renewable production and residential electric cost results suggests that energy policy decisions do indeed involve costly economic trade-offs rather than simply the identification of dominant policy outcomes as one might find in a game theoretic approach to this issue.

5.3 Energy Efficiency, Political Economy, and the Real Estate Market

The notion that political ideology may materially influence real estate market outcomes is not new. Within a general finance context, numerous authors have found evidence suggesting direct correlations between political cycles, corporate campaign contributions, and stock returns both domestically and abroad (e.g., Huang 1985; Foerster and Schmitz 1997; Santa-Clara and Valkanov 2003; Cooper et al. 2010; Belo et al. 2013). More directly applicable within a real estate context, Ramchander et al. (2009) examine 35 years of U.S. REIT returns and find an array of complex inter-relations. In particular, they find stronger political cycle return relations when: (1) the Federal Reserve pursues an expansionary monetary policy under Republican administrations; (2) during the final 2 years of a President's term as society prepares to select a new leader and chart a new course or direction for the future; and (3) when the executive and legislative branches of government are controlled by the same political party (i.e., unity), thus increasing the ability of politically motivated actors and legislators to enact meaningful, substantive change.

Building upon these foundations, Harrison and Seiler (2011b) investigate potential political ideology effects on real estate market valuations at a more micro level. Specifically, they investigate whether rental rate premiums accruing to environmentally certified (LEED and/or EnergyStar) office buildings vary along with the political ideology of the local market area in which the structure is located. After presenting evidence that both grant programs and property tax incentives providing economic support for "green" building projects are significantly more prevalent in "Blue" counties than in their "Red" counterparts, they document robust green lease premiums across the nation. Interestingly, these lease rate premiums also vary systematically along political ideology lines, with green premiums of nearly 6% accruing to certified office buildings in politically Democratic/liberal areas, while premiums of less than 2% prevail in more politically conservative/Republican locations.

Taking this analytical framework one step further, Harrison and Seiler (2011a) replicate their core analysis on a sample of industrial warehouse facilities—a property type unlikely to benefit from direct customer interaction and, therefore, of potentially less importance from an environmental "branding" perspective. On the other hand, given the high intensity of use at such facilities, energy-efficiency issues may be uniquely important from a cost perspective. As with their previous findings on office buildings, their evidence suggests that industrial warehouses in politically liberal areas are approximately 2.5 times more likely to be LEED and/or EnergyStar certified. Furthermore, while substantial (approximately 8%) lease rate premiums are found for certified warehouse facilities in "Blue" counties, certified warehouses actually exhibit discounted lease rates in politically conservative "Red" areas. Taken together, these results strongly suggest that political ideology is a material and value-relevant component of the commercial real estate market place.

5.4 Key Policy Implications, Framework Design, and Ongoing Challenges

Against this backdrop, policymakers must continue to evaluate and implement policy solutions which are desired by, or at least acceptable to, their key constituents. At the same time, businesses and other real estate market participants must flexibly and forcibly respond to any changes in their regulatory and/or operating environment. In this final section of the chapter, we discuss those key environmental and energy policy issues that are likely to shape the continuing development of real property markets into the near future.

5.4.1 The International Experience

While much of the preceding discussion centered on U.S. results, these issues have broader economic implications throughout both the developed and developing world. Of note, increased environmental awareness has led to a proliferation of alternative green energy and building certification programs around the world. While most of these program certifications are available globally, firms tend to focus on certification programs developed and popularized in their domestic markets. These programs include the well-publicized Leadership in Energy and Environmental Design (LEED), EnergyStar, and Pearl certification programs in the U.S., Building Research Establishment Environmental Assessment Method (BREEAM) certification in the U.K., European Union Energy Performance Certificates across continental Europe, Greenstar certification in Australia, and the Green Pyramid rating system in Egypt (Abdel Aleem et al. 2015). Similar to the Harrison and Seiler (2011a, b) results outlined above, Brounen and Kok (2011) provide international evidence that political ideology matters by demonstrating that the adoption of Energy Participation Certificates (EPCs) in Holland is directly related to both public sentiment regarding green initiatives and the "Green" party vote share in recent elections. To the extent the adoption of environmentally friendly, energy-efficient building design and construction processes are driven by ideological values rather than inherent cost savings or productivity advantages, the economic viability and sustainability of such reforms is dramatically weakened. While political pressure may effectively force private enterprise to internalize the costs of public goods provision in the short-run, long-run competitive pressures from the financial marketplace provide an important check and balance on that process.

5.4.2 Challenges for Policymakers: Political Atmosphere and Policy Trade-Offs

As with much of our political arena today, energy and housing policy decisions are becoming highly politicized. This politicization is evident along multiple dimensions, and while enhanced energy efficiency is clearly achievable, inevitably trade-offs must occur. While some consumption gains accrue simply to more efficient building design and construction, many analysts contend that a significant fraction of building-related energy consumption is driven by the choice of building characteristics and/or the ultimate tenant uses of the facility. For example, Esteri (2016) estimates that over 80% of the indirect effects of building energy usage are driven by the choice of building characteristics, while Xu (2013) similarly finds that annual building electrical consumption varies tremendously by intended use. More specifically, educational facilities use less energy than office buildings, which in turn use significantly less energy than shopping malls and hotel/lodging properties. As such, while building energy consumption represents a large component of the market, there may be significant limitations to the ability of energy-efficiency programs to affect change without materially altering the nature of underlying business operations.

On a related note, Valenzuela et al. (2014) argues that energy consumption patterns vary across demographic, socio-economic, and housing characteristics and attributes, and further contends that much of this variation is related to the differential needs and desires of either owners versus renters, or high-end versus low-end consumers. Consistent with this paradigm, Ahmed et al. (2013) find that low-income poverty-level households have a relatively high price-elasticity of demand (and low-income elasticity of demand) for energy consumption, while Barry (2015) finds a significant geographic variation in the frequency of energy retrofit adoption. More specifically, energy retrofits are typically much more common in urban, as opposed to rural, areas. One potential driver of this geographic concentration is the lack of education and awareness of energy use and consumption patterns, as these positive feedback tools are often missing in rural communities.

Within this context, Grandclement et al. (2015) suggest that energy-efficient buildings must either harmonize or balance energy efficiency versus comfort. Optimal outcomes from an economic perspective will trade-off conflicting goals of multiple stakeholders, and often require intensive negotiations to achieve desired outcomes. Complicating these efforts is a noticeable and growing rift between high- and moderate-energy consumers who often hold vastly different perceptions of conservation across these groupings (Hara et al. 2015). Effective policy solutions and innovations must recognize these differential end-user needs, and generic one-size fits all policy dictates focused exclusively on the building stock are unlikely to be optimal from a societal welfare perspective. The presence of politically motivated actors and market participants with strongly held, conflicting ideologies promise to keep these issues front and center in helping to shape the continuing evolution of commercial real estate markets.

5.4.3 *Impediments to Sustainable Development: Cost Concerns and Conflicting Results*

Along with higher lease rates and property values, green building advocates frequently cite on-going cost savings and productivity advantages as key benefits of pursuing environmental certification and other energy-efficiency initiatives. For example, Goering (2009), Choi (2009) and Watson (2009) all report that LEED certified buildings use substantially less energy (10–35%) than their non-certified counterparts, and further argue that additional building operating expenses are also reduced. Additional evidence on the benefits of green buildings is provided by Miller et al. (2009), who report that employee productivity is approximately 1% higher in such buildings, with employees taking nearly three less sick days per year. On the other hand, much of the development industry continues to believe that green development initiatives are either: (1) prohibitively expensive to build, operate, and/or maintain or (2) produce benefits which cannot be directly captured by the building owners and/or operators. Further complicating the effective analysis of these issues, the lack of unambiguous, reliable data and a time series of consistent results across multiple markets often leads to conflicting policy implications. For example, Kontokosta (2015) argues that data limitations, information asymmetries, and alternative benchmarking and certification programs which do not sufficiently measure, model, or prioritize the efficiency of energy consumption patterns hamper the efficacy of broad-based energy-efficiency initiatives across the commercial real estate industry, as firms may choose to prioritize certification and public recognition over true efficiency gains. In addition, Esteri (2016) argues that because the bulk of indirect energy costs are driven by the choice of building attributes, planners can and should encourage energy progress through adopting development policies and programs that favor compact housing. On the other hand, Xu (2013) finds that building size is not related to the intensity of energy consumption, but rather is driven by the intended use of the tenant. Under this scenario, compact housing initiatives would have relatively little impact on overall energy consumption unless such smaller facilities effectively serve to limit the scope or intensity of the economic activity undertaken by end users of the space.

Additional roadblocks to the further market acceptance and penetration of energy-efficient buildings include the expected costs of ongoing monitoring and maintenance of new technology, concerns over the reliability and market acceptance of green building products and systems, and litigation risk associated with the potential future loss of certification or unrealized energy-efficiency gains if emerging technologies develop slower or less reliably than anticipated (Anderson 2008; D'Arelli 2008; Del Percio 2008; Jones and Vyas 2008; Addae-Dapaah et al. 2009). Given the highly politicized atmosphere in which many of these policy discussions are taking place, without clear, unambiguous answers to many of these concerns, optimal policy solutions promise to remain elusive.

5.4.4 *Implications for City, Urban, and Regional Planning*

Finally, as energy-efficiency considerations continue to gain attention, it is likely that these debates and discussions will have potentially dramatic spillover effects with respect to urban and regional planning. For example, while Gudipudi et al. (2016) report that increased population density is positively related to the aggregate level of greenhouse gas emissions, the slope of this relation is less than unity. As such, doubling the population within a given spatial area indeed increases emissions, but will not double them. Thus, given a constant population, increased "sprawl" may well contribute to increased overall emissions levels via inefficient commuting. Relatedly, Yin et al. (2013) find that nearly 20% of energy consumption (in Kumamoto, Japan) is attributable to "mobility goals" or transportation issues. To the extent such results are robust and generalizable, we may well expect to see continued efforts among city and regional planners to limit urban sprawl and/or further encourage the development, use, and expansion of mass transit alternatives. Given the urban–rural divide highlighted by the Pew Research Center (2014), where conservatives and liberals hold vastly different views on the most desirable community attributes and development patterns, alternative policy approaches toward limiting and managing sprawl are virtually guaranteed to continue being shaped by ideological pressures.

5.5 Conclusion: Costs and Benefits of Energy-Efficient Buildings

Energy-efficiency initiatives within the building and commercial real estate industry represent an on-going and persistent source of conflict within political and policy circles. While virtually all parties agree that buildings represent a significant source of both energy consumption and their associated environmental costs, optimal policy trade-offs and solutions often appear to be driven by political ideologies and objectives. While such trade-offs are not new, and in fact represent the vital and efficient functioning of a Democratic process, the hyper-partisan and polarized state of the U.S. electorate today leads to divergent market outcomes across jurisdictions characterized by competing ideological views. This chapter documented significantly higher reliance upon the use and generation of renewable energy sources in politically liberal (a.k.a. "Blue") states, while "Red" states were found to exhibit significantly lower (residential) electricity rates. A review of the limited existing literature suggests that such patterns may not be unique to the U.S., while potential policy debates, differences, and conflicts may be exacerbated by the lack of adequate research data and findings on the long-run costs and benefits of renewable building products, processes, and/or marketing and branding efforts. These stark differences in both energy market outcomes and their associated policy implications hold a significant potential importance with respect to commercial real estate markets, as evolving political trends could materially reshape the construction, development, and urban planning process in unforeseen ways. As such, today's real estate professional must be finely attuned to not only the direct costs and benefits of provisioning space to the market, but must also continue to be mindful of the political component of the entitlement, permitting, and planning process.

References

Abdel Aleem, S.H.E., A.F. Zobaa, and H.M. Abdel Mageed. 2015. Assessment of Energy Credits for the Enhancement of the Egyptian Green Pyramid Rating System. *Energy Policy* 87: 407–416.

Addae-Dapaah, K., L. Hiang, and N.Y.S. Sharon. 2009. Sustainability of Sustainable Real Estate Development. *Journal of Sustainable Real Estate* 1 (1): 203–225.

Amhed, R., K. Jones Stater, and M. Stater. 2013. The Effect of Poverty Status and Public Housing Residency on Residential Energy Consumption in the U.S. *Energy Studies Review* 20 (1): 1–33.

Anderson, B.D. 2008. Green Building Representation and the Emerging Potential for Securities Fraud Liability. *Real Estate Issues* 33 (3): 53–58.

Barry, N. 2015. Rural America: Perceptions of Residential Energy Retrofits. *Cityscape: A Journal of Policy Development and Research* 17 (3): 233–238.

Belo, F., V.D. Gala, and J. Li. 2013. Government Spending, Political Cycles, and the Cross Section of Stock Returns. *Journal of Financial Economics* 107 (2): 305–324.

Brounen, D., and N. Kok. 2011. On the Economics of Energy Labels in the Housing Market. *Journal of Environmental Economics and Management* 62 (2): 166–179.

Choi, C. 2009. Removing Market Barriers to Green Development: Principles and Action Projects to Promote Widespread Adoption of Green Development Practices. *Journal of Sustainable Real Estate* 1 (1): 107–138.

Cooper, M.J., H. Gulen, and A.V. Ovtchinnikov. 2010. Corporate Political Contributions and Stock Returns. *Journal of Finance* 65 (2): 687–724.

D'Arelli, P. 2008. Selling and Governing the Green Project: Owner Risks in Marketing, Entitlement and Project Governance. *Real Estate Issues* 33 (3): 15–21.

Del Percio, L. 2008. Legal Issues Arising Out of Green Building Legislation. *Real Estate Issues* 33 (3): 59–64.

Egging, R. 2013. Drivers, Trends, and Uncertainty in Long-Term Price Projections for Energy Management in Public Buildings. *Energy Policy* 62: 617–624.

Estiri, H. 2016. Household Energy Consumption and Housing Choice in the U.S. Residential Sector. *Housing Policy Debate* 26 (1): 231–250.

Foerster, S.R., and J.J. Schmitz. 1997. The Transmission of US Election Cycles to International Stock Returns. *Journal of International Business Studies* 28 (1): 1–13.

Goering, J. 2009. Sustainable Real Estate Development: The Dynamics of Market Penetration. *Journal of Sustainable Real Estate* 1 (1): 167–201.

Grandclement, C., A. Karvonen, and S. Guy. 2015. Negotiating Comfort in Low Energy Housing: The Politics of Intermediation. *Energy Policy* 84: 213–222.

Gudipudi, R., T. Fluschnik, A.G.C. Ros, C. Walther, and J.P. Kropp. 2016. City Density and CO_2 Efficiency. *Energy Policy* 91: 352–361.

Hara, Keishiro, Michinori Uwasu, Yusuke Kishita, and Hiroyuki Takeda. 2015. Determinant Factors of Residential Consumption and Perception of Energy Conservation: Time-Series Analysis by Large-Scale Questionnaire in Suita, Japan. *Energy Policy* 87: 240–249.

Harrison, D., and M. Seiler. 2011a. The Political Economy of Green Industrial Warehouses. *Journal of Sustainable Real Estate* 3 (1): 44–67.

Harrison, D., and M. Seiler. 2011b. The Political Economy of Green Office Buildings. *Journal of Property Investment and Finance* 29 (4/5): 551–565.

Huang, R.D. 1985. Common Stock Returns and Presidential Elections. *Financial Analysts Journal* 41 (2): 58–61.

Jones, P., and U.K. Vyas. 2008. Energy Performance in Residential Green Developments: A Florida Case Study. *Real Estate Issues* 33 (3): 65–71.

Kontokosta, C.E. 2015. A Market-Specific Methodology for a Commercial Building Energy Performance Index. *Journal of Real Estate Finance and Economics* 51 (2): 288–316.

Miller, N.G., D. Pogue, Q.D. Gough, and S.M. Davis. 2009. Green Buildings and Productivity. *Journal of Sustainable Real Estate* 1 (1): 65–89.

Pew Research Center. 2014. *Political Polarization in the American Public*, June.

Ramchander, S., M. Simpson, and J. Webb. 2009. Political Cycles, Partisan Orientation, Gridlock, and REIT Returns. *Journal of Real Estate Portfolio Management* 15 (2): 115–128.

Santa-Clara, P., and R. Valkanov. 2003. The Presidential Puzzle: Political Cycles and the Stock Market. *Journal of Finance* 58 (5): 1841–1872.

Valenzuela, C., A. Valencia, S. White, J.A. Jordan, S. Cano, J. Keating, J. Nagorski, and L.B. Potter. 2014. An Analysis of Monthly Household Energy Consumption among Single-Family Residences in Texas, 2010. *Energy Policy* 69: 263–272.

Watson, R. 2009. Industry Insight: The Green Building Impact Report 2008. *Journal of Sustainable Real Estate* 1 (1): 241–243.

Xu, P. 2013. Commercial Building Energy Use in Six Cities in Southern China. *Energy Policy* 53 (1): 76–89.

Yin, Y., S. Mizokami, and T. Maruyama. 2013. An Analysis of the Influence of Urban Form on Energy Consumption by Individual Consumption Behaviors from a Microeconomic Viewpoint. *Energy Policy* 61: 909–919.

Author Biography

Dr. David M. Harrison Professor and Howard Phillips Eminent Scholar Chair in Real Estate, College of Business Administration, University of Central Florida. His research focuses primarily on real estate investment trusts and mortgage markets, and his research publications have appeared in a variety of journals, including: Real Estate Economics, Journal of Real Estate Finance and Economics, Journal of Real Estate Research, Journal of Urban Economics, and the Financial Review.

CHAPTER 6

An Analysis of LEED Certification and Rent Effects in Existing U.S. Office Buildings

Jordan Stanley and Yongsheng Wang

6.1 Introduction

Energy efficiency and sustainability of commercial buildings is an important part of efforts to improve environmental protection and sustainable living in the United States. The U.S. Green Building Council (USGBC) has led this effort by organizing the Leadership in Energy and Environmental Design (LEED) certification program to recognize sustainable practices in building design, construction, and operation. This program is open to all types of buildings—commercial, industrial, and even residential. So far, commercial office buildings are the main

The original version of this chapter was revised: For detailed information please see Erratum. The erratum this chapter is available at https://doi.org/10.1057/978-1-137-57446-6_11

J. Stanley (✉)
Department of Economics, Syracuse University, Syracuse, NY, USA
e-mail: jstanley@syr.edu

Y. Wang
Department of Economics and Business, Washington and Jefferson College, Washington, PA, USA
e-mail: wysqd01@gmail.com

N.E. Coulson et al. (eds.), *Energy Efficiency and the Future of Real Estate*, DOI 10.1057/978-1-137-57446-6_6

participants. The number of LEED-certified (henceforth "LEED") office buildings increased significantly across the country over the past decade. Meeting the LEED requirements can yield energy-efficiency benefits, which in turn can reduce operating costs. The notion of energy efficiency may also be highly valued by the public, and corporate campaigns have included green initiatives for building construction and operation. Past research has examined the effect of LEED certification on rents—prior studies, such as Eichholtz et al. (2010) and Fuerst and McAllister (2011), have found rental premia for LEED buildings. An interesting notion is whether these rental premia come from the LEED process (such as building renovations and energy-efficiency improvements), from the signal of being officially labeled "LEED," or a combination of the two. How LEED is valued in the real estate market as well as if and how this valuation changes over time are also important aspects to consider.

This study examines LEED commercial office buildings in major (as defined by metropolitan GDP) U.S. cities using a difference-in-differences method with a sample determined by propensity-score matching. Based on our knowledge, this is the first comprehensive study focusing on office buildings certified as LEED for Existing Buildings (LEED-EB or LEED-EBOM) that employs this method. The findings of this study reveal the impact of LEED certification in a more-controlled environment than in previous studies. Specifically, we wish to determine if there exists a designation effect of LEED on rent—if and to what extent being officially certified "LEED" matters. Building owners presumably expect profit gains when making the decision to register for, and eventually attain, LEED certification. In general, profit gains can come through increased revenue or decreased costs. In the context of LEED, energy efficiency can cut operating costs, which in turn could lead to lower rents being charged. Revenue could increase if the building improvements or green labeling of LEED allows higher rents to be charged (Peterson and Gammill 2010).

The estimated 5 – 8% rental premium of LEED office buildings over similar non-LEED buildings found in this analysis is comparable to estimates found in earlier studies; however, the focus of this paper is on the effect of LEED over time. We want to find out whether the change in rental rate growth for LEED properties after official certification differs from that of the comparison group when controlling for group and time effects. In other words, we want to know whether LEED properties have higher rents because of the policy, or because of some other unobserved factors attributable to LEED buildings, regardless of when they become certified. If rental premium increased based on the signal of certification or official completion of the necessary property improvements and management, one would expect to see a statistically significant positive policy effect.

The main results of this study find a statistically significant negative policy effect—rent for LEED buildings compared to similar non-LEED buildings decreases on average by about 3–4% points following official certification. In our most closely matched sample, the total effect of LEED certification on rents is slightly less than a 1% premium. One potential explanation for this would be a reduction in operating expenses from improved energy efficiency allowing LEED buildings to charge lower rent. Another explanation is real estate market conditions, such as the 2008 recession or LEED saturation in major cities, affecting market valuation of official LEED certification. Overall, our results imply that LEED certification alone does not lead to an increase in rental premium.

Before discussing the present analysis, it will be useful to provide background information on LEED, discuss economic mechanisms, and summarize past literature.

6.2 Background Information on LEED

LEED was created by the USGBC in 1998 to better measure the practices of green construction and building operation through a point system. Interest in the program has greatly increased since its initiation. As of August 2014, there are more than 60,000 commercial buildings participating in the LEED program.[1] A LEED rating can be assigned to either the entire building or a certain portion of the structure. In some instances, part of a building is eligible to have a higher rating than the entire structure. There are five categories in the LEED rating system: building design and construction, interior design and construction, building operations and maintenance, neighborhood and development, and homes.[2] Florance et al. (2010) showed that the top five property types (based on either square footage or market cap) are office, retail, industrial, health care, and multi-family homes; however, the proportion of industrial, health care, and multi-family homes are small among all LEED buildings.

It is possible to certify both a newly constructed structure and an existing one. Figure 6.1 shows the number of LEED listings for new construction and existing buildings. Among all certified buildings, 48.6% are existing properties (see Fig. 6.1). This high percentage of certified existing buildings embodies the philosophy of USGBC that focuses on

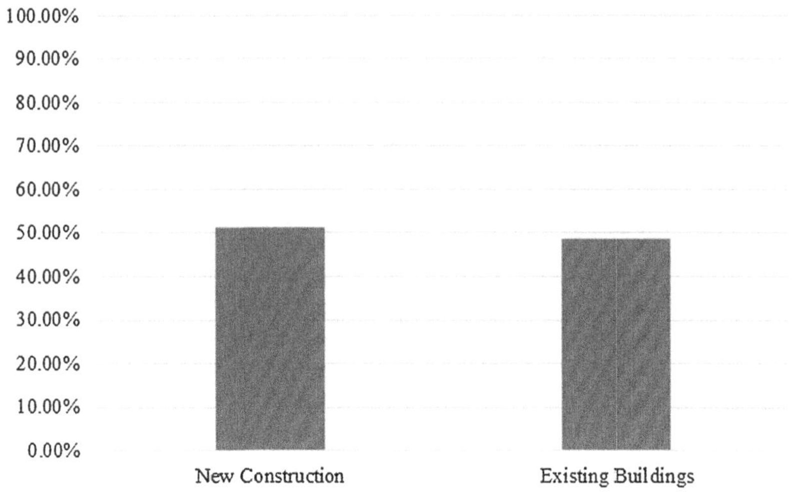

Fig. 6.1 LEED certification for new construction and existing buildings. *Data Source* USGBC (2014)

long-term, sustainable building practices. LEED-EB places emphasis on the operation and management of a property and does not need to be accomplished through major design initiatives or large renovations (Blumberg 2012). Throughout the lifetime of a certified structure, it is eligible to apply for a higher level of LEED certification with newly added green features and practices. To accomplish the mission of green building, existing buildings provide the most potential, and further expansion of the program is possible beyond the current situation.

There are four levels of LEED certification: Certified, Silver, Gold, and Platinum. LEED is a point-based system—different green practices of a building will earn different points. The major credit categories of LEED certification include the following: integrative process during the predesign period, location and transportation, materials and resources, water efficiency, energy and atmosphere, sustainable sites on ecosystem and water impact, indoor environmental quality, innovation, regional priority, smart location and linkage, neighborhood pattern and design, green infrastructure, and buildings. The points required for each level of certification are 40–49 for Certified, 50–59 for Silver, 60–79 for Gold, and 80 and above for Platinum.[3]

6.3 The Economics of LEED

LEED certification can have several economic consequences for building owners, tenants, investors, and geographic areas. LEED buildings can have positive externalities for building occupants and the local community. Completing certain LEED credits can improve neighborhoods in ways, such as rainwater management, reduced pollution, and better waste and hazardous material disposal. Other LEED credits benefit building occupants by improving indoor air quality, light pollution, and thermal comfort.[4] Such improvements can have positive effects on employee productivity and retention [see Miller et al. (2009), among others]. Investment in sustainable real estate, such as LEED buildings, offers potential future benefits for investors, as such buildings are better equipped to handle energy price increases or heightened government regulation (Reichardt et al. 2012, p. 7).

For a building owner who seeks to maximize profit, participation in the LEED program can affect profits through costs or revenue. As LEED is not a mandatory program, one can assume that the expected benefits of LEED outweigh the expected costs for a building owner who decides to pursue certification. There are costs to earning LEED certification; however, the resulting energy-efficiency improvements can greatly reduce operating expenses. Such cost savings could be significant when factoring in maintenance costs, improved building longevity, and the potential for energy price increases or new government mandates or regulations in the future.

Considering revenue, if and how LEED is valued in the real estate market can be a major factor in the decision-making process for a building owner interested in LEED. LEED certification can increase revenue if renters are willing to pay more for green labeling or the accompanying property improvements. If this is the case and owners are able to capitalize on renter valuation of LEED, one would expect (all else being equal) to see higher rents in a commercial property following official certification.[5] The amount of space matters as well. Available square footage can affect rent and thus revenue—the scarcity or abundance of LEED space could affect market valuation.

Profit ramifications could vary over time, and building owners could make decisions based on expectations in the long run. In the short term, LEED certification costs (e.g., making the necessary renovations) could exceed the initial cost savings of energy efficiency. Higher rents could be charged to offset these initial costs, or owners may be unable to increase rent. How the market values LEED is important and could vary over time. "Greengoods" are typically assumed to be normal goods, meaning that a strong economy could increase willingness to pay higher rent for LEED space while weaker economic conditions could reduce that willingness to pay. LEED presence is another potential factor. If a property is one of few LEED buildings in an area, willingness to pay for space in such a building may be high. As more buildings become LEED, a rent premium associated with certification could be reduced by this increased supply. If LEED becomes the norm, any rent premium that existed when LEED was "special" could diminish or disappear completely. These factors could also relate to the structure of local real estate markets—market power (i.e., the ability to charge higher rents) could be lower during recessions or when the supply of LEED buildings is high.

It is also worth noting that energy-efficiency improvements are not solely dependent on participation in the LEED program. A building could certainly improve its energy efficiency without seeking LEED certification or any other energy-efficiency labeling. LEED certification (or other green labeling, such as ENERGY STAR) simply provides a signal to the market that the given property meets some energy-efficiency standard.[6] Receiving a label, such as LEED or ENERGY STAR, informs the market that a building is energy efficient. An important distinction is whether the actual energy efficiency or the label itself is valued in the market.

The economic factors associated with LEED certification can have implications on energy policy. The attractiveness of LEED from both owner and renter perspectives is important to consider. For example, if building operators need to receive higher rent in order to make the certification process worth the cost, there must be renters willing to pay such a premium. Otherwise, building operators may not find LEED certification (or continued certification) attractive. Policy matters are complicated by unobserved costs and benefits of energy savings. It can be difficult to determine welfare effects, and differences will exist among market participants (Alcott and Greenstone 2012). Alcott and Greenstone (2012) note that while investment inefficiencies may exist, they likely vary across consumers. The authors recommend targeted policies with information disclosure being one example. This recommendation is also suggested in Peterson and Gammill (2010). In 2010, California and Washington, D.C. mandated ENERGY STAR rating disclosures before any major real estate transaction. Such policies could induce more investment in energy efficiency to increase a building's attractiveness, while more informed decision making from tenants and buyers can improve the value of energy-efficient properties (Peterson and Gammill 2010).

In sum, economic factors, such as certification costs, energy-efficiency benefits, real estate market conditions, and the valuation of green buildings, are all important considerations regarding LEED certification and its potential impacts.

6.4 Literature Summary

This overview will emphasize research that investigates rent or sales premia associated with LEED certification. Such analysis often focuses on commercial buildings; however, there are studies looking at other market segments, such as single-family residences and multi-family properties [see Bond and Devine (2016), among others]. The general consensus is that LEED buildings have a rent or sales price premium compared to non-LEED buildings. The estimated values of the rental premium associated with LEED mostly fall between 5 and 15%. The past work has ranged from national analysis to major markets. Typically, the data source is CoStar, a large commercial real estate database.

In the past, hedonic analysis has often been employed in real estate studies. Examples of such studies involving LEED include Fuerst and McAllister (2008), Fuerst and McAllister (2011), Das and Wiley (2014), Miller et al. (2008), and Wiley et al. (2010). Other studies, such as Dermisi (2013), employ fixed effects models. More relevant to the present analysis are studies which employed propensity scores or difference-in-differences techniques. Propensity-score matching (PSM) has been utilized in the LEED literature in studies, such as Reichardt (2014), Robinson and Sanderford (2015), and Eichholtzet et al. (2010). Propensity-score matching helps to reduce heterogeneity in the sample by pairing LEED properties with similar non-LEED properties. Difference-in-differences is a technique which has been previously used in this literature in studies, such as Reichardt et al. (2012). Difference-in-differences controls for group and time effects to isolate a specific treatment (policy) effect. The exact nature of our methodology and comparisons to the past techniques will be discussed in greater detail shortly.

The present analysis adds to the past research in this area and offers several refinements. The combination of PSM and difference-in-differences is, to our knowledge, a technique which has not been employed in a past analysis of LEED and rental premium in office buildings. The difference-in-differences approach controls for time and group effects to better estimate the effect of official LEED certification, while PSM helps make the treatment and comparison properties more similar along observable dimensions. This combination of techniques improves upon past work in several ways. Employing hedonic analysis determines an implicit price for LEED, but this may be affected or driven by other building characteristics. Through PSM, we can better examine the specific impact of LEED on rent by comparing properties which are more similar along important observable dimensions. Difference-in-differences allows us to look at the effect of certification over time, providing a more complete investigation of LEED compared to more static estimations seen in cross-sectional and fixed effects analysis. In addition to our methodological choices, our selection of LEED-EB for office buildings in major U.S. markets provides a focused analysis on a major segment of LEED properties. This focus allows for a more controlled sample through which the precise effects of LEED certification can be determined.

6.5 Data and Methodology

6.5.1 Data

The time period analyzed in this study is from 2008 through 2012, and the data are observed quarterly. These years have been selected for a few reasons. The number of green buildings tripled during this time period.[7] In particular, the number of LEED-EB certifications sharply increased in 2009 and continued to grow (Blumberg 2012). Furthermore, the LEED certification process underwent updates in the late 2000s. Focusing on 2008 and beyond provides a better picture of the current LEED system.

The cities used in this study were determined based on metropolitan area data from the U.S. Bureau of Economic Analysis (BEA). By focusing on a sample of large urban economic centers, this study can reduce the heterogeneity one would expect to encounter if sampling from a wide range of cities. The commercial real estate market may still differ between cities, but there would be wider variance when comparing small

Table 6.1 List of cities in the data sample

Atlanta, GA	Minneapolis, MN
Baltimore, MD	New York, NY
Boston, MA	Philadelphia, PA
Chicago, IL	Phoenix, AZ
Dallas, TX	Portland, OR
Denver, CO	San Diego, CA
Detroit, MI	San Francisco, CA
Houston, TX	San Jose, CA
Los Angeles, CA	Seattle, WA
Miami, FL	Washington, DC

Note These are the top 20 cities based on metropolitan GDP in 2012. Due to a lack of LEED properties with adequate data availability, Boston and Detroit are dropped from the final sample

cities to larger ones. Therefore, the properties included in this study's sample are from central cities in large, urban areas—specifically U.S. cities ranked among the top 20 metropolitan gross domestic products (GDP). The urban areas included in our sample also account for all of the top cities for LEED certification in the United States as of December 2012.[8] Table 6.1 lists the cities in the data sample.

Particular building information for this study is from the CoStar real estate database. We construct a panel data set following the same office buildings over time. CoStar provides property characteristics for commercial real estate in the United States. It is typically the property data source for studies in the commercial real estate literature. The variable of interest for this study is rent, specifically the total gross rent per square foot.

The LEED sample was selected based on location in one of our sample cities and property data availability for 2008 through 2012. In order to have multiple observations before and after certification, our LEED properties are those certified after 2008 but no later than Quarter 1 of 2012. The LEED buildings were then crosschecked via the USGBC's Green Building Information Gateway—an online search engine for green building activity.[9] Properties were only kept if there was no LEED certification prior to the quarter of LEED-EB certification during our sample years. The comparison properties come from CoStar and were selected based on property data availability and zip code.

Summary statistics for the CoStar sample are included in Table 6.2. This sample includes properties with missing quarters of data. These summary statistics are included to show how the data look in general

Table 6.2 CoStar property summary statistics

Variable	*Observations*	*Mean*	*Standard deviation*	*Minimum*	*Maximum*
Rent ($/sq. ft)	27,897	27.36	10.67	6.5	99.55
Age (years)	27,840	39.79	26.92	1	141
Stories	27,880	14.84	12.91	1	110
Renovated	27,900	0.41	0.49	0	1
Years since renovation	27,896	5.91	10.68	0	137
Land (acres)	27,760	2.71	4.41	0.03	61
RBA (sq. ft.)	27,880	298,379.9	480,478.7	5732	14,000,000
LEED	27,900	0.14	0.3504552	0	1
ENERGY STAR	27,900	0.61	0.4875883	0	1

Note Data are from CoStar for the top 20 U.S. cities in terms of metropolitan GDP. "Renovated", "LEED", and "ENERGY STAR" are binary variables. The inconsistent number of observations is due to the inclusion of some properties with missing values

before the sample is narrowed to properties with consistently available data.[10] While it may be the case that these properties could possess different characteristics from those with inconsistent data availability, the summary statistics do not show a major difference in available observable characteristics between those with complete data and those with incomplete data. We assume that any unobserved characteristics would not systematically differ between the treatment and comparison groups with and without sufficient data. For the analysis, the sample of comparison properties is narrowed following propensity-score matching. These steps will be discussed in more detail shortly. Summary statistics for the unmatched sample are split by group (buildings that ever become LEED and those who do not) in Tables 6.3 and 6.4. For the unmatched sample, it is evident that LEED buildings on average have higher rents than non-LEED buildings. Furthermore, LEED buildings are typically newer and larger, and are also more likely to be ENERGY STAR certified.[11]

6.5.2 *Methodology*

The core methodology utilized in this study is a difference-in-differences approach. Difference-in-differences has been used in the LEED literature in such studies as Reichardt et al. (2012). Difference-in-differences helps address potential endogeneity concerns by controlling for group

Table 6.3 Summary statistics for unmatched sample of LEED buildings

Variable	*Observations*	*Mean*	*Standard deviation*	*Minimum*	*Maximum*
Rent ($/sq. ft)	4000	31.72	11.30	11.5	99.55
Age (years)	4000	29.52	16.46	1	106
Stories	4000	26.09	14.89	3	71
Renovated	4000	0.34	0.47	0	1
Years since renovation	4000	4.19	7.47	0	49
Land (acres)	3940	3.13	35.96	0.28	41
RBA (sq. ft.)	4000	573,070.7	357,696.1	40,000	1,700,000
ENERGY STAR	4000	0.95	0.2179722	0	1

Note Data are from CoStar. "Renovated", "LEED", and "ENERGY STAR" are binary variables. The inconsistent number of observations is due to the full sample including some properties with missing values

Table 6.4 Summary statistics for unmatched non-LEED buildings

Variable	*Observations*	*Mean*	*Standard deviation*	*Minimum*	*Maximum*
Rent ($/sq. ft)	23,897	26.64	10.38	6.5	87.27
Age (years)	23,840	41.51	27.93	1	141
Stories	23,880	12.95	11.51	1	110
Renovated	23,900	0.42	0.49	0	1
Years since renovation	23,896	6.20	11.10	0	137
Land (acres)	23,820	2.64	4.09	0.03	61
RBA (sq. ft.)	23,880	252,368.1	483,060.5	5732	14,000,000
ENERGY STAR	23,900	0.55	0.50	0	1

Note Data are from CoStar. "Renovated", "LEED", and "ENERGY STAR" are binary variables. The inconsistent number of observations is due to the inclusion of some properties with missing values

and time effects in order to isolate the potential average treatment effect. Cross-sectional studies do not investigate changes over time and often fail to account for unobservable differences between treatment and comparison groups. Hedonic regressions are often employed in real estate studies; however, this technique may produce estimation difficulties due to multicollinearity. For example, LEED status may be related to rent but also affected by the age of the building. Hedonic estimation of the contribution of LEED status to rent may thus be inadequate.

We use LEED-EB certification as our treatment variable with the official designation date representing the timing of the treatment. We seek to determine if being officially designated LEED results in a rental premium—in essence, we want to see if the name signal of "LEED" is worth anything in and of itself.[12] A key requirement for a difference-in-differences approach is that treatment and comparison groups do not have differential trends before the treatment is administered. Figure 6.2 shows the quarter-to-quarter trends for the whole sample. It shows that, while the levels of rent differ, the trends for the treatment and comparison groups are quite similar over time even as more of the treatment sample becomes LEED certified. Figure 6.3 shows the rent trends for the matched sample when normalizing around the quarter of certification. The data do not show an anticipatory rent increase leading up to

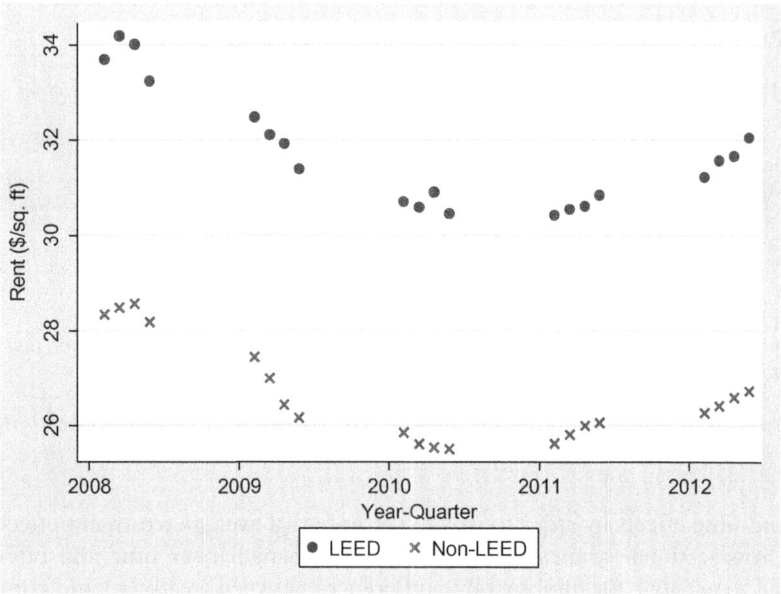

Fig. 6.2 Rent trends for LEED and non-LEED properties 2008 through 2012. *Note* Rent values are in dollars per square feet and are averaged by group and quarter. "LEED" and "Non-LEED" represent whether or not a property became LEED-EB at any point between 2009 Q1 and 2012 Q1 but was not previously certified as any form of LEED

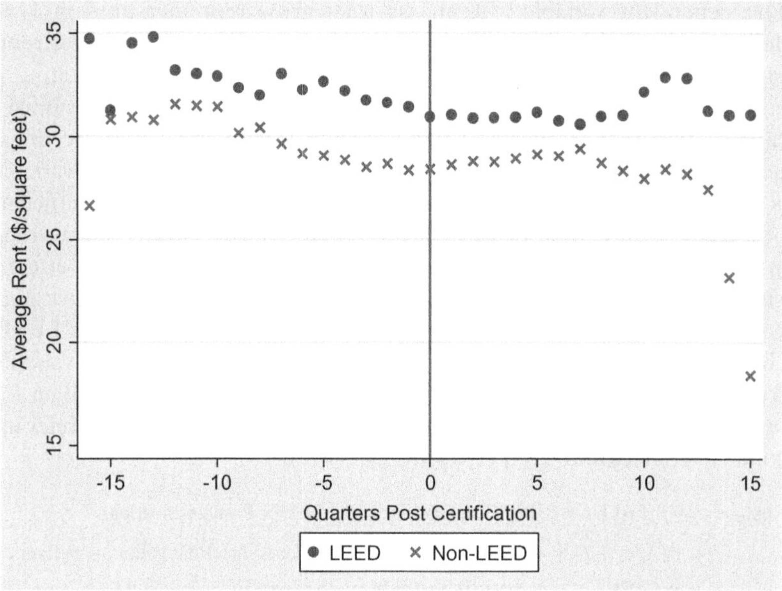

Fig. 6.3 Rent trends for LEED and non-LEED properties pre/post-certification. *Note* Rent values are in dollars per square feet and are averaged by group and quarter. "LEED" and "non-LEED" represent whether or not a property became LEED-EB at any point between 2009 Q1 and 2012 Q1 but was not previously certified as any form of LEED. "Quarters Post Certification" represents the difference between the observation quarter and the quarter of certification (or, the matched partner's quarter of certification). The matched data are from the "Without Replacement" sample

official LEED certification. Pre-certification trends are similar comparing LEED and non-LEED properties. Immediately after certification, LEED rents are steady, while non-LEED rents increase slightly. However, after roughly 2 years of certification, LEED rents increase, while non-LEED rents decrease. As buildings in our sample became certified between 2009 and 2011, this delayed rise in rents could simply signify the economy's recovery and a change in the valuation of "green" market goods.

The baseline form for our difference-in-differences regressions is

$$\text{Ln(Rent)}_{it} = \alpha + \beta_1 \text{LEED}_i + \beta_2 \text{PostCertification}_t + \beta_3 \text{LEED} \times \text{PostCertification}_{it} + \varepsilon_{it}. \tag{6.1}$$

The dependent variable, "Rent," is total gross rent measured in U.S. dollars—our preferred specifications use the logarithm of total gross rent. For the independent variables, "LEED" is a binary variable indicating if a given property i ever becomes LEED; "PostCertification" is a binary variable that is 0 if quarter t is before the treatment (LEED certification) and 1 if after treatment; and "LEED × PostCertification" variable is the interaction of "LEED" and "PostCertification". Our coefficient of interest is β_3 as this represents the average policy effect—the average impact of LEED certification after controlling for group and time effects. Finally, α is the constant term and ε is the error term. For intuitive purposes, we will later refer to the LEED group indicator variable as "LEED Group" and the interaction term as "LEED Policy." The latter variable represents the effect official certification has on rent when controlling for both group and time effects. Additional specifications add on relevant control variables and fixed effects to Eq. (6.1):

$$\begin{aligned}\text{Rent}_{it} = {}& \alpha + \beta_1\text{LEED}_i + \beta_2\text{PostCertification}_t + \beta_3\text{LEED} \times \text{PostCertification}_{it} \\ & + \beta_4\text{Age}_i + \beta_5\text{Stories}_i + \beta_6\text{Renovated}_i + \beta_7\text{YearsSinceRenovation}_i + \beta_8\text{Land}_i \\ & + \beta_9\ln(\text{RBA}_i) + \beta_{10}\text{ENERGY STAR}_i + \beta_{11}\text{CityGDP}_i + \beta_{12}\text{CityUnemployment}_i \\ & + \beta_{13}\text{CityFE}_i + \beta_{14}\text{YearQuarterFE}_i + \beta_{15}\text{PropertyFE}_i + \varepsilon_{it}.\end{aligned} \tag{6.2}$$

The property-related variables are "Land" (measured in acres), "Stories", "ENERGY STAR certification" (binary variable if property is certified before or within sample years), "Age" (in years), "Renovated" (binary variable indicated if a building has been renovated), "Years since Renovation," and "Rentable Building Area (RBA)." "Age" is calculated as the year of observation minus the year built. "Years since renovation" is either the year of observation minus the year of renovation (if the building had been renovated) or 0. "Rentable building area" is the total area (in square feet) in the building that may be occupied by tenants as well as any associated common areas.[13] Since ENERGY STAR is not the focus of this analysis, we simply treat it as a binary variable to indicate non-LEED green initiative. In several specifications, variables representing local economic conditions are included. Annual metropolitan GDP and unemployment rate are the specific measures employed. The GDP data come from the U.S. Bureau of Economic Analysis, while the unemployment rate data are from the Bureau of Labor Statistics. Different specifications also add in fixed effects (the "FE" variables in Eq. 6.2" for city, year-quarter, and property. It is possible that rent at a given point in time is affected by time-invariant city conditions (e.g., local real estate market), general market conditions during that particular quarter-year, or unobserved characteristics unique to that particular property.

A drawback of using this methodology in our setting is that LEED certification is neither mandatory nor uniform in implementation date. LEED certification comes about because buildings both seek out and earn the designation; it is not inherently random, nor is it mandated by a governing body. Certain characteristics could affect who becomes LEED and when they do so, and these characteristics could also have some effect on rent. From a more mechanical perspective, a clear divide between pre- and post-periods for the treatment group does not exist in our setting, since properties become LEED at different times. The "PostCertification" binary variable is straightforward for our LEED properties, but it is not readily apparent how we should determine such a variable for the comparison properties in the context of our analysis. To address these issues, we additionally employ propensity-score matching (PSM).

PSM has been used in the sustainable building certification literature in studies, such as Deng et al. (2012) and Eichholtz et al. (2010). PSM determines a "propensity score" that represents the likelihood of treatment based on assorted observable characteristics. By then matching propensity scores between treatment and comparison groups, one can improve comparability between the groups along important observable dimensions. The dependent variable here is an indicator variable for whether or not a building became LEED-EB between 2008 and 2012. Using the sample with no repeated properties, we generate propensity scores through a probit regression of becoming LEED on observable property characteristics (see descriptions under Eq. 6.2) at the beginning of our sample (2008 Quarter 1):

$$\begin{aligned}\text{Prob(LEED)} = {} & \alpha_0 + \delta_1\text{Age} + \delta_2\text{Stories} + \delta_3\text{Renovated} + \delta_4(\text{YearsSinceRenovation}) \\ & + \delta_5\text{Land} + \delta_6\ln(\text{RBA}) + \delta_7\text{ENERGY STAR} + \mu_0.\end{aligned} \tag{6.3}$$

After we have the estimated coefficients, we determine the predicted value of "LEED" based on the actual property characteristics of each building. This predicted value of "LEED" (which is between 0 and 1) is the propensity score. Once propensity scores are calculated, each LEED property is matched to a comparison property with a similar propensity score.

Table 6.5 LEED certification probit regression results

Variable	*Coefficient estimate*
Stories	0.0025
	(0.006)
Land	−0.001
	(0.009)
ENERGY STAR	1.010***
	(0.169)
Building age	−0.009***
	(0.003)
Renovated	−0.113
	(0.150)
Years since renovation	0.005
	(0.012)
ln(RBA)	0.703***
	(0.111)
Constant	−10.43***
	(1.311)
Observations	1386

Note *** indicates statistical significance at the 1% level, ** for 5% level, * for 10% level; Standard errors are included in parentheses; Data are for 2008 Q1; The dependent variable is a binary variable taking on "0" if the building does not become LEED within our sample and "1" if it does; "ENERGY STAR" is a binary variable; ln(RBA) is ln(Rentable Building Area); "Renovated" indicates is a binary variable represented whether or not the building was renovated after its construction; "Years Since Renovation" is the interaction of "Renovated" and the number of years since renovated; "Building Age" is the age of the building in years; "Land" is in acres

Table 6.5 includes results of the probit regression which determines the propensity scores. Several observable characteristics appear to be important predictors of the decision to become LEED; the variables for ENERGY STAR, age of the building, and rentable building area have estimated coefficients that are statistically significant. It makes intuitive sense that younger, larger, and more green-thinking buildings would opt to become LEED. Figure 6.4 shows the distribution of the propensity scores split by LEED and non-LEED buildings for the full sample. For our purposes, we want overlap in the propensity scores between treatment and comparison properties. There does not appear to be a sharp divide between the treatment and comparison groups in the predicted likelihood (based on observable building characteristics) of becoming LEED. Some properties that became LEED have a low predicted

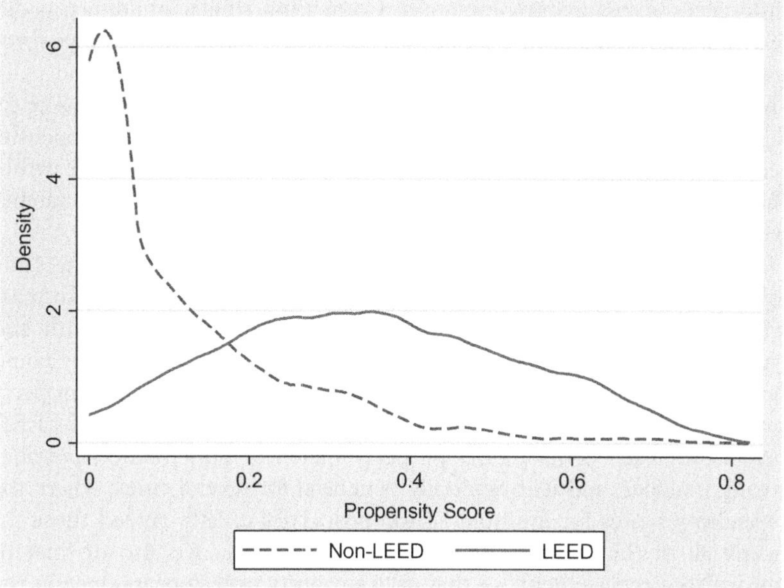

Fig. 6.4 Propensity score distributions by LEED and non-LEED properties. *Note* Propensity score is the predicted probability of becoming LEED. Propensity scores were generated using 2008 Quarter 1 values for property characteristics. The property characteristics included in the regression are building age, stories, renovation status, years since renovation (if renovated), land, the logarithm of rentable building area (RBA), and ENERGY STAR certification. "Non-LEED" means that the building differences-in-differences not become LEED, while "LEED" means that the building first received LEED certification between 2009 Q1 and 2012 Q1

probability, while some non-LEED buildings would have been expected to have become LEED based on the probit results. The matching produces pairs of buildings which are similar in building characteristics and predicted LEED certification but different in actual LEED certification. While the range of the overlap is large, the concentration of non-LEED properties is at a lower level of propensity score than that for LEED buildings (see Fig. 6.4).

In the main analysis, we restrict matching to within city.[14] Our PSM focuses on property characteristics, but we also wish to control for differences across geographic areas. Comparing similar buildings in different areas could still neglect important sources of variation, so we force our matches to be between properties in the same city. For the main analysis, we do not limit the matches to smaller geographic areas (e.g., zip codes) as such a restriction produces more variance in propensity scores. Furthermore, some of the intra-city matches actually occur within the same zip code. Still, as a check, we create a sample using matches within zip codes.

We opt to not match solely on geography, as properties in the same location could have drastically different building characteristics. Instead, we perform the nearest propensity-score neighbor matching with and without replacement. With replacement, one comparison property could be matched to multiple treatment properties. A comparison property can be duplicated and assigned the relevant "pre"- and "post"-LEED periods for each of its LEED property matches. This method provides strong matches, and it is especially beneficial for several cities, where the propensity scores for multiple LEED properties greatly exceed those for nearly all of the non-LEED buildings. As a check, we also do matching without replacement, so that each property only appears once in the sample.[15]

Using PSM strengthens our difference-in-differences approach. Our comparison group now consists of properties that did not become LEED but, based on observable property characteristics, were about as likely as their LEED property counterparts to do so. Crucial to our difference-in-differences strategy, we now have clear pre/post-periods for each matched pair. Summary statistics for the matched samples split by LEED status are included in Table 6.6 and 6.7. Table 6.6 contains statistics for the "With Replacement" sample, while Table 6.7 shows the statistics for the "Without Replacement" sample. PSM greatly reduces the heterogeneity seen in the full sample between LEED and non-LEED buildings (compare these tables to Tables 6.3 and 6.4). Figures 6.5 and 6.6 show the LEED and non-LEED rent trends over time for both matched samples. Compared to the full sample (see Fig. 6.2), the matched samples show LEED and non-LEED properties becoming closer in rent over time. This is especially true in the "With Replacement" sample (see Fig. 6.5). LEED buildings still show higher rent on-average compared to non-LEED properties; however, the difference diminishes over time.

Our methodology still cannot fully address the non-random selection of properties who opt to become LEED. As noted earlier, properties

Table 6.6 Summary statistics for "With Replacement" matching sample

Variable	*Observations*		*Mean*		*Standard deviation*		*Minimum*		*Maximum*	
	LEED	*Non-LEED*	*LEED*	*Non-LEED*	*LEED*	*Non-LEED*	*LEED*	*Non-LEED*	*LEED*	*Non-LEED*
Rent ($/sq. ft)	3940	3940	31.77	30.65	11.38	10.32	11.5	8	99.55	73.92
Age (years)	3940	3940	29.53	27.68	16.55	14.95	1	2	106	104
Stories	3940	3940	26.09	25.65	14.95	17.42	3	3	71	110
Renovated	3940	3940	0.34	0.34	0.47	0.47	0	0	1	1
Years since renovation	3940	3940	4.24	3.62	7.51	6.50	0	0	49	28
Land (acres)	3940	3940	3.13	3.00	5.96	5.10	0.28	0.14	41	43.34
RBA (sq. ft.)	3940	3940	577,133	565,981	358,045	516,355	51,000	32,101	1,700,000	3,800,000
Energy Star	3940	3940	0.96	0.94	0.20	0.23	0	0	1	1

Note Data are from CoStar. "Renovated", "LEED", and "ENERGY STAR" are binary variables. All LEED properties are existing office buildings which were first certified LEED between 2009 Q1 and 2012 Q1. Non-LEED properties are matched within city and allowing for replacement—i.e. each LEED property is matched to its nearest propensity score neighbor by city

Table 6.7 Summary statistics for "Without Replacement" matched sample

Variable	*Observations*		*Mean*		*Standard deviation*		*Minimum*		*Maximum*	
	LEED	*Non-LEED*	*LEED*	*Non-LEED*	*LEED*	*Non-LEED*	*LEED*	*Non-LEED*	*LEED*	*Non-LEED*
Rent ($/sq. ft)	3940	3940	31.77	29.15	11.38	10.16	11.5	8	99.55	73.92
Age (years)	3940	3940	29.53	29.14	16.55	17.04	1	2	106	104
Stories	3940	3940	26.09	21.69	14.95	14.81	3	3	71	110
Renovated	3940	3940	0.34	0.37	0.47	0.48	0	0	1	1
Years since renovation	3940	3940	4.24	4.18	7.51	6.79	0	0	49	28
Land (acres)	3940	3940	3.13	3.86	5.96	7.16	0.28	0.14	41	61
RBA (sq. ft.)	3940	3940	577,133	477,626	358,045	402,791	51,000	32,101	1,700,000	3,800,000
Energy Star	3940	3940	0.96	0.96	0.20	0.20	0	0	1	1

Note Data are from CoStar. "Renovated", "LEED", and "ENERGY STAR" are binary variables. Non-LEED properties were matched to LEED properties based on propensity score. Non-LEED properties are matched within city without allowing for replacement—i.e. each LEED property is matched one-to-one to a non-LEED property by city

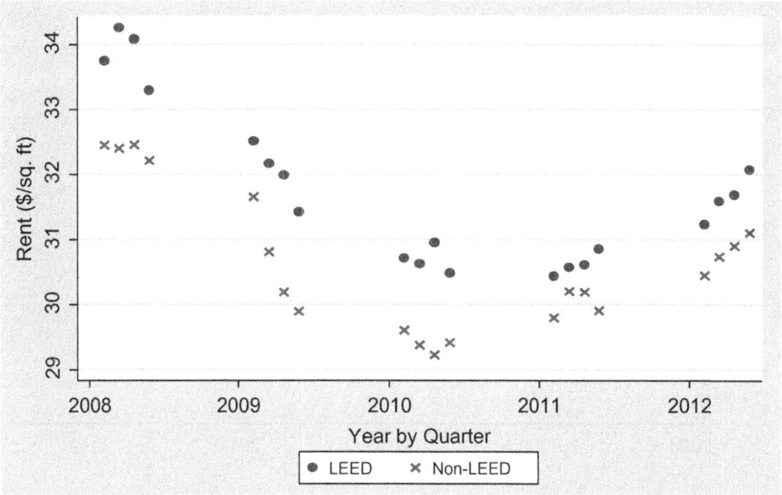

Fig. 6.5 Comparison of rent trends by LEED status for "With Replacement" sample. *Note* Rent values are in dollars per square feet and are averaged by group and quarter. "LEED" and "Non-LEED" represent whether or not a property became LEED-EB at any point between 2009 Q1 and 2012 Q1 but was not previously certified as any form of LEED. "With Replacement" means that non-LEED properties could be matched to multiple LEED properties and thus included multiple times in the sample

becoming LEED must expect some benefits (e.g., higher rents) to certification. While the exact reservation price is unknown, some non-LEED properties may expect positive (though not large enough) returns, while others may not see any value to LEED certification. Therefore, properties that choose not to become LEED may in fact have a willingness to pay of zero—effectively a corner solution.[16] If this is the case, our estimated coefficients could be biased. In our matched sample, most properties have earned ENERGY STAR certification at some point, so one could assume that our sample group generally sees some value in energy-efficiency certification. However, this perceived value may or may not apply to LEED—properties may feel that LEED has merit but is not worth the extra cost to them, or they may have a willingness to pay of zero.

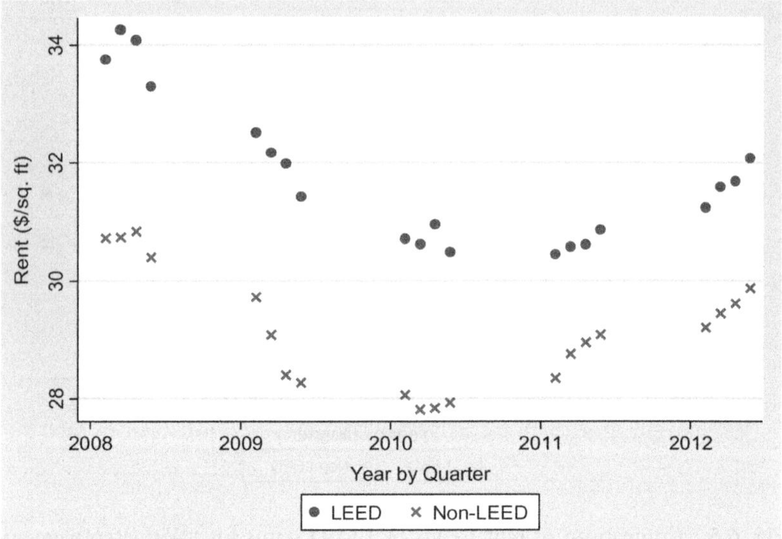

Fig. 6.6 Comparison of rent trends by LEED status for "Without Replacement" sample. *Note* Rent values are in dollars per square feet and are averaged by group and quarter. "LEED" and "Non-LEED" represent whether or not a property became LEED-EB at any point between 2009 Q1 and 2012 Q1 but was not previously certified as any form of LEED. "Without Replacement" means that each non-LEED property could only be matched to one LEED property

In sum, our methodology addresses endogeneity concerns that have often been overlooked in the literature. We improve upon the approaches in the past studies to address these concerns by combining difference-in-differences with propensity-score matching. Our timeframe of analysis represents the biggest boom in LEED certification in the U.S., and our sample of cities includes the most LEED-heavy metropolitan areas in the country.

6.6 Results

We run several specifications for the regression analysis. The methodology is the same across specifications—a difference-in-differences regression with a propensity-score-matched sample (either "With Replacement" or "Without Replacement"). The control variables do

Table 6.8 Regression results for logarithm of total gross rent using "With Replacement" sample

	(1)	(2)	(3)	(4)	(5)
Variables	*Ln(Rent)*	*Ln(Rent)*	*Ln(Rent)*	*Ln(Rent)*	*Ln(Rent)*
LEED policy	−0.0343	−0.0495**	−0.0420*	−0.0442*	−0.00362
	(0.0262)	(0.0225)	(0.0223)	(0.0229)	(0.0198)
LEED group	0.0492	0.0569**	0.0519**	0.0516**	
	(0.0378)	(0.0255)	(0.0234)	(0.0240)	
Post certification	−0.0151	0.0333*	0.0203	0.0209	0.00327
	(0.0188)	(0.0197)	(0.0186)	(0.0190)	(0.0128)
Age			−0.00223***	−0.00210***	0.0490***
			(0.000767)	(0.000773)	(0.0150)
Stories			0.00228**	0.00206*	
			(0.00114)	(0.00114)	
Ln(RBA)			0.0455	0.0495*	
			(0.0284)	(0.0284)	
Land acres			−0.00171	−0.00171	
			(0.00137)	(0.00139)	
Renovated			−0.0722**	−0.0771***	
			(0.0294)	(0.0296)	
Years since renovation			0.00208	0.00192	−0.00342**
			(0.00187)	(0.00191)	(0.00133)
Ln(City GDP)				0.769***	0.729**
				(0.284)	(0.288)
City unemployment rate				1.778**	1.759*
				(0.880)	(0.914)
Constant	3.377***	3.361***	2.809***	−5.792*	−6.197**
	(0.0309)	(0.0269)	(0.347)	(3.156)	(3.129)
Observations	7880	7880	7880	7680	7680
R-squared	0.006	0.546	0.599	0.600	0.871

Note *** indicates statistical significance at the 1% level, ** for 5% level, * for 10% level; standard errors are in parentheses and are all clustered by property; Columns (2) through (4) include fixed effects for city and year-quarter; Column (5) includes property fixed effects; "LEED Group", "Post Certification", and "LEED Policy"are all binary variables; "LEED Policy" is "LEED Group" times "Post Certification"; ln(RBA) is ln(Rentable Building Area). "With Replacement" means that a comparison property could be matched to multiple LEED properties

differ across specifications, and most specifications include fixed effects for city and year-quarter. The regression analysis is performed using total gross rent values in levels, as well as in logarithmic form.[17] Due to the

Table 6.9 Regression results for logarithm of total gross rent using "Without Replacement" sample

	(1)	(2)	(3)	(4)	(5)
Variables	*Ln(Rent)*	*Ln(Rent)*	*Ln(Rent)*	*Ln(Rent)*	*Ln(Rent)*
LEED policy	−0.00982	−0.0259	−0.0295*	−0.0296*	−0.0288**
	(0.0239)	(0.0169)	(0.0162)	(0.0161)	(0.0139)
LEED group	0.0912***	0.0978***	0.0771***	0.0771***	
	(0.0336)	(0.0201)	(0.0189)	(0.0188)	
Post certification	−0.0258	0.0291	0.0221	0.0228	0.0145
	(0.0163)	(0.0185)	(0.0167)	(0.0167)	(0.0111)
Age			−0.00215***	−0.00215***	0.0315***
			(0.000634)	(0.000633)	(0.0106)
Stories			0.00197*	0.00197*	
			(0.00101)	(0.00101)	
Ln(RBA)			0.0520**	0.0520**	
			(0.0230)	(0.0230)	
Land acres			−0.00201*	−0.00201*	
			(0.00116)	(0.00116)	
Renovated			−0.0471*	−0.0476*	
			(0.0271)	(0.0270)	
Years since renovation			0.00135	0.00140	−0.00276***
			(0.00161)	(0.00159)	(0.000967)
Ln(City GDP)				0.900***	0.881***
				(0.243)	(0.248)
City unemployment rate				1.268*	1.211
				(0.765)	(0.784)
Constant	3.329***	3.312***	2.696***	−7.247***	−7.325***
	(0.0244)	(0.0227)	(0.280)	(2.706)	(2.786)
Observations	7880	7880	7880	7880	7880
R-squared	0.019	0.557	0.601	0.603	0.875

Note *** indicates statistical significance at the 1% level, ** for 5% level, * for 10% level; standard errors are in parentheses and are all clustered by property; Column (4) includes city fixed effects; Column (5) includes property fixed effects; "LEED Group", "Post Certification", and "LEED Policy" are all binary variables; "LEED Policy" is "LEED Group" times "Post Certification"; ln(RBA) is ln(Rentable Building Area). "Without Replacement" means that a comparison property could not be matched to multiple LEED properties

intuitive comparability of results and past styling in the literature, only the logged specifications are included and discussed. Results are presented in Tables 6.8 and 6.9.

For the most part, the results are similar across specifications with slight differences between the two matched samples. We include five specifications that correspond to the five columns in Tables 6.8 and 6.9. The standard errors in all specifications are clustered by property. The dependent variable is the logarithm of total gross rent. Table 6.8 covers the "With Replacement" sample, while Table 6.9 regards the "Without Replacement" sample. Column (1) contains results from the baseline difference-in-differences regression. The only variables included are the group indicator (LEED Group), the time dummy variable (Post Certification), and the interaction term (LEED Policy). Column (2) adds in dummy variables for city (e.g., Atlanta) and year-quarter (e.g., 2009 Q2). Column (3) adds property-level control variables, to the specification in Column (2). These property variables are land (in acres), stories, age (in years), years since renovation, and the logged value of rentable building area (in square feet). Note that the "ENERGY STAR" variable used in the matching process has been excluded as almost the entire matched sample is ENERGY STAR.[18] Column (4) is specification (3) adding in both city-level economic indicator variables (GDP and unemployment rate). Column (5) contains the results for a specification adding in property fixed effects. Our preferred specification is that seen in Column (4) as it represents the specification controlling for the most variation aside from the property fixed effects specification.[19]

The results of the regression analysis imply a strong LEED group effect across specifications. The estimated group effect is about 5% for the "With Replacement" sample and around 8% for the "Without Replacement" sample. The estimated coefficient for the "LEED Group" variable is statistically significant at the 5% significance level for all specifications in the "With Replacement" sample and at the 1% level for the "Without Replacement" sample. This slight difference between samples makes intuitive sense—the "With Replacement" group has greater similarity between treatment and comparison groups, so the group effect should be smaller and less significant. The coefficient estimates are comparable to many of the premium estimates in the literature. For example, Fuerst and McAllister (2011) estimate a 6% rental premium for LEED buildings. A 6% rental premium is also found in Eichholtzet et al. (2010).

The focus of our paper is on the effect of official LEED certification on rental premium. The LEED group effect roughly implies a 5–8% rent premium per square-foot; however, the question in this study is whether any change in rental rate growth for LEED properties is significantly different than that of the non-LEED comparison group when controlling for group and time effects. In other words, we want to know whether LEED properties have higher rents because of the treatment (LEED certification), or because of some other unobserved factor(s) attributable to LEED buildings regardless of when they become certified. For example, if a LEED rental premium was based on the signal of certification, one would expect to see a significant positive policy effect following certification. Controlling for other factors, the estimated effect in our analysis is a reduction in rent of about 3% on-average for the "without replacement" sample [see Column (4) in Table 6.8] and a reduction close to 4.5% on-average for the "with replacement" sample [see Column (4) in Table 6.8]. For our preferred specification, the results are statistically significant at the 10% level in both samples. When looking at the total effect of LEED, LEED properties on-average still possess a rent premium over similar non-LEED buildings; however, based on our results, this premium diminishes after official certification.

This effect can be seen in the raw data. Recall that Figs. 6.5 and 6.6 show trends in rent for our matched samples split by LEED group. The LEED buildings show higher rent throughout the sample; however, the gap between the two groups gets smaller over time as more of the LEED properties become certified. When accounting for timing of certification (see Fig. 6.3), LEED buildings also show higher rents on-average. Immediately following the certification quarter, the matched non-LEED properties show an increase in rent compared to roughly constant rent for their LEED counterparts. After almost 2 years of certification, LEED rents increase, while non-LEED rents in the sample decrease. One potential explanation is that the actual implementation and maintenance of LEED practices is indeed more important to renters than simply the "green" label. Based on our sample years (2008 through 2012), the trend seen in the data could also be due to economic recovery in the real estate market. When economic conditions were weaker, renters may be less willing to pay for LEED spaces relative to similar non-LEED spaces.

We run several additional regressions as robustness checks. First, we perform a placebo test, where we switch the treatment to "never LEED" to see if the results are complementary to our main findings. Indeed, the "never LEED" coefficient estimates are comparable in size and statistical significance to the main results and opposite in sign (see Table 6.10). The estimated effect of "never LEED" is a net negative (the "policy" effect is positive but not large enough to overcome the group effect).

Table 6.10 Regression results for placebo test using "Never LEED" as treatment

	(1)	(2)	(3)	(4)
Variables	*Ln(Rent)*	*Ln(Rent)*	*Ln(Rent)*	*Ln(Rent)*
Never LEED policy	0.0343003	0.0495**	0.0420*	0.0417*
	(0.0262)	(0.0224988)	(0.0223079)	(0.0224)
Never LEED group	−0.0492054	−0.0568938**	−0.0519**	−0.0517**
	(0.0378)	(0.0255195)	(0.0234)	(0.0233)
Post "Certification"	−0.0494***	−0.016223	−0.0217378	−0.0217833
	(0.0183)	(0.0199)	(0.0193721)	0.0193964
Age			−0.0022278***	−0.00223***
			0.0007672	0.000767
Stories			0.002278**	0.002277**
			0.0011366	0.0011368
Ln(RBA)			0.0455443	0.0455888
			0.0284259	0.0284284
Land acres			−0.0017127	−0.0017103
			0.001371	0.0013708
Renovated			−0.0722**	−0.0731**
			0.0294	0.029249
Years since renovation			0.002178	0.0021674
			0.0018746	0.0018499
Ln(City GDP)				0.77894***
				0.2841812
City unemployment rate				1.70109**
				0.840209
Constant				
	3.4260***	3.41740***	2.8609***	−5.7939*
	(0.0217715)	(0.0217583)	0.3515738	3.155292
Observations	7880	7880	7880	7880
R-squared	0.0056	0.5458	0.5987	0.6000

Note *** indicates statistical significance at the 1% level, ** for 5% level, * for 10% level; standard errors are in parentheses and are all clustered by property; Columns (2) through (4) include city and year-quarter fixed effects; "Post Certification", and "LEED Policy" are all binary variables; "LEED Policy" is the "LEED Group" variable times "Post Certification"; ln(RBA) is ln(Rentable Building Area). "With Replacement" means that comparison property could be matched to multiple LEED properties

A second check involves restricting matching to within zip codes—placing greater emphasis on locational rather than constructional similarities.[20] The results for the "With Replacement" sample are included in Table 6.11. The coefficient signs on the LEED variables remain the same; however, the magnitudes are smaller and the estimated effects are statistically insignificant. This finding fits with the results of Reichardt et al. (2012) which follows a difference-in-differences design (without

Table 6.11 Regression results for logarithm of total gross rent using "With Replacement" sample matched within zip code

	(1)	*(2)*	*(3)*	*(4)*
Variables	*Ln(Rent)*	*Ln(Rent)*	*Ln(Rent)*	*Ln(Rent)*
LEED policy	−0.0166	−0.0149	−0.00968	−0.0134
	(0.0259)	(0.0184)	(0.0177)	(0.0183)
LEED group	0.0337	0.0336	0.0113	0.0117
	(0.0368)	(0.0260)	(0.0234)	(0.0237)
Post certification	−0.0453**	0.00112	−0.0121	−0.0196
	(0.0188)	(0.0214)	(0.0198)	(0.0203)
Age			−0.00274***	−0.00233***
			(0.000750)	(0.000723)
Stories			0.00297**	0.00437***
			(0.00141)	(0.00145)
Ln(RBA)			0.0381	0.0280
			(0.0334)	(0.0348)
Land acres			0.000677	0.000940
			(0.00137)	(0.00136)
Renovated			−0.0361	−0.0442
			(0.0301)	(0.0303)
Years since renovation			0.00152	0.00103
			(0.00136)	(0.00137)
Ln(City GDP)				1.209***
				(0.239)
City unemployment rate				1.357* (0.793)
Constant				
	3.400***	3.385***	2.933***	−10.30***
	(0.0293)	(0.0271)	(0.403)	(2.651)
Observations	7440	7440	7440	6560
R-squared	0.009	0.541	0.600	0.608

Note *** indicates statistical significance at the 1% level, ** for 5% level, * for 10% level; standard errors are in parentheses and are all clustered by property; propensity score matching done within zip codes; Column (4) includes city fixed effects; "Post Certification", and "LEED Policy" are all binary variables; "LEED Policy" is the "LEED Group" variable times "Post Certification"; ln(RBA) is ln(Rentable Building Area). "With Replacement" means that comparison property could be matched to multiple LEED properties. Matching in this sample is limited to comparison properties within a LEED property's zip code

PSM) and finds no statistically significant impact of LEED on rent (or vacancy rates) over time. The overall effect of LEED certification estimated in our regressions using zip code matches is close to zero—there is a slightly positive rent premium (the group effect) that is essentially cancelled out by the negative policy effect of official certification [see

Column (4) of Table 6.11]. Recalling the main analysis, the preferred specification in our "With Replacement" sample yielded a total estimated impact of LEED on rents of under 1%. Taken as a whole, the results when matching LEED properties to similar non-LEED properties imply rent premiums which are close to zero.

A final check seeks to gauge the role of market saturation in our main findings. Using the LEED Project Directory from the USGBC, we count the number of certified LEED projects in a city for each of the years in our sample.[21] We then include two variables—one to estimate the effect of LEED saturation on rent for all properties and the second to estimate any additional effect of LEED saturation on rents for certified LEED buildings (Certified LEED Building Count interacted with the LEED-Post Certification interaction term). Results are included in

Table 6.12 Regression results accounting for city LEED saturation

	(1)	*(2)*	*(3)*	*(4)*
Variables	*Ln(Rent)*	*Ln(Rent)*	*Ln(Rent)*	*Ln(Rent)*
LEED policy	−0.04171*	−0.0422582*	−0.0069919	0.0687504
	(0.0224)	0.0216263	0.0441447	0.1287585
LEED group	0.0516433**	0.0518**	0.0512545**	0.0514724**
	0.0233425	(0.0231833)	0.0232991	0.0231467
Post "Certification"	0.0199765	0.0204222	0.0145195	0.016033
	0.018554	0.0182843	0.0200894	0.0195659
Certified LEED count	0.0001113		0.0002579	
	0.0001813		0.000257	
Ln(Certified LEED count)		0.0899***		0.0872***
		(0.0305781)		(0.0317)
Certified LEED count × LEED policy			−0.0002488	
			(0.000287)	
Ln(Certified LEED count) × LEED policy				−0.02327
				(0.0271)
Age	−0.0022***	−0.002244***	−0.002240***	−0.0022575***
	(0.0007671)	0.0007671	0.0007677	0.0007663
Stories	0.002277**	0.0022728**	0.0022025*	0.002208*
	0.001137	0.0011365	(0.0011475)	0.0011357

(continued)

Table 6.12 (continued)

	(1)	(2)	(3)	(4)
Variables	*Ln(Rent)*	*Ln(Rent)*	*Ln(Rent)*	*Ln(Rent)*
Ln(RBA)	0.0455873	0.0457101	0.0468323	0.0468*
	0.0284317	0.0284111	0.028521	0.0283
Land acres	−0.0017103	−0.0017046	−0.0017	−0.0016421
	0.001371	0.0013705	(0.0014)	0.0013823
Renovated	−0.0731073**	−0.0752**	−0.0735738**	−0.0752**
	(0.0292386)	0.0292249	0.0292633	0.02929
Years since renovation	0.0021665	0.0023642	0.0021966	0.0023718
	0.0018475	0.0018391	0.0018463	0.0018448
Ln(City GDP)	0.7252803**	0.8417***	0.7276327**	0.8988***
	0.3069322	0.2699345	0.3065369	0.2858934
City unemployment rate	1.5478*	2.404074***	1.5870**	2.5760***
	0.7966146	0.8061342	0.8053366	(0.8356)
Constant	−5.264992	−7.043886***	−5.323735	−7.673446**
	3.374776	(2.9334)	(3.373641)	3.095537
Observations	7880	7880	7880	7880
R-squared	0.6001	0.6023	0.6005	0.6027

Note *** indicates statistical significance at the 1% level, ** for 5% level, * for 10% level; standard errors are in parentheses and are all clustered by property; All columns include city and year-quarter fixed effects; "Certified LEED Count" is the number of certified LEED buildings by city and year; "Post Certification", and "LEED Policy" are all binary variables; "LEED Policy" is the "LEED Group" variable times "Post Certification"; "With Replacement" means that comparison property could be matched to multiple LEED properties

Table 6.12. When only including the "Count" variable, the estimated policy effect of LEED certification on rent hardly changes. The coefficient on the "Count" variable is positive, implying that the number of LEED buildings in a city is positively related to average rents [see Columns (1) and (2) of Table 6.12]. LEED saturation is seen to have a negative (though statistically insignificant) effect on LEED buildings post-certification [see Columns (3) and (4) of Table 6.12]; however, the addition of this variable renders the LEED policy effect estimates statistically insignificant. Overall, these checks further imply that LEED certification has a non-positive effect on rents over time. Furthermore, market saturation appears to be an important aspect in the real estate valuation of LEED certification.

6.7 Discussion and Conclusion

This study examines LEED office buildings from 2008 to 2012 in major U.S. cities by comparing them to similar non-LEED office buildings within their city. It uses PSM to pair similar properties and then employs a differences-in-differences approach to isolate the impact of LEED certification by controlling for time and group effects. Based on our results, a 5–8% rental premium for LEED buildings existed in the sample; however, this estimated premium decreases by an average decline of 3–4% points following official LEED certification. This decline could be indicative of reduced operating expenses associated with energy efficiency. It could also imply shifts in real estate market valuation of LEED due to recessionary factors or increasing LEED presence in a geographic area.

Our findings differ from some of those in the previous LEED literature. While we still see an overall rental premium in our main analysis, our policy effect estimates are often negative and never both positive and statistically significant. It should be noted that the negative policy effect estimate is strongest when utilizing the most-closely matched comparison group in our most-controlled model [see Column (4) in Tables 6.8 and 6.9]. In addition, our sample of cities consists of large economic centers with high concentrations of LEED buildings. The number of LEED buildings was rapidly increasing in our sample years and cities, and increased competitiveness can drive down rents (Baker and Chinloy 2014). Therefore, the reduced (or unaffected) premium we find following official certification may not reflect the impact of LEED in less green-saturated real estate markets.

Another note is that our time period of analysis coincides with a recession. If we expect green goods to be normal, the willingness to pay for LEED would be reduced in a weak economy. We strived to partially address this concern by having our "pre" period be within the recessionary period rather than the years before the downturn, but it is still possible that the time period of our analysis influences the results. The role of ENERGY STAR is also important to consider. As nearly our entire matched sample is ENERGY STAR regardless of LEED status, the smaller premium following LEED certification may imply that general energy efficiency is more important than formal "LEED" designation. In a recession, there may be less willingness to pay for a higher level of energy efficiency when comparable buildings exist. Reichardt et al.

(2012) find that the rental premium for sustainable building certification rose from 2006 to 2008 but fell during the recession.

Regardless, a reduction in rental premium would not necessarily mean that LEED is a bad business decision. Becoming LEED could also be based on an assessment of the potential long-term benefits. The decline in rent following official certification seen in our analysis may be related to the cost savings associated with energy efficiency. If operating expenses are lower, this could lead to lower rents being charged.[22] Past research by the USGBC as well as academic studies has found greatly reduced operating expenses in LEED buildings (see Reichardt (2014), among others). While we were unable to do so with our current data, a stronger analysis of energy efficiency and cost saving associated with LEED would be a desirable follow-up to the present study. Analyzing other investment-related aspects of LEED would also be an interesting research foray. For example, it is possible that LEED could relate to the idea of Corporate Social Responsibility.[23]

Our findings can be connected to several policy implications. First, while determining why properties become LEED is beyond the scope of our analysis, the reasons are quite important in light of our results. Assuming profit-maximizing decision-making, the benefits of LEED must outweigh the costs of becoming certified. This expected benefit likely comes from some change in real estate valuation (e.g., rent increase) or a reduction in costs. If rents are indeed unaffected or even reduced following LEED certification, future building owners who elect to become LEED (or those who are already LEED) must have other reasons to pursue (continue) energy-efficient property development. Again, assuming that building owners seek LEED certification for financial gain of some kind, cost saving may be the mechanism. The lower rents we see in our results following official certification and the continued expansion of the LEED program could support this supposition. In line with the past work [e.g., Alcott and Greenstone (2012) or Peterson and Gammill (2010)], perhaps information inadequacies are to blame—better information disclosure and valuation processes could improve the value of LEED properties and increase rents.

A final point pertains to the relationship between LEED and real estate markets. As previously noted, the estimated effect of LEED on rent could be due to market conditions. Buildings continued to certify LEED during the recession, but, based on our results, there was a non-positive effect on rental premium following official certification. From a policy perspective, the intent of LEED is not to raise rents—the purpose is to improve energy efficiency. Sustainability is a long-term concept, and the present market valuation may be less relevant for a program like LEED. The continued popularity of LEED means both that building owners still view certification as worthwhile (in some regard) and that energy efficiency is increasingly becoming the norm. Therefore, the nature of the market valuation of LEED could have changed. Building owners, particularly during a recession or in a LEED-saturated city, may opt for certification based on expectations of increased energy cost savings, eventual increases in rent, or future shifts in standards—both in terms of real estate characteristics and government regulations. Further investigation into the reasons, building owners decide to pursue and renew LEED certification could be beneficial to both researchers and policy makers. Other potential avenues for future research on LEED include the different subsystems (e.g., New Construction) and levels of certification, the relative values of certain LEED credits, the possible effects of changes to the LEED system over time, and effects of LEED certification on other outcomes.

Notes

1. USGBC. http://www.usgbc.org/articles/what-green-building (Retrieved on 08/15/2014) (USGBC 2014).
2. USGBC. http://www.usgbc.org/leed#rating (Retrieved on 08/19/2014).
3. USGBC. http://www.usgbc.org/leed#rating (Retrieved on 08/19/2014).
4. The LEED credit library can be found at http://www.usgbc.org/credits.
5. The ability to alter rent will depend on the structure of the market. Those with market power may be able to capitalize preferences for LEED into charging higher rent, while those with little market power may not be able to change rents so readily.
6. While both are voluntary, a key difference between LEED and ENERGY STAR is that LEED points are earned directly through actions while ENERGY STAR eligibility is based on a score calculated from energy consumption performance relative to peers See https://www.energystar.gov/buildings/facility-owners-and-managers/existing-buildings/earn-recognition/energy-star-certification for more information on ENERGY STAR scores.
7. http://www.usatoday.com/story/news/nation/2012/10/24/green-building-leed-certification/1650517/ (USA TODAY 2013).

8. http://www.usgbc.org/resources/leed-project-stats-ranked-cities-and-states (USGBC 2012).
9. See www.gbig.org for more information.
10. Most properties with missing rent values were excluded from the sample. Buildings with missing quarters of data were included if a total gross rent value could be directly determined from other rental values. For example, consider a property with one quarter that does not have a total gross rent value. If direct gross rent was available and all other total gross rent values matched the corresponding direct gross rent value (perhaps because the property had no sublet rent), the missing total gross rent value would be corrected under the formula total gross rent = direct gross rent.
11. For commercial buildings, LEED and ENERGY STAR have different focuses. LEED focuses more on the entire building process and relationship with the surrounding environment. ENERGY STAR focuses more on operation. Details of ENERGY STAR for commercial buildings can be accessed on www.energystar.gov.
12. One limitation is that LEED is indeed a process, and some benefits could emerge before the official certification. For example, efficiency measures taken in adhering to LEED guidelines in order to eventually meet certification requirements could have effects before the property is officially designated LEED. These efficiency measures could improve operating performance and affect rental rates with or without LEED designation. It is also possible that building operators set rent higher after LEED registration but before certification due to renovations or the anticipated LEED designation. To address these concerns, our focus is solely on the actual LEED designation.
13. Rentable building area (RBA). http://www.costar.com/about/glossary.aspx?hl=R (Retrieved on 08/19/2014) (CoStar 2014).
14. For example, consider property A and property B that are both in city C. Say that property A and property B are estimated to have been equally likely to become LEED but only property A does so. These would then be "matched"—we assign the "PostCertification" variable for property A to property B as well. Our goal is to examine if and how rent changes over time vary between LEED and non-LEED properties.
15. Some of the matches do not change. For others who now share a nearest neighbor, we form subgroups within a given range of propensity scores such that the numbers of LEED and non-LEED buildings in the subgroup are equal and as comparable as possible. Then we randomly match properties in each subgroup and assign the appropriate "PostCertification" values.
16. Krishnamurthy, C. K. B. and B. Kriström (2016).

17. A relevant question would be how, if at all, vacancy rate relates to rent and LEED status. We ran the same regressions using vacancy rate as the dependent variable and found no statistically significant effect of LEED. These results are excluded from the present paper but are available upon request.
18. Regression results are nearly identical with or without including the "ENERGY STAR" indicator.
19. The property fixed effects have little impact on the main results for the "Without Replacement" sample, and present the disadvantages of covering repeated properties in the "With Replacement" sample as well as preventing our desire to estimate the LEED group effect.
20. This matching requires more non-LEED properties to be repeated in the sample.
21. The variable is a running count. So, the 2008 count includes the number of LEED buildings certified in 2008 or earlier, the 2009 count is the number of LEED buildings certified in or before 2009, and so on.
22. Baker and Chinloy (2014).
23. Eichholtz et al. (2010).

Acknowledgements We appreciate comments from Dr. Ed Coulson from the University of Nevada, Las Vegas, and participants at the International Association for Energy Economics (IAEE) European Energy Policy Conference in Rome, Italy, in 2014. We also thank anonymous referees for their helpful comments and questions. Any errors or omissions are our own.

References

Allcott, H., and M. Greenstone. 2012. Is There an Energy Efficiency Gap? *The Journal of Economic Perspectives* 26 (1): 3–28.

Baker, H. Kent, and Peter Chinloy 2014.*Private Real Estate Markets and Investment*. Oxford: Oxford University Press.

Blumberg, David. 2012. LEED in the U.S. Commercial Office Market: Market Effects and the Emergence of LEED for Existing Buildings. *Journal of Sustainable Real Estate* 4: 23–47.

Bond, Shaun A., and Avis Devine. 2016. Certification Matters: Is Green Talk Cheap Talk? *Journal of Real Estate Finance and Economics* 52: 117–140.

CoStar. 2014. *Rentable Building Area*. http://www.costar.com/about/glossary.aspx?hl=R. Accessed 19 Aug 2014.

Das, Prashant, and Jonathan A. Wiley. 2014. Determinants of Premia for Energy-Efficient Design in the Office Market. *Journal of Property Research* 31 (1): 64–86.

Deng, Y., Z. Li, and J. Quigley. 2012. Economic Returns to Energy-Efficient Investments in the Housing Market: Evidence from Singapore. *Regional Science and Urban Economics* 42 (3): 506–515.

Dermisi, S. 2013. Performance of Downtown Chicago's Office Buildings Before and After Their LEED Existing Buildings' Certification. *Real Estate Finance* 29 (5): 37–50.

Eichholtz, P., N. Kok, and J. Quigley. 2010. Doing Well by Doing Good? Green Office Buildings. *American Economic Review* 100 (5): 2492–2509.

Florance, A., N. Miller, R. Peng, and J. Spivey. 2010. Slicing, Dicing, and Scoping the Size of the U.S. Commercial Real Estate Market. *Journal of Real Estate Portfolio Management* 16 (2): 101–118.

Fuerst, F., and P. McAllister. 2008. Green Noise or Green Value? Measuring the Price Effects of Environmental Certification in Commercial Buildings. MPRA Paper No. 11446. Munich, Germany: University Library of Munich.

Fuerst, F., and P. McAllister. 2011. Green Noise or Green Value? Measuring the Effects of Environmental Certification on Office Values. *Real Estate Economics* 39 (1): 45–69.

Krishnamurthy, C. K. B., and B. Kriström. 2016. Determinants of the Price-Premium for Green Energy: Evidence From an OECD Cross-Section. *Environmental and Resource Economics* 64: 173–204.

Miller, Norm, Jay Spivey, and Andrew Florance. 2008. Does Green Pay Off? *Journal of Real Estate Portfolio Management* 14 (4): 385–400.

Miller, N., D. Pogue, Q.D. Gough, and S.M. Davis. 2009. Green Building and Productivity. *Journal of Sustainable Real Estate* 1 (1): 65–91.

Peterson, Kristian, and Ross Gammill. 2010. The Economics of Sustainability in Commercial Real Estate. *IMFA Foundation White Paper.*

Reichardt, A., F. Fuerst, N. Rottke, and J. Zietz. 2012. Sustainable Building Certification and the Rent Premium: A Panel Data. *Journal of Real Estate Research* 34 (1): 99–126.

Reichardt, Alexander. 2014. Operating Expenses and the Rent Premium of ENERGY STAR and LEED Certified Buildings in the Central and Eastern US. *The Journal of Real Estate Finance and Economics* 49 (3): 413–433.

Robinson, Spenser J., and Andrew R. Sanderford. 2015. Green Buildings: Similar to Other Premium Buildings? *The Journal of Real Estate Finance and Economics* 52: 99–116.

United States Green Building Council. 2012. LEED Project Stats – Ranked Cities and States. http://www.usgbc.org/resources/leed-project-stats-ranked-cities-and-states . Accessed 15 Aug 2014.

United States Green Building Council. 2014. *LEED Rating Systems.* http://www.usgbc.org/articles/what-green-building. Accessed 15 Aug 2014.

United States Green Building Council. 2014. *What is Green Building?* http://www.usgbc.org/leed#rating. Accessed 19 Aug 2014.

USA TODAY. 2013. *In U.S. Building Industry, Is It Too Easy To Be Green?* http://www.usatoday.com/story/news/nation/2012/10/24/green-building-leedcertification/1650517/. Accessed 15 Aug 2014.

Wiley, J., J. Benefield, and K. Johnson. 2010. Green Design and the Market for Commercial Office Space. *Journal of Real Estate Finance and Economics* 41 (2): 228–243.

Authors' Biography

Mr. Jordan Stanley Ph.D. Candidate in Economics, Department of Economics, Syracuse University. His research focuses on environmental economics. He is a graduate of Washington and Jefferson College.

Dr. Yongsheng Wang Associate Professor of Economics, Director of Financial Economics, Washington and Jefferson College. He is also a visiting scholar at the graduate school of public and international affairs at the University of Pittsburgh. His research focuses on energy economics and real estate economics. His past research was funded by LUCE Foundation, Freeman Foundation, Heinz Endowments, and NIST (Department of Commerce).

CHAPTER 7

Energy Efficiency and Green Building Markets in Japan

Jiro Yoshida, Junichiro Onishi and Chihiro Shimizu

7.1 Introduction

This chapter presents a review of the existing studies on Japanese green buildings and a new empirical analysis of the relation between office rents, green building labels, and the actual energy use. Economic analysis of green buildings started with studies on the US market. Early studies use the US data and identify positive associations between green building labels and property prices (e.g., Eichholtz et al. 2009). Higher property prices can be a result of

The original version of this chapter was revised: For detailed information please see Erratum. The erratum to this chapter is available at https://doi.org/10.1057/978-1-137-57446-6_11

J. Yoshida (✉)
The Pennsylvania State University, University Park, State College, PA, USA
e-mail: jiro@psu.edu

J. Onishi
Xymax Real Estate Institute Corporation, Chiyoda-ku, Tokyo, Japan
e-mail: junichiro@xymax.co.jp

C. Shimizu
Nihon University, Chiyoda-ku, Tokyo, Japan
e-mail: shimizu.chihiro@nihon-u.ac.jp

N.E. Coulson et al. (eds.), *Energy Efficiency and the Future of Real Estate*, DOI 10.1057/978-1-137-57446-6_7

higher rental rates (e.g., Eichholtz et al. 2009) and higher occupancy rates (e.g., Fuerst and McAllister 2009, 2011a, b; Wiley et al. 2010). Subsequent studies use data from other countries and generally find consistent results (e.g., Deng et al. 2012; Zheng et al. 2012; Devine and Kok 2015).

A question still remains as to what causes the positive association between green building labels and property prices. There are several possible reasons for value premiums in green buildings (Yoshida 2009). First, socially conscious consumers may positively view green labels and pay higher prices when they buy houses (Aroul and Hansz 2012; Dastrup et al. 2012; Bruegge et al. 2016; Fuerst and Shimizu 2016). Similarly, socially conscious firms may pay higher rents for benefits in their corporate social responsibility strategy (Eichholtz et al. 2010; Miller et al. 2008; Pivo and Fisher 2010; Fuerst and McAllister 2011a; Devine and Kok 2015; Eichholtz et al. 2016). Second, property buyers may be willing to pay a higher price or rent because green buildings give them direct cost savings. For example, better heat insulators and more energy-efficient equipment can reduce operating costs for the property owner. The cost efficiency of a building can be associated with a high price (Laquatra 1986; Dian and Miranowski 1989; Gilmer 1989; Brounen and Kok 2011; Deng et al. 2012; Aydin et al. 2016). Third, public policy programs can provide consumers with subsidies or tax incentives to reduce user costs. The building price reflects both current and expected future policies. Fourth, developers may charge a higher price for green buildings due to a larger cost of development (Yoshida and Shimizu 2012; Dippold et al. 2014). However, green technologies can result in a value discount if the total life-cycle cost for a potential owner is larger (Borenstein 2008). Several studies report the absence of a green price premium (Fuerst and McAllister 2011b; Jaffee et al. 2011; Yamagata et al. 2011; Deng and Wu 2014; Freybote et al. 2015) and a price discount for residential properties (Zheng et al. 2012; Yoshida and Sugiura 2015).

However, most studies do not disentangle possible causes except for a few studies. Eichholtz et al. (2013) show that increased energy efficiency is fully capitalized into rents and asset values. Yoshida and Sugiura (2015) study Japanese condominiums and find that the long-life design is associated with price premiums, but the use of renewable energy and recycled materials and water is associated with price discounts.

This study presents two empirical findings. First, we show that the observed building features that are associated with sustainability are effective in reducing the actual consumption of electricity and water. These sustainability features include a zone air conditioning system, a card-key security system, and a recent building renovation. We also find that buildings with green labels are associated with less consumption of electricity and water after controlling for the observed sustainability features. Green labels are determined on the basis of a long list of green building features. Thus, these features that we do not observe in our data have an additional effect on the reduction of the energy and resource consumption. This is one of a few studies about the actual energy consumption for green buildings. Although a large number of engineering studies confirm the energy efficiency of green building features, the energy efficiency does not guarantee the actual reduction of energy consumption. It is because users may actually increase the energy consumption because of lower energy and water costs. Our finding confirms that green buildings contribute to the reduction of the consumption of electricity and water.

Second, we show that a rent premium observed for green buildings is paid by tenants not for a brand associated with green building labels but for material benefits of green buildings regarding lower costs of energy and water. When the usage of electricity and water is omitted in a rent estimation equation, green building labels have a significant positive effect on office rents. However, when we include the usage of electricity and water, the coefficient on green building labels becomes insignificant whereas the coefficients on the usage of electricity and water are statistically significant. Green building labels are an important factor that determines the actual usage of electricity and water, and they indirectly affect office rents through the effects of electricity usage and water usage. However, green building labels themselves do not have a direct effect on office rents.

The remainder of this chapter is organized as follows. In the next two sections, we explain Japanese green building labels and the extant studies on green buildings in Japan. In Empirical Strategy section, we specify hedonic regression models. In Data section, we summarize the data on the transaction prices and green building labels used in this study. Results section presents the empirical analysis and a discussion of the results. The last section concludes the study.

7.2 Green Building Labels in Japan

Energy efficiency has gained much attention in Japan since the oil crisis in the 1970s. The Act on the Rational Use of Energy (which is commonly known as "Energy Conservation Act") was enacted in 1979. The act imposed regulations on energy-intensive factories and widely prevalent household equipment such as vehicles, refrigerators, and air conditioners. Since then, the energy efficiency of the targeted sectors and equipment significantly improved and exceeded the world standard. The scope of the act was subsequently expanded, and stronger measures were introduced. However, the act did not cover buildings until 2005. Even by this 2005 revision, only large buildings exceeding 2000 square meters in floor space are regulated.

Preceding the revision to the Energy Conservation Act, a national green building certification called CASBEE was launched in 2001. It was approximately 10 years after BREEAM was launched in the UK and 5 years after LEED was launched in the USA. As BREEAM and LEED, CASBEE adopts a multifaceted approach to assessing sustainability. It evaluates various sustainability aspects including (1) indoor environment, (2) quality of services, (3) outdoor environment on site, (4) energy, (5) resources and materials, and (6) off-site environment. CASBEE provides a comprehensive measure called BEE (Building Environment Efficiency), which is the ratio of the value of "environmental quality (Q)" to the value of "environmental load (L)." At the end of March 2015, 16,471 buildings were certified. In 2012, a variation of CASBEE called CASBEE Real Estate was launched. This is a simplified version of CASBEE and designed to reduce the time and cost of evaluation. Table 7.1 summarizes green building labels in Japan and major countries.

The Tokyo Metropolitan Government launched its own comprehensive green building program (Tokyo Green Building Program, or TGBP henceforth) in 2002 on the basis of the Basic Plan for Environmental Protection (BPEP) launched in 1997 and the Tokyo Metropolitan Environmental Security Ordinance enacted in 2000. The government requires owners of large buildings to submit Green Building Plans and subsequently releases the submitted plan and related materials on its website. Since 2005, the developers of large-scale condominium projects are required to announce their itemized green scores to potential buyers. Although evaluations are mandated only to large construction or renovation projects exceeding 5000 m^2 in floor area, owners of smaller buildings can voluntarily participate in the program. The evaluated green factors are as follows: (1) energy conservation such as the reduction of thermal loads and the use of renewable energy, (2) resource efficiency such as the use of eco-friendly materials and long-life building design, (3) environmental protection such as water recycling and planting, and

Table 7.1 Selected green building labels

		LEED	*Energy star*	*BREEAM*	*EPCs*	*HQE*	*GRESB*	*Greenstar*	*NABERS*
Used in this study		–	–	–	–	–	–	–	–
Country		USA	USA	UK	UK	France	Netherlands	Australia	Australia
Organization		US Green Building Council	US Government (EPA)	Building Research Establishment	UK Government	HQE Association	GRESB	Green Building Council of Australia	Australian Government
Since		1998	1995	1990	2006	1996	2010	2003	1990
Target		Buildings	Buildings	Buildings	Buildings	Buildings	Firm	Buildings	Buildings
Focus		Comprehensive	Energy efficiency	Comprehensive	Energy efficiency	Comprehensive	Comprehensive	Comprehensive	Energy efficiency
Output		4 Ranks	Energy star ≥ 75	5 Ranks	8 Ranks	4 Ranks	4 Quadrants	6 Ranks	5 Ranks
Evaluated items	Building and equipment	○	–	○	○	○	–	○	–
	Operation	○	○	○	–	–	○	○	○
	Water	○	–	○	–	○	○	○	○
	Material	○	–	○	–	○	–	○	–
	Interior	○	–	○	–	○	○	○	○
	Site and surroundings	○	–	○	–	○	–	○	–
	Transport	○	–	○	–	–	–	○	–
	Waste	○	–	○	–	○	–	○	○
	Contamination	○	–	○	–	○	–	○	–
		CASBEE	CASBEE Real Estate	DBJ Green Building Certificate	SMBC Sustainable Building Assessment	TGBP	BELS		
Used in this study		○	○	○	○	–	–		
Country		Japan	Japan	Japan	Japan	Japan	Japan		
Organization		Japanese Government (MLIT)	Japanese Government (MLIT)	Development Bank of Japan	Sumitomo Mitsui Bank Corporation	Tokyo Metropolitan Government	Japanese Government (MLIT)		

(continued)

Table 7.1 (continued)

		LEED	*Energy star*	*BREEAM*	*EPCs*	*HQE*	*GRESB*	*Greenstar*	*NABERS*
Since		2001	2012	2011	2011	2002	2014		
Target		Buildings	Buildings	Buildings	Buildings	Buildings	Buildings		
Focus		Comprehensive	Comprehensive	Comprehensive	Comprehensive	Comprehensive	Energy efficiency		
Output		5 Ranks	4 Ranks	5 Ranks	6 Ranks	Scores on 22 items	5 Ranks		
Evaluated items	Building and equipment	○	○	○	○	○	○		
	Operation	–	○	–	○	–	–		
	Water	○	○	○	○	○	–		
	Material	○	○	–	○	○	–		
	Interior	○	○	○	○	○	–		
	Site and surroundings	○	○	○	○	○	–		
	Transport	○	○	○	○	–	–		
	Waste	–	–	○	○	○	–		
	Contamination	○	–	–	○	–	–		

(4) mitigation of the heat island phenomenon such as waste heat reduction and the use of solar-reflective materials. For each factor, a positive score (1, 2, 3, etc.) is awarded if a building satisfies the program's higher standards. Receiving no point indicates that the building performs no better than an ordinary building.

More recently, Development Bank of Japan and Sumitomo Mitsui Banking Corporation started in 2011 their own green building certification programs. These banks were the first Japanese banks to become members of the United Nations Environment Programme Finance Initiative. These programs evaluate even broader sustainability measures. For example, the DBJ certificate is based on (1) ecology, (2) amenity, (3) community, (4) risk management, and (5) partnership among stakeholders. Its evaluation process is simpler and quicker than for other programs.

7.3 Extant Studies on Japanese Green Buildings

In this section, we review the extant studies on Japanese green buildings. Although the majority of studies are non-academic or engineering studies, there are several academic studies about the economic analysis of green buildings.[1] We review Yoshida (2009, 2010, 2012), Yoshida and Sugiura (2010, 2015), Yoshida and Shimizu (2012), Fuerst et al. (2013), Nakayama et al. (2015), and Fuerst and Shimizu (2016).[2]

Yoshida (2009, 2010, 2012) and Yoshida and Sugiura (2010, 2015) use transaction price data for both new and pre-owned condominiums in Tokyo and data for buildings assessed in the Tokyo Green Building Program (TGBP). Using a matched sample, they test whether green condominiums are traded at a premium and whether each green factor in the label affects property prices differently. Yoshida and Sugiura (2010, 2015) first demonstrate theoretically that a green building can be initially priced at a discount but eventually priced at a premium if green buildings feature a longer economic life and a larger life-cycle cost due to replacements of expensive equipment. They empirically confirm this theoretical prediction; green condominiums are initially traded at lower prices than comparable non-green condominiums but are traded at a premium after 2 years because depreciation rates for green buildings are lower.

Yoshida (2009, 2010, 2012) and Yoshida and Sugiura (2010, 2015) further investigate whether green factors affect property prices differently. Positive price differences are associated with a long-life design, which is an architectural design that results in a longer economic life of the building through easier renovations and conversions. This result makes sense because a long-life design reduces an owner's life-cycle costs by facilitating maintenance, renovation, and conversion. According to an engineering study, the benefit of the long-life design is as large as a 38% reduction in life-cycle costs in Japan, where the average life of a residential building is only 26 years. In contrast, energy and resource efficiency, such as water recycling, the use of eco-friendly materials, and the use of renewable energy, are associated with negative price differences. The use of eco-friendly materials and water recycling will increase future maintenance expenses and capital expenditures. For example, eco-friendly materials are significantly less durable, and a water-recycling system for a small building is four times more costly than public sewage services. These future benefits and costs are capitalized into the initial price of a condominium.[3]

Yoshida and Shimizu (2012) and Fuerst et al. (2013) estimate premia in both asking and transaction prices for newly developed green condominiums in Tokyo. They merge a unique transaction dataset that includes both asking and transaction prices with other datasets that contain homebuyer characteristics, developer, and development project characteristics. Homebuyer characteristics include annual income, the age of household head, occupation (employment status, job function, and industry), household size, the number of children, and the identifier for first-time buyers. Development project characteristics include scale, location characteristics, and building characteristics. The estimation result of hedonic models reveals that the average asking price for condominiums with a green label is approximately 5% higher than that for comparable condominiums without a label. In other words, the developers of green condominiums ask a significantly higher price. However, actual transaction prices are approximately 4% lower than asking prices. They find that wealthier and higher income buyers pay a larger premium for green condominiums, both in absolute and in relative terms. In contrast, buyers with below-median income pay a smaller price premium. Thus, the green condominium is a normal good.

Fuerst and Shimizu (2016) find that the effect of green labels on condominium prices varies by income group. They divide buyers into four income groups and estimate a hedonic price equation separately for each income group. A green building premium in asking price increases with income (from 4 to 8% of the asking price for non-green buildings). Similarly, a percentage premium in transaction price is mainly driven by households with above-average income. Because more affluent people buy expensive condominiums, a price premium in monetary value is even more pronounced. This is the first study to demonstrate that higher income buyers value green features more although the marginal value of energy cost saving would be smaller for them.

Nakayama et al. (2015) study green premium in office rent in Tokyo. Using the hedonic approach, they show that green office rents are 4.39% higher than comparable non-green office rents. They further create five strata with respect to the propensity score for green buildings and estimate a rent premium in each stratum. Buildings are relatively large and new in the stratum with the highest propensity score whereas buildings are older and smaller in the low-score strata. They do not find a significant rent premium except for a stratum with the second highest propensity score. Thus, a rent premium for green office buildings is not uniform across different building sizes and ages.

7.4 Empirical Strategy

We first estimate the following equation about monthly energy usage at the building level:

$$\ln Z_{ijt} = \alpha G_i + \boldsymbol{X}_i'\boldsymbol{\beta} + \delta_t + \lambda_j + \varepsilon_{ijt}, \tag{7.1}$$

where $\ln Z_{ijt}$ denotes the energy usage of building i located in submarket j in month t, G_i denotes a dummy variable for green building labels, $\boldsymbol{X}_i$ denotes a vector of building characteristics, δ_t denotes month fixed effects, λ_j denotes submarket fixed effects, and ε_{ijt} denotes the error term. The dependent variable Z_{ijt} is either electricity usage (total kWh for the past year) or water usage (m^3 for the past year). Office space characteristics $\boldsymbol{X}_i$ consist of gross building floor area, the number of stories above ground, building age, the walking time to the nearest railway/subway station, management fee (per month per square meter), maintenance costs, capital expenditures (5-year average per square meter), dummy variables for recent building renovation, a zone air conditioning system, and a card-key security system.[4] We specify 50 submarkets in Tokyo's 23 wards. These submarkets include premier business centers such as Marunouchi, Otemachi, Shinjuku, Shibuya, Nihombashi, and Roppongi. The parameters of interest are α, which represents the effect of green building labels, and the elements of $\boldsymbol{\beta}$ that are related with sustainability.

Second, we estimate an office rent equation for newly contracted leases:

$$\ln R_{ijt} = \alpha G_i + \boldsymbol{X}_i'\boldsymbol{\beta} + \boldsymbol{Z}_i'\boldsymbol{\gamma} + \delta_t + \lambda_j + \mu_{ijt}, \tag{7.2}$$

where $\ln R_{ijt}$ denotes the natural logarithm of the rent contracted at quarter-year t for office space i located in submarket j, $\boldsymbol{Z}_i$ denotes a vector of building-level energy usage variables, δ_t denotes quarter-year fixed effects, λ_j denotes submarket fixed effects, and μ_{ijt} denotes the error term. Since the unit of observations i is lease contracts, we adjust the standard errors for clusters at the building level. The parameters of interest are α, which represents the effect of green building labels, the elements of $\boldsymbol{\beta}$ that are related with sustainability, and $\boldsymbol{\gamma}$, which represents the effect of energy usage. In particular, we test whether green building labels have an effect on office rents after controlling for energy usage and sustainability features. If labels have a positive effect, it is the rent premium caused by green labels themselves, not by energy cost savings. A possible reason for such a rent premium is the tenant firms' social responsibility considerations.

7.5 Data

We combine three datasets in this study: green building labels, office buildings and leases, and operating costs of buildings. We use green building labels given by CASBEE, CASBEE Real Estate, the DBJ Green Building Certificate, and the SMBC Sustainable Building Assessment. There are several reasons to use these labels among other labels. First, these labels are given to individual buildings. Several other labels are given to owners or building portfolios. By using labels for buildings, we can combine the label status and other information about rent, operation, and building characteristics. Second, these labels are given by a third party on the basis of objective criteria. For example, CASBEE was developed by a research committee consisting of academia, industry, and national and local governments. After the assessment system was determined, the Institute for Building Environment and Energy Conservation (IBEC) has been implementing CASBEE. The IBEC has certified 11 private assessor organizations to ensure rigorous implementations of the program. Other labels that we use also adopt a rigorous approach to designing and implementing certificates. Third, the assessment criteria for these labels are not just energy efficiency but very comprehensive. The criteria include waste reduction, interior environmental quality for users, and operating policies. There are 90 buildings with the DBJ Green Building Certificate, 77 buildings with CASBEE, 36 buildings with CASBEE Real Estate, and 8 buildings with the SMBC Sustainable Building Assessment as of November 2014. We construct a dummy variable (G_i) that takes the value of one if a building has any of these four labels.

The office rent data are taken from the new lease contract database of Xymax, Inc. The existing studies typically use asking rents because of their availability. However, there are significant differences between asking rents and contracted rents (Fuerst et al. 2013). Our use of the contracted rents is an advantage of this study. Rents in the database are gross rents, which include operating expenses. In Japan, operating expenses do not fluctuate much over time. Building characteristics include building size (e.g., total floor area), building age, the type of air conditioning system, distance to the nearest railway station, submarket, and lease contract date. To study relatively homogeneous properties, we restrict our sample to the leases contracted between January 2013 and December 2014 in buildings greater than or equal to 300 Tsubo (992 m^2) located in the 23 wards in Tokyo.

The operating expense data are obtained from the property management database of Xymax, Inc. The database includes the building-level information about property management fees, maintenance cost, monthly electricity usage, and monthly water usage. We exclude buildings that use district heating and cooling system (DHC) because electricity usage is not comparable between buildings with DHC and without DHC.

Tables 7.2 and 7.3 show the definition and summary statistics of variables, respectively. The sample size is 480 lease contracts in 169 buildings. These contracts include 22 leases in green buildings, which account for 5% of the entire sample. The average monthly rent in the sample is 4801 yen per m^2. The average building in the sample is a 22-year-old, 10-story building with 9344 m^2 of gross building area and located 4 min from the nearest station. Approximately, 90% of the buildings have a card-key security system, and 85% have a zone air conditioning system.

Table 7.2 List of variables

Variable	*Definition*	*Unit*
Contract rent	Monthly rents for new lease contracts	Yen/m^2
Green label dummy	=1 if a building has a green label	–
Gross building area	Gross building area of the building	m^2
Building age	Number of years since construction	Year
Number of stories above ground	Number of stories above ground	Stories
Time to the nearest station	Time to walk to the building from the nearest station	Min
Zone air conditioning dummy	=1 if a building uses a zone air conditioning system	–
Card-key system dummy	=1 if a building uses a card-key security system	–
Building renovation dummy	=1 if a building was renovated within X years	–
Lease quarter-year dummies	A set of dummy variables for the quarter-year when a lease was contracted	–
Submarket dummies	A set of dummy variables for 50 submarkets in Tokyo 23 wards	–
Maintenance cost	Monthly maintenance costs per square meter paid by a tenant	Yen/m^2
Repair cost	Repair costs per square meter during the past 5 years	Yen/m^2
Electricity usage	Monthly average amount of electricity usage during the past year per square meter	kWh/m^2
Water usage	Monthly average amount of water usage during the past year per square meter	m^3/m^2

7.6 Result

Table 7.4 shows the estimation result of Eq. (7.1) about energy usage. Columns (1) and (2) show the results for log electricity usage per gross building area. In column (1), the coefficient on green label dummy is negative but not statistically significant. When gas usage dummy is included (column (2)), the coefficient becomes statistically significant at the 5% level. The use of electricity is approximately 10% lower in green buildings. Other building characteristics that are related with sustainability also affect the electricity usage: A zone air conditioning system, a card-key security system, and recent building renovation have statistically significant negative effects. Total gross building area has a negative coefficient, which indicates scale economies. The coefficient on the gas usage

Table 7.3 Summary statistics

Variable	*N*	*Mean*	*St. Dev.*	*Min*	*Max*
Contract rent	480	4801.55	1762.20	1966.25	16,649.60
Green label dummy	480	0.05	0.21	0.00	1.00
Gross building area	480	9343.66	15,048.94	1000.53	97,978.74
Number of stories above ground	480	10.11	4.92	4.00	34.00
Time to the nearest station	480	3.64	2.24	0.00	14.00
Building age	480	22.31	10.54	0.00	53.00
Zone air conditioning dummy	480	0.85	0.36	0.00	1.00
Card-key system dummy	480	0.90	0.30	0.00	1.00
Building renovation dummy	480	0.13	0.34	0.00	1.00
Maintenance cost	344	231.15	96.69	77.88	629.44
Repair cost	377	12,362.80	10,398.91	1037.17	45,708.58
Electricity usage	165	22.18	7.06	10.18	37.66
Water usage	162	0.11	0.05	0.02	0.28

dummy is positive. However, this coefficient may not entirely represent a causal effect because buildings with more electricity usage may use gas as a supplementary source of energy.

Columns (3) and (4) show the results for log water usage per gross building area. The green building label dummy has a statistically significant negative effect; approximately, 17.2% smaller amount of water is used in green buildings (column (4)).[5] Other sustainability-related building characteristics also decrease water usage (a zone air conditioning system, a card-key security system, and recent building renovation). Scale economies are not observed with respect to the entire building area, but a negative coefficient on the number of stories indicates that scale economies exist with respect to the size of each floor.

We confirm that sustainability-related features of the building are effective in reducing energy and water consumption. In addition, additional green building features represented by green building labels are also effective in the reduction of energy and water consumption. These effects on energy and water consumption are an equilibrium outcome of tenants' consumption behavior. Thus, we find that the actual tenants do not waste more electricity or water when these goods are cheaper to obtain. A limitation of this analysis is that the detailed tenant information is not available. Thus, we cannot analyze whether a less consumption of energy and water is caused by a change in tenant behavior or by selection. It is possible that environmentally conscious tenants select into

Table 7.4 Result of energy usage regressions

		Dependent variable			
		Log electricity usage		*Log water usage*	
		(1)	*(2)*	*(3)*	*(4)*
Green_label	Green label dummy	−0.038 (0.049)	−0.101** (0.050)	−0.239*** (0.074)	−0.189** (0.074)
log(GBA)	Log gross building area	−0.031** (0.012)	−0.076*** (0.015)	−0.039** (0.017)	0.004 (0.020)
Story	Number of stories above ground	0.011** (0.005)	0.010** (0.005)	−0.014** (0.006)	−0.013** (0.006)
Age	Building age	−0.003** (0.001)	−0.004*** (0.001)	−0.004** (0.002)	−0.003 (0.002)
Minute	Time to the nearest station	0.025*** (0.005)	0.034*** (0.005)	0.033*** (0.007)	0.020*** (0.008)
Individual_air_conditioning	Zone air conditioning dummy	−0.150*** (0.042)	−0.123*** (0.042)	−0.120*** (0.045)	−0.123*** (0.045)
Machine_security	Card-key system dummy	−0.313*** (0.044)	−0.267*** (0.044)	−0.406*** (0.058)	−0.443*** (0.058)
Renewal	Building renovation dummy	−0.146*** (0.036)	−0.143*** (0.035)	−0.266*** (0.050)	−0.258*** (0.049)
Occupancy	Occupancy rate	0.003*** (0.001)	0.003*** (0.001)	0.006*** (0.001)	0.005*** (0.001)
Gas_dummy	Gas usage dummy		0.197*** (0.035)		−0.173*** (0.045)
Constant	Constant	3.546*** (0.151)	3.820*** (0.158)	−1.197*** (0.203)	−1.444*** (0.212)
Time	Submarket fixed effects	Yes	Yes	Yes	Yes
Area	Month fixed effects	Yes	Yes	Yes	Yes
Observations	Observations	2126	2126	1132	1132
Adjusted R^2	Adjusted R^2	0.424	0.433	0.583	0.589
F statistic	F Statistic	22.445***	22.897***	22.687***	22.861***

This table shows the regression result of Eq. (7.1). Data are a panel of monthly observations at the building level. In parentheses are standard errors that are the White heteroscedasticity-consistent standard errors. Significance at the 0.1, 0.05, and 0.01 levels is indicated by *, **, and ***, respectively green buildings and consume a smaller amount of energy but other tenants of non-green buildings do not reduce consumption.

Table 7.5 shows the estimation result of Eq. (7.2) about the natural logarithm of office rents. Column (1) shows the result of the baseline model that includes building characteristics but does not include variables for operating expenses. The estimated coefficient on green label is 0.217 and statistically significant at the 5% level. On the basis of this coefficient, office rents are 26.7% higher for green office buildings than for otherwise similar non-green office buildings.[6] A positive rent premium is consistent with the result obtained by Eichholtz et al. (2009). However, the size of the premium is larger than their estimate for the USA (6%). The coefficients on other variables show the following result. Office rents are higher when a building is newer, larger, taller, and located closer to the nearest railway/subway station.

Column (2) shows the result when we include log maintenance and repair costs. The coefficient on log maintenance costs is not statistically significant but the coefficient on log repair costs is positive and significant at the 5% level. Maintenance costs are daily expenditures such as cleaning whereas repair costs are longer term capital expenditures. Another variable for long-term capital investments is the renovation dummy. Its coefficient is not statistically significant but the point estimate is positive. Thus, capital expenditures tend to increase office rents. In this specification, the coefficient on green building labels slightly increases to 0.236 and is statistically significant at the 1% level.

However, the coefficient on green building labels becomes significantly smaller and statistically insignificant when we include electricity or water usage. In column (3), when we include the log electricity usage, the coefficient on electricity usage is negative and statistically significant, but the coefficient on green labels decreases to 0.030 and becomes insignificant. Similarly, in column (4) when we include the log water usage, the coefficient on the green labels is 0.010 and not statistically significant. When we include the log usage of both electricity and water (column (5)), the coefficients on these variables are statistically significant and the adjusted R-squared increases to 0.801. The green label coefficient remains insignificant.

Column (6) shows the result when we include all variables mentioned above. The model has the largest explanatory power with the adjusted R-squared of 0.805. Among the variables about building operations,

Table 7.5 Result of rent regressions

	(1)	(2)	(3)	(4)	(5)	(6)
Green label dummy	0.217** (0.089)	0.236* (0.124)	0.030 (0.103)	0.010 (0.111)	0.060 (0.092)	0.096 (0.097)
Log gross building area	0.052* (0.028)	0.085** (0.033)	0.073 (0.049)	0.035 (0.046)	0.083* (0.043)	0.058 (0.062)
Number of stories above ground	0.011** (0.005)	0.003 (0.008)	−0.013 (0.018)	0.005 (0.024)	−0.002 (0.017)	−0.000 (0.017)
Time to the nearest station	−0.030*** (0.009)	−0.045*** (0.012)	−0.019 (0.025)	−0.033 (0.021)	−0.011 (0.020)	−0.013 (0.020)
Building age	−0.008*** (0.002)	−0.011*** (0.003)	−0.012* (0.007)	−0.008 (0.006)	−0.011* (0.006)	−0.009 (0.008)
Zone air conditioning dummy	0.079 (0.055)	0.038 (0.121)	−0.247*** (0.087)	−0.157* (0.091)	−0.184** (0.087)	−0.212 (0.135)
Card-key system dummy	−0.004 (0.081)	0.095 (0.125)	0.080 (0.108)	−0.040 (0.100)	0.168 (0.111)	0.189 (0.134)
Building renovation dummy	0.045 (0.053)	0.095 (0.083)	0.031 (0.140)	0.205 (0.150)	0.014 (0.111)	0.018 (0.134)
Log maintenance costs		−0.034 (0.067)				−0.046 (0.170)
Log repair costs		0.059** (0.028)				−0.018 (0.057)
Log electricity usage			−0.209** (0.099)		−0.309*** (0.102)	−0.305*** (0.112)
Log water usage				0.098 (0.068)	0.159** (0.065)	0.170** (0.070)
Constant	8.103*** (0.258)	7.571*** (0.565)	8.733*** (0.715)	8.528*** (0.619)	8.985*** (0.571)	9.571*** (0.826)
Submarket fixed effects	Yes	Yes	Yes	Yes	Yes	Yes
Quarter-year fixed effects	Yes	Yes	Yes	Yes	Yes	Yes
Observations	480	332	165	162	162	158
Adjusted R^2	0.758	0.775	0.779	0.769	0.801	0.805

This table shows the regression result of Eq. (7.2). In parentheses are standard errors that are the White heteroscedasticity-consistent standard errors adjusted for clusters defined by buildings. Significance at the 0.1, 0.05, and 0.01 levels is indicated by *, **, and ***, respectively variables for the electricity and water usage have statistically significant effects on office rents. The estimated coefficient is −0.305 on the log electricity usage and 0.170 on the log water usage, both of which are statistically significant at least at the 5% level. A 1% reduction in electricity usage is associated with 0.305% higher rents, and a 1% reduction in water usage is associated with 0.170% lower rents. The opposite signs of these effects may look puzzling at first. However, water usage for office properties is mainly for the common area and its costs are already added on to the gross rent. Thus, rents are higher for buildings with more water usage. In contrast, electricity usage significantly varies by tenant, and tenants reimburse part of electricity cost to the owner. Thus, buildings that use efficient electric appliances offer savings in tenants' electricity costs. Tenants are willing to accept a rent premium for these energy-efficient buildings, and the owners of these buildings use the rent premium to pay for the cost of investment in energy efficiency. In this case, less use of electricity is associated with a higher rent.

In contrast, the coefficient on green labels is 0.096 and not statistically significant. As Table 7.4 shows, green building labels affect the actual usage of electricity and water. Thus, the office rents are indirectly affected by green building labels through the effects of electricity usage and water usage. However, green building labels themselves do not have a direct effect on office rents. The significant rent premium for green buildings found in the baseline model (column (1)) indicates tenants' larger willingness to pay. However, they pay a rent premium not for a brand associated with green building labels but for material benefits of green buildings regarding lower costs of energy and water.

7.7 Conclusion

This chapter presents a review of the extant studies on Japanese green buildings and a new empirical analysis of the relation between office rent, green building labels, and actual energy use. In our new empirical analysis, we provide evidence as to what causes the positive association between green building labels and office rents. We first show that sustainability-related features of the building are effective in reducing the actual consumption of electricity and water. After controlling for the effect of these observed sustainability-related features, we find that green labels have separate effects on the reduction of the consumption of electricity and water. Thus, various green features required by green building labels are effective in saving energy and water usage. However, green labels do not have a direct effect on office rents once we control for the effect of electricity and water usage. A rent premium observed for green buildings is paid by tenants not for a brand associated with green building labels but for material benefits of green buildings regarding lower costs of energy and water.

Notes

1. For a list of green building studies in Japan, see: http://ynakajolabo.meikai.ac.jp/ronbun01.html.
2. There are other economic studies about sustainability. However, their focus is not on green buildings but rather on green spaces, views, and amenities (e.g., Yamagata et al. 2016).
3. Suzuki and Oka (1998) estimate the life-cycle energy consumption and CO_2 emission of office buildings in Japan from an architectural engineering perspective.
4. The area of typical floor is also available but not used because it is collinear with gross building floor and the number of stories. Similarly, a dummy for raised floor is not used because it is highly correlated with building age.
5. The percentage difference is calculated as exp(−0.189)–1.
6. The percentage difference in rents is calculated by exp(0.237)–1.

References

Aroul, R.R., and J.A. Hansz. 2012. The Value of "Green:" Evidence from the First Mandatory Residential Green Building Program. *Journal of Real Estate Research* 34 (1): 27–49.

Aydin, E., D. Brounen, and N. Kok. 2016. Capitalization of Energy Efficiency in the Housing Market. Working Paper.

Borenstein, S. 2008. The Market Value and Cost of Solar Photovoltaic Electricity Production. UCEI Working Paper CSEM WP, 176.

Brounen, D., and N. Kok. 2011. On the Economics of Energy Labels in the Housing Market. *Journal of Environmental Economics and Management* 62 (2): 166–179.

Bruegge, C., C. Carrion-Flores, and J.C. Pope. 2016. Does the Housing Market Value Energy Efficient Homes? Evidence from the Energy Star Program. *Regional Science and Urban Economics* 57: 63–76.

Dastrup, S.R., J.G. Zivin, D.L. Costa, and M.E. Kahn. 2012. Understanding the Solar Home Price Premium: Electricity Generation and "Green" Social Status. *European Economic Review* 56 (5): 961–973.

Deng, Y.H., and J. Wu. 2014. Economic Returns to Residential Green Building Investment: The Developers' Perspective. *Regional Science and Urban Economics* 47: 35–44.

Deng, Y.H., Z.L. Li, and J.M. Quigley. 2012. Economic Returns to Energy-Efficient Investments in the Housing Market: Evidence from Singapore. *Regional Science and Urban Economics* 42 (3): 506–515.

Devine, A., and N. Kok. 2015. Green Certification and Building Performance: Implications for Tangibles and Intangibles. *Journal of Portfolio Management* 41 (6): 151–164.

Dian, T.M., and J. Miranowski. 1989. Estimating the Implicit Price of Energy Efficiency Improvements in the Residential Housing Market-A Hedonic Approach. *Journal of Urban Economics* 25: 52–67.

Dippold, T., J. Mutl, and J. Zietz. 2014. Opting for a Green Certificate: The Impact of Local Attitudes and Economic Conditions. *Journal of Real Estate Research* 36 (4): 435–473.

Eichholtz, P., N. Kok, and J. M. Quigley. 2009. Why Do Companies Rent Green? Real Property and Corporate Social Responsibility. Berkeley Program on Housing and Urban Policy Working Papers, W09-004.

Eichholtz, P., N. Kok, and J.M. Quigley. 2010. Doing Well by Doing Good? Green Office Buildings. *American Economic Review* 100 (5): 2492–2509.

Eichholtz, P., N. Kok, and J.M. Quigley. 2013. The Economics of Green Building. *Review of Economics Statistics* 95 (1): 50–63.

Eichholtz, P.M.A., N. Kok, and J.M. Quigley. 2016. Ecological Responsiveness and Corporate Real Estate. *Business and Society* 55 (3): 330–360.

Freybote, J., H. Sun, and X. Yang. 2015. The Impact of LEED Neighborhood Certification on Condo Prices. *Real Estate Economics* 43 (3): 586–608.

Fuerst, F., and P. McAllister. 2009. An Investigation of the Effect of Eco-Labeling on Office Occupancy Rates. Working Papers in Real Estate & Planning, No. 2009–2008, University of Reading.

Fuerst, F., C. Shimizu, and J. Yoshida. 2013. The Investment Value of Green Buildings in Japan. *European Real Estate Society (ERES)* 265.

Fuerst, F., and P. McAllister. 2011a. Green Noise or Green Value? Measuring the Effects of Environmental Certification on Office Values. *Real Estate Economics* 39 (1): 45–69.

Fuerst, F., and P. McAllister. 2011b. The Impact of Energy Performance Certificates on the Rental and Capital Values of Commercial Property Assets. *Energy Policy* 39 (10): 6608–6614.

Fuerst, F., and C. Shimizu. 2016. Green Luxury Goods? The Economics of Eco-Labels in the Japanese Housing Market. *Journal of the Japanese and International Economics* 39: 108–122.

Gilmer, R.W. 1989. Energy Labels and Economic Search. *Energy Economics* 11 (3): 213.

Jaffee, D., R. Stanton, and N. Wallace. 2011. Energy Factors, Leasing Structure and the Market Price of Office Buildings in the U.S. Working Paper.

Laquatra, J. 1986. Housing Market Capitalization of Thermal Integrity. *Energy Economics* 8 (3): 134–138.

Miller, N., J. Spivey, and A. Florance. 2008. *Does Green Pay Off?* Unpublished Manuscript.

Nakayama, Y., A. Yoshida, and J. Onishi. 2015. The Importance of Sustainability Management in the Future Real Estate Market. *ARES Journal* 25: 58–63.

Pivo, G., and J.D. Fisher. 2010. Income, Value and Returns in Socially Responsible Office Properties. *Journal of Real Estate Research* 32 (3): 243–270.

Suzuki, M., and T. Oka. 1998. Estimation of Life Cycle Energy Consumption and CO_2 Emission of Office Buildings in Japan. *Energy and Buildings* 28 (1): 33–41 (Elsevier).

Wiley, J.A., J.D. Benefield, and K.H. Johnson. 2010. Green Design and the Market for Commercial Office Space. *Journal of Real Estate Finance and Economics* 41 (2): 228–243.

Yamagata, Y., D. Murakami, H. Seya, M. Tsutsumi, and Y. Kawaguchi. 2011. An Analysis of Spatio-Temporal Effect of Green Building Rating on Real Estate Price. *JAREFE Journal* 2011 (2): 23–39.

Yamagata, Y., D. Murakami, T. Yoshida, T. Seya, and S. Kuroda. 2016. Value of Urban Views in a Bay City: Hedonic Analysis with the Spatial Multilevel Additive Regression (SMAR) Model. *Landscape and Urban Planning* 151: 89–102.

Yoshida, J. 2009. The Economic Value of Green Buildings. The Japan Economic Research Institute Monthly, June.

Yoshida, J. 2010. Price of Green Buildings: An Empirical Study of Condominiums in Tokyo. Final Report, Ministry of Land, Infrastructure, Transport, and Tourism of Japan.

Yoshida, J., and A. Sugiura. 2010. Which Greenness is Valued? Evidence from Green Condominiums in Tokyo. SSRN 1636426.

Yoshida, J. 2012. The Price of Green Buildings: Empirical Analysis using Tokyo Condominium Data Between 2009 and 2011, 68 pp. Final Report, Tokyo Association of Real Estate Appraisers, December.

Yoshida, J., and C. Shimizu. 2012. The Effect of a Green Building Certificate on New Condominium Prices in Japan. *The Quarterly Journal of Housing and Land Economics* 83: 18–29.

Yoshida, J., and A. Sugiura. 2015. The Effects of Multiple Green Factors on Condominium Prices. *Journal of Real Estate Finance and Economics* 50 (3): 412–437.

Zheng, S.Q., J. Wu, M.E. Kahn, and Y.H. Deng. 2012. The Nascent Market for "Green" Real Estate in Beijing. *European Economics Review* 56 (5): 974–984.

Authors' Biography

Dr. Jiro Yoshida Associate Professor of Business, the Smeal College of Business, Penn State University. He also serves as Research Associate at Columbia Business School, Senior Fellow at Policy Research Institute of the Ministry of Finance of Japan, and Research Fellow at the Housing Research and Advancement Foundation of Japan. His area of research includes asset pricing, real estate finance, and macroeconomics. He is a Weimer School Postdoctoral Honoree at Homer Hoyt Institute, and a recipient of the dissertation award from American Real Estate and Urban Economics Association and Fulbright Scholarship. He received his B.Eng. from the University of Tokyo, his M.S. from MIT and UC Berkeley, and his Ph.D. from UC Berkeley.

Mr. Junichiro Onishi Manager, Xymax Real Estate Institute Corporation, a subsidiary of a leading asset and property management company in Japan. He is responsible for office market analysis, joint projects with Kyoto University, and seminars for property owners. He received his B.Eng. from Tokyo Institute of Technology.

Dr. Chihiro Shimizu Professor, College of Sports Science, Nihon University in Japan. He also serves as Research Affiliate at Center for Real Estate at MIT. His area of research includes applied econometrics, machine learning, and real estate economics. He received his B.A. and M.S. from Nihon University and Ph.D. from the University of Tokyo.

CHAPTER 8

Paths of Green Building Technology in China

Yu Zhou

8.1 Introduction

As China becomes the world's largest source of greenhouse gases (GHG), and amid mounting domestic concerns on air pollution, Chinese government has prioritized low-carbon development. In 2009, China pledged to reduce the carbon intensity by 40–45% per GDP unit by 2020, and in 2015 updated that pledge to 60–65% reduction by 2030 in the Sino-US agreement.[1] Building is a key area in which to accomplish such goals. Since 2006, China has developed a green building (GB) program with impressive growth. Yet, GB remains a small fraction of the construction market. In particular, technological choices of the GB program have become contested ground where "being green" runs the risk of becoming a cover for luxury high-tech deployment. Luxury bias and upscale construction

The original version of this chapter was revised: For detailed information please see Erratum. The erratum to this chapter is available at https://doi.org/10.1057/978-1-137-57446-6_11

Y. Zhou (✉)
Department of Earth Science and Geography, Vassar College,
Poughkeepsie, USA
e-mail: yuzhou@vassar.edu

N.E. Coulson et al. (eds.), *Energy Efficiency and the Future of Real Estate*, DOI 10.1057/978-1-137-57446-6_8

shadow many GB projects in China to this day, resulting in GB projects demanding more rather than less energy than ordinary buildings.

This chapter examines the technological changes in Chinese GBs based on three major GB programs: LEED designed by US Green Building Council; China's own Green Star program issued by the Ministry of Housing and Urban Rural Development (MOHURD); and passive building system originating from Germany. The chapter first reviews the emergence of China's GB program, paying attention to the influence of globalization and the Chinese government's desire to forge an indigenous technological path of GB. Using results from an analysis of China's green building stock, a survey of 121 architects in China's developed regions, and interviews with governmental officials, real estate developers, brokers, and property management firms throughout China[2] between 2013 and 2016, I argue that the best opportunity for GB in China is focusing on promoting ultra-low-energy passive building technology. Such technology will have broad market appeal as it ties the improvement of users' living experience with substantial energy savings, thus promoting interest among users, developers, and building professionals. It will also take advantage of China's massive building material and construction industry, and motivate them to environmentally friendly upgrades. The Chinese government has already realized the potential for passive technology, as it highlights such technology in the latest policy directive on GB.[3] Overall, I argue that it is important for GBs to shift from the emphasis on signature high-tech equipment to affordable and enduring quality construction. Such an approach is much more feasible in China now after more than a decade of GB development under LEED and the Green Star program, since these two standards have laid down the solid foundation for suppliers of building technology and skilled professionals. The overall slowdown of the housing market since 2014 also provides an opportune time for high quality and enduring construction to have better market appeal.

8.2 Building Systems and Technological Choices

Green building technology refers to a bundle of technology that can lower a building's environmental impact. It is a complex field where standardization common in other technological areas hardly applies. A localized approach is of paramount importance. This is because, first, the environmental performance of buildings is determined not by the application of an individual piece of technology, but also by the integration of many products and systems: architectural designs, construction materials, heating and ventilation systems, water systems, electrical systems, landscaping, construction, and maintenance protocols are all contributing factors. Thus, local applications will greatly affect the overall building performance. This is quite different from, say, information technology, for which prevailing global standards and evolution paths are well established. Second, the efficacy of building technology is influenced by the local environment and user habits. For example, the efficiency of solar and geothermal technology depends on the local micro geology and climate patterns. District heating developed in northern Europe can be efficient under a centralized heating regime in cold climate. However, it would be less useful in southern China where decentralized and varied heating system is the norm. Central air-conditioning system similarly may be more efficient than individual air conditioning (AC) all operating full time, but uses more energy if individual ACs are only turned on for a short period as commonly the case in China. As the expectations on comfort level differ in China and advanced countries, what is considered energy saving in the West may actually demand more energy in China. Third, because building materials and equipment are typically bulky and hard to transport, the costs and quality of a specific building technology depend on the quality of localized supplies, customization, and implementation. Given all of these variations, it is necessary to develop a locally appropriate GB technological standard and approach.

China has been the world's largest construction site for the past 20 years, and has thus received considerable attention from global corporations and architecture design firms.[4] One can find a diverse and even bewildering array of building technology suppliers from all over the world in China. This has created a rich field of experimentation, selections, and integration, but also demands skilled local selection of technology and adapting it to the specifics of local buildings. China's short history of GB development is fraught with the tendency to select technology for visibility and upscale development instead of sustainability. Elsewhere, I argue that China's GB program has to confront the "development first" mentality of the local governments, and engage and educate a wide range of stakeholders, including developers, building professionals, and the public.[5] Such engagement is not only necessary to expand and sustain GB momentum; it is also valuable for identifying the most attractive and affordable technology in the mainstream building market. The involvement with the public, for example, will help the building professionals to locate the balance between environmental benefits, such as energy efficiency, and quality of life benefits, such as better indoor air quality. While the reliance on technological intervention (even energy-efficient ones) to achieve a high-comfort level is counterproductive for the goal of lower carbon intensity, the program of passive houses currently emerging in China may provide a plausible alternative as it advocates quality construction, indigenous building material supply, and local adaptability with extremely high energy efficiency and excellent indoor environment.

8.2.1 Green Building Promotion in China

The decade of the 2000s marks the beginning of GB development in China. Before 2000, governmental branches, research institutes, architects, and NGOs made experimental and haphazard exploration on energy- and water-efficient construction techniques. Since 2000, the Chinese government has lent its powerful support behind the efforts as it views buildings as a key venue to meet China's pledge to lower carbon intensity. Studies have shown that building energy consumption accounts for 46.7% of the total energy consumption in China, and 60% of carbon emissions in cities come from maintaining buildings' functions.[6] Presently, China's per capita building energy consumption is among the lowest in the world, one-fifth of Japan and South Korea, and one-third of EU countries (Fig. 8.1). However, it is a result not of better green building technology but a low standard of living. For example, about 600 million Chinese people live in climate zones characterized by hot summers and cold winters. This zone has over 80 days when the average

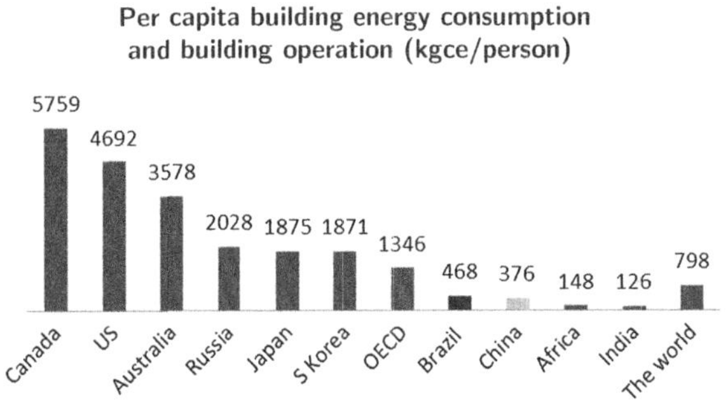

Fig. 8.1 International building energy consumption. *Source* NRDC 2012

daily temperature dips below 10 °C. Historically, no heating provisions have been provided in this area[7] and the thermal insulation building envelope is mostly very poor.[8] With rising incomes, heating and air-conditioning demand will inevitably grow. Without quality buildings, either the costs of energy will be prohibitively high or quality of life will continue to suffer. It is not surprising that the Chinese government views greening Chinese buildings as an urgent task.

The Chinese state has implemented both mandatory and voluntary measures to promote GB. Since 2000, MOHURD has increased the new building mandate to require 50–65% more energy efficiency than the basic standard in the 1980s. However, even with the raised standard, the efficiency level only matched the level of Germany in the 1990s. In 2006, MOHURD issued its first voluntary GB rating system which measures site planning, energy use, land use, water conservation, and internal air quality.[9] It certifies buildings up to three stars, which represent the best environmental performance. Provinces or provincial-level municipalities are responsible for evaluating one- or two-star projects, while the MOHURD and its associated agent certify three-star projects. This standard has been localized to every province and has expanded to include different types of buildings. The hope of the Green Star certification is to encourage more capable real estate developers to study and invest in more advanced environmentally friendly technology. To promote the GB adoption rate, on January 1, 2013, the State Council issued the Green Building Action Plan,[10] setting the goal that by 2015, 20% of all new buildings have to be green, and all newly built public buildings and affordable housing financed by the state have to be green certified. The two-star and three-star buildings would be eligible for local government subsidies and planning priorities (although such subsidies only existed in a few richest provinces or municipalities).[11] The provincial governments are required to develop their own action plans to be at least compatible with that of the central government.[12]

The state attention to GB has had remarkable effects. Figure 8.2 shows the dramatic increase in the number of GB projects and floor space in China after 2010. LEED and Green Star labels are the two most mainstream standards in China, but they are applied to very different building types (Fig. 8.3). The divergence demonstrates the contested nature of technological selection. As I will elaborate later, LEED was introduced to China earlier and was associated with prestigious architecture firms and landmark projects. It is seen as a more upscale,

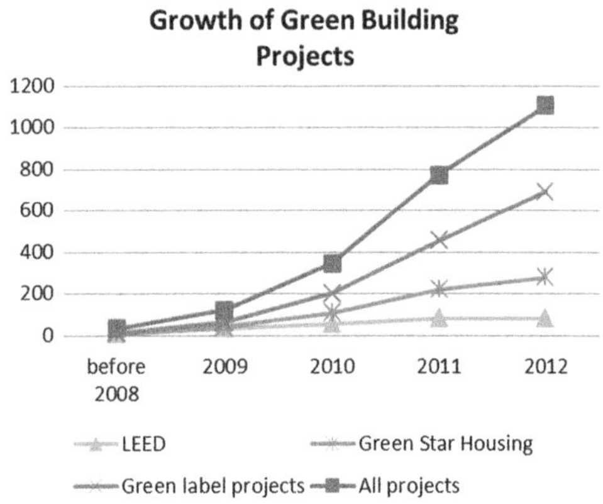

Fig. 8.2 Growth of green buildings, 2008–2012

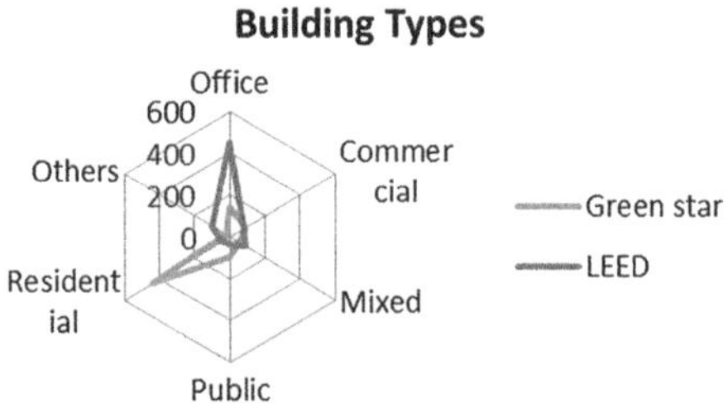

Fig. 8.3 LEED and China's green building label

internationally approved badge of honor on corporate social responsibilities, and thus tends to be applied to high-end offices and commercial complexes hosting foreign corporations and upper-class clientele as well as prominent public landmarks. The moderate growth of LEED is only because a growing list of buildings is still going through the lengthy certification processes. The domestic Green Star standard is applied to more mainstream residential and public buildings. Measured by both number and floor space, new GBs in 2012 have exceeded all the previous years combined and the growth continues into 2015.[13] Yet, in total, GBs remain a minor fraction of the total construction areas.

Elsewhere, I argue that China's Green Star program suffers from overreliance on the top–down administrative system and bureaucratic quotas.[14] Such an approach is effective in mandating developers to meet the minimal requirement of GB, but would have trouble encouraging the construction of high-quality GBs. The top–down approach also makes it difficult to sustain the momentum for GBs once the official attention shifts away. The trend since 2014 has indeed confirmed this pattern. As the Chinese government heightened its mandatory requirement for publicly funded projects to be GBs, the financial incentives for high-level GBs remain limited or did not materialize in most parts of China, More of the GB growth occurred in one-star building to meet the minimal requirement. By 2015, the share of three-star GBs declined from almost one-third in 2013 to 19% in 2015.[15] While the mandatory expansion of one-star GBs is a positive development as it is akin to raising the building code, it is also clear that China needs an alternative engine for the development and application of high-quality GBs. I argue that the stage now is set for a passive building system development in China. The following sections trace the change of GB approaches in the two major GB programs (LEED and Green Star), analyze how each has affected China's construction industry, and explain why a passive building system will gain currency in the coming years.

8.3 Changes in GB Technology in China

8.3.1 LEED: Pioneering Green Building Technology in China

China's initial motivation for GB development was not to lower buildings' carbon footprint, but to learn efficient Western building technology to improve quality and comfort level of buildings. Tellingly, it was the Bureau of Science and Technology of MOHURD that took the helm of the GB program. The earliest demonstration of GB buildings in China was mostly based on LEED standard developed by the United States Green Building Council.[16] As China entered an era of large-scale construction, building material and construction methods changed rapidly. LEED brought into China state-of-the-art energy-efficient technologies such as geothermal pump systems, solar electricity, and other high-performance materials and equipment such as low-E windows and wall insulation. Grand MOMA in Beijing, for example, was among the earliest LEED Gold projects designed by American architect Steven Holl, built between 2003 and 2009. The project featured one of the largest geothermal cooling and heating systems in the world, as well as a highly thermal-insulated building envelope. The construction process also reduced construction pollution and waste handling. The project received several international awards in 2009 and 2010.[17] Steven Holl also designed Vanke's headquarter in Shenzhen, the first LEED Platinum building in South China, with customized exterior shading, permeable courtyard surface, among others.

Given that such a GB technology was almost completely absent in China during the early 2000s, much of the equipment had to be imported or custom-made. This means that LEED projects in China are almost always premium and landmark buildings. Raffles City in Chengdu, a LEED Gold certified building designed by Steve Holland completed in 2014, is a flamboyant multi-use complex featuring geothermal wells and large ponds to harvest and recycle rainwater, as well as high-performance glazing and energy-efficient equipment.[18]

While LEED buildings in China clearly attract international and local attention, they are not necessarily greener, because these buildings are based on the comfort level of the West which is much higher than commonly found in China. For example, while most Chinese office buildings rely on natural ventilation, LEED buildings are almost always sealed to ensure constant indoor temperature and humidity through mechanical intervention. It is not surprising that a LEED-certified building would typically demand more energy than its China's counterparts. One Beijing planner commented in my interviews: "Nowadays, green buildings always use more energy. Why should the Chinese government promote it?" GrandMOMA, as an upscale LEED building example, features a swimming pool, luxury shops, and international schools. Raffles City is also a symbol of conspicuous consumption, with human spaces and local vegetation relegated to marginal positions. The engulfing scales—and sterile, cold, and geometric appearances of some LEED projects—make it difficult for average observers to figure out what is so "green" about these buildings. The association between LEED, prestige, and technology also creates a persistent impression that GB can only be achieved through expensive technology. Such exclusivity became even more conspicuous in residential buildings. In a LEED-certified apartment complex, the Alpha International Community in Nanchang, capital of relatively poor inland province of Jiangxi the developer markets the building to have constant indoor temperature throughout the year with 8-month heating and cooling, in a region where most houses do not have heating provisions in the winter. This apartment complex is also twice as expensive as the compatible buildings in the area and has twice the management fee, signaling its exclusive nature.[19]

In some cases, the upscale development piled up so many high-tech features that it backfired, because the building technique was not well localized, or the building material was low quality, or the systems were poorly implemented. Landsea Group (朗诗集团), a leading real estate developer that brands itself with high-tech GBs, has run into several highly publicized controversies as its buildings are found to have water leaks and mold problems from the hydronic piping system built into the walls and floors to maintain indoor temperature.[20] The residents were also troubled by the fact that they were not allowed to open windows as it would damage the temperature control system of the building. Several reports characterize such a green technology as strategies for earning a premium, and called out Landsea GBs as "fake-green." Such controversies greatly undermine the confidence of the market in the promises of GB. Given that homes are the single most important asset of Chinese households, the controversies surrounding GBs could bring huge damages to their prospects in the housing market.

Despite these problems, LEED should still be credited for introducing to China a collection of promising GB technologies. As LEED projects proliferated, China's domestic production of GB technology and implementation capacity also grew. For example, before LEED, the geothemal system was not used in China, but it has now become so common that China is now among the world's largest market of geothemal systems, with double-digit growth every year.[21] Manufacturers of high-performance windows have also emerged, mostly for export, but also for the domestic market. Research in China, a industrial research institute, reports that China only had 5.9 million m^2 of the best energy-saving glass in 2009, and it grew to 50 million in 2015 with a forecasted rapid capacity expansion down the road.[22]

8.3.2 China's Green Star Program: Spreading GB Technology

Mindful of the association between LEED, luxury, and high-tech equipment, MOHURD has opted to develop China's own green building certification rather than copying the LEED system. The Green Star evaluation stresses practical, and passive approaches in the hope of controlling costs. Qiu Baoxing (2013), head of MOHURD until 2015, citing research from 213 GB projects, suggests that the average increased cost of 'building green' is ¥31/m^2 for one-star housing, ¥88/m^2 for two-star housing, and ¥196/m^2 for three-star housing—all costs that can be recovered in 2–6 years.[23] Other researchers also confirmed the moderate added costs of Green Star buildings.[24] Figure 8.3 shows that Green Star is a more mainstream standard in China.

However, the luxury association persists even for Green Star buildings. Most building professionals I interviewed, with the exception of a few leaders in China's green building promotion, continue to assume that GBs must come with some sort of signature active technology, such as solar panel tops, geothermal pumps, etc. I compared the unit sale price and management fee of 330 green apartments paired with similar apartment complexes nearby and found that the green apartments cost on average almost ¥2000, or 20% higher, and management fee cost 36% higher than the conventional ones, far exceeding the cost differential cited by MOHURD. Since the management fee levels typically correlate with the perceived status of a particular residential complex, this indicates that green housing complexes are built to be higher end.[25]

Developers choose an upscale approach to GBs to gain visibility and a fatter profit margin. An economic-efficiency analysis of GB homes in Shanghai[26] reveals that the residents typically pay a premium for GBs which cannot be paid off in energy savings. Developers draw a better profit margin in such buildings due to the premium paid by residents. Yet, such relationship can only work in the high-end home, so developers would deploy luxury and visible technology to maintain the premium regardless of the environmental outcomes. Interviews with housing brokers in Beijing suggested: "Average home buyers do not generally respond to overall environmental sensibility. But they respond to fancy equipment, so it is easier to make a sales pitch if advanced equipment is installed." As the building industry China in the 1990s and 2000s entered a state of upgrading, green building technology became just one of the high-tech fads in the market. Needless to say, such luxury bias runs counter to the purpose of reducing building energy consumption.

The lack of interest in reducing building energy consumption is also shown by the types of GB labels developers applied. There are two types of Green Star certifications: design certification and operation certification. The latter is awarded after the buildings are in operation for 1 year so to show that the buildings indeed meet the energy-efficiency criteria. By 2015, only 6.3% of GB certification was in operation, and the rest was all in design, creating doubt of the true outcome of designed GBs.[27] A report from the National Research Defense Council shows that the intensity of China's building energy consumption continued to grow

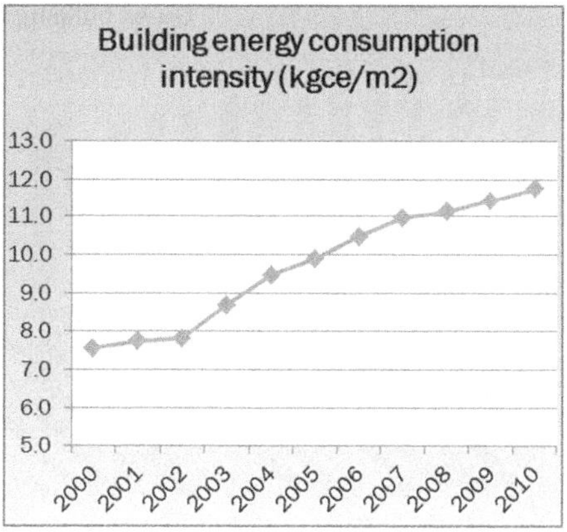

Fig. 8.4 Building energy consumption intensity, 10,000 t coal equivalent. *Source* NDRC, 2012

after 2000, only with moderately slower rate, indicating that buildings on average are consuming more energy on per unit base despite the GB promotion (Fig. 8.4).[28]

Despite the shortcomings of China's GB programs, what is indisputable is the fact that the promotion of more energy-efficient construction through voluntary and mandatory programs, since 2005 has transformed China's building material industry, with more environmentally friendly building material and equipment available and affordable supplies. In 2014, I surveyed 121 architects in 13 provinces or municipalities to assess the most common approaches in GB. Here are the results ranked by popularity (Fig. 8.5).

The most commonly used techniques tend to be passive technologies, such as enhanced natural ventilation, energy saving windows and insulated walls, individual household utility measurements, etc. The top preference of natural ventilation should be noted as it shows that Chinese users overall unlike western users are far less used to an artificial indoor climate created by sealed building envelope. There is considerable room for improvement, however. For example, better wall insulation is 'frequently used' by less than half of the respondents: external shade, and green roofing and walls are still rare. Some environmentally sensible practices, such as recycling building material, selling apartments with finished interiors rather than unfinished casts, and using green building material and pre-fabricated concrete, are still far from being the standard practices.

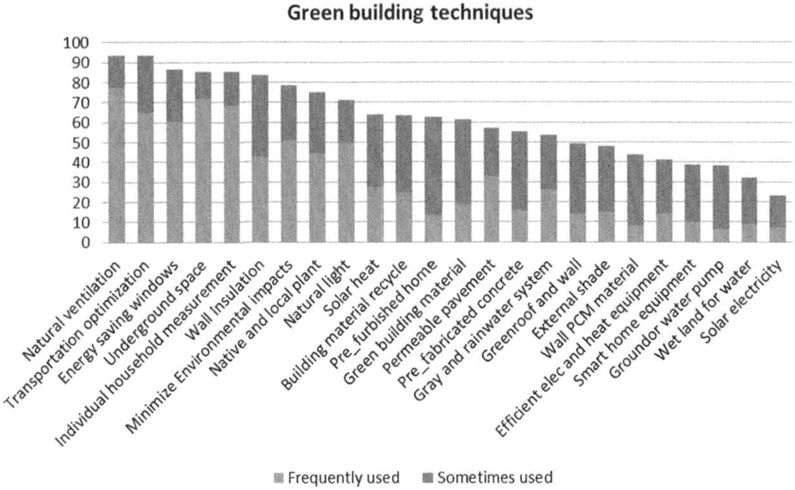

Fig. 8.5 Prevalence of green building techniques. *Source* Author's survey

The active, high-tech solutions, although highly visible, are actually among the least often used, partly because of costs and other integration problems. The most commonly used active technology is solar heating. It is quite affordable and the systems have been installed in many rural and urban homes across China. Interviews also suggested that groundwater pump systems are becoming more common, although their use varies depending on the local climates and characteristics of the sites. Some architects suggested that given the risk of thermal pollution with water-based pumps, the implementation of geothermal is or should be subjected to a special approval process. Overall, technological systems such as geothermal are still costly. I visited one of the newly built large residential/office complexes in Beijing in 2014. The managers suggested that the geothermal system could provide only 10% savings for the swimming pool heating in the club house within this complex. All equipments had to be imported, so the purchase and maintenance costs were high. Photovoltaic is used the least frequently in China, in great part because of the difficulty of integrating the panels with the power grid. However, the Chinese government has issued a series of new policies since 2013 to encourage distributive solar energy,[29] which may pave the way for more solar installation in the future.

Given the size and growth of China's building industry, there is no question that it has ample room for experimentations and deployment of all sorts of GB technology, yet the most sensible approach remains to promote high-quality passive technology for the mainstream market. It is important for the building professionals and Chinese public to realize that performance of the buildings does not stem from how much cutting-edge technology was installed, but from the quality of the building material and the construction. The experience of Chinese GB promotion also shows that energy saving alone would not be sufficient to mobilize buyers and developers. It is also not realistic to expect that state subsidies can support such a size of the market for a sustained period. Multiple take-holders have to be mobilized to popularizing GB technology. Chinese public are clearly interested in and willing to pay for better living experiences. Elsewhere, I argue that Green Star paid too little attention to integrating the public preferences of buildings into the label, as the top–down bureaucratic approaches have trouble considering experiences at the ground level. The challenge of China's GB expansion is to meet the expectations of more comfortable living without increasing energy consumption. Fortunately, the passive building provides a promising answer.

8.3.3 Passive House System: Combine Comfortable Living with Energy Saving

Passive houses, which have spread from Germany to other European countries since the 1990s, represent the highest energy performance buildings. The first passive house was built in Darmstadt, Germany in 1990 and achieved over 90% of energy saving as compared to its conventional counterparts in central Europe at the time through its tightly sealed building envelope and air exchange system.[30] In addition to saving energy, passive houses were also proven to have comfortable living conditions for the residents. The EU in 2010 passed legislation that requires all new buildings in member states to meet nearly zero energy standards as shown by passive houses, by 2020.[31]

China has been working with the German Energy Agency (DENA) since 2009 to introduce the passive house system into China. A demonstration project was brought in by the City of Hamburg called Hamburg House at the Shanghai World Expo in 2010. As an exhibit installment without long-term users, the building provided a test ground for the feasibility of such buildings in China, especially during the hot and humid Shanghai summer. While Hamburg House did not gain much public attention, it has set off the experiment of building passive houses in China. MOHURD and private developers have collaborated with DENA or the Passive House Institute (the leading design and solution provider for passive houses in Germany) to build demonstrative projects in China. For example, Landsea Group (朗诗集团) commissioned German architect Peter Ruge Architekten to build an apartment/hotel complex "Bruck" in its R&D park in Zhejiang province, the heart of China's densely populated Yangtze River delta, a hot-summer and cold-winter climate zone.[32] Such demonstrative projects provided much needed data for Chinese architects to study and evaluate the performance of building material and equipment, identify problems and formulate solutions. Kong et al. (2016), among others, tested the thermal performance of this building in winter and found that it provided a satisfactory indoor environment when it was occupied.[33] By 2016, my interviews at MOHURD suggested that China has 44 different passive building projects either completed or under construction, covering a variety of climate zones and building types.

One of the most noticeable projects is a residential building Zaishuiyifang (在水一方) in Qinhuangdao, Hebei province in Northern China. Unlike predominant low-rise passive houses in Europe, this building is an 18-story high-rise, totaling 6467 m^2,[34] more typical of Chinese residential complexes. The building was jointly designed by DENA and Bureau of Science and Technology under MOHURD, and the construction had to meet the stringent standards of the German passive house. The developer himself moved into the apartment, while it was under construction to examine and give feedback about the real living experience. In order for this example to be replicable, most of the building material and equipment was sourced domestically, although some key components had to be imported from Germany. MOHURD tested the building extensively after the completion and after residents moved in. They found that the indoor temperature and air quality met the standards for passive buildings. Since the residents tend to open windows in the summer, the apartments have higher room temperature and humidity than the German designing standards. However, it is important that the users can control the home environment and it is up to the users to find the comfortable balance of indoor environment and energy saving. MOHURD test shows that the building was able to provide a comfortable living experience with 80% reduction of heating and 40% reduction of cooling costs than the conventional new buildings in the area at a 10.5% higher cost.[35] As the buildings are designed to be much more enduring than common Chinese buildings, MOHURD engineers expect the costs to decline once such buildings become the mainstream. Overall, the results support the feasibility of passive building systems in China. Stephan Kohler, DENA's Chief Executive, in presenting DENA certification to this building on October 2013, was quoted to say that "It is the first practical and consistent example of an entire building project from planning to completion that shows how efficient houses can be realized with the means available and under the economic circumstances prevalent in China."[36] Based on the experiences of this building, Hubei province drafted China's first standard for passive buildings for the province. More demonstration projects are in the works from this developer and others.

While the passive building system is clearly at the early stages in China, it is promising as a way to address the shortcomings of LEED and Green Star standards. LEED in China is too elite to be adopted into the mainstream building market, and China's Green Star does not take user experiences into sufficient consideration and thus has trouble motivating the market. The advantages of passive buildings are the following. First, they represent a much needed correction for the Chinese building industry from a mindless pursuit of newer and higher technology, to a return to the basics of quality construction. Passive houses are not a collection of fancy technology and do not typically have exotic exterior. However, they are built to last through detail-oriented, thoughtful construction processes with careful supervision and skilled work by engineers and workers. MOHURD has long tried to promote passive technology, but it runs into the headwind of the of real estate developers' preference of deploying showy technology to gain premium. Passive buildings highlight the ability of passive approaches in ensuring building quality and energy performance, and lifting the term "passive" to the forefront of user and builder consciousness. This can help to correct the misleading faith that the Chinese public has placed on high-end technology.

Second, passive buildings have a proven record of comfortable living despite their ultra-low-energy usage. This will be critical for meeting the quality-of-life demands in China while attending to environmental sustainability. Given that housing is the single biggest asset in most Chinese households, a comfortable living experience is essential to mobilize buyers. Many Chinese residents in south China are not accustomed to high-powered artificial climate intervention in heating and cooling, the gentle and natural approach of passive buildings is, therefore, much more appealing. By insulating the buildings against external environment, passive buildings also offer two other attractive features in Chinese market: cleaner indoor air, and excellent noise reduction. The Chinese public is highly concerned with the air pollution problem. Since the air-exchange system in passive buildings can filter out the harmful particles and stabilize the oxygen level of the indoor air, it can bring significant health benefits for residents. In addition, Chinese urban environments are noted for their high noise level, and passive buildings are excellent for minimizing external noise. More importantly, passive buildings, if done right, allow users to have control of ventilation, which is critical for Chinese users. As Chinese users can open and close windows at will rather than being forced to fit into building requirements, they can learn the best ways to find his/her own balance of comfort level and energy costs. These advantages, combined with significant energy savings, have the potential to draw considerable enthusiasm in the Chinese market.

Third, China has the world's largest building material industry in need of an upgrade. LEED has brought an individual building technology system into China, but the expansion of passive building construction can lead to comprehensive changes of this industry to be more environmental friendly and energy efficient. During the development of passive building demonstration projects, Chinese builders have found that while quality building materials are available domestically, they are few and far between. Those that exist often depend on export markets. In fact, both Europe and United States import quality building material such as doors and glasses from China, but it is an area of frequent trade disputes, which create an uncertain environment for high-quality building material makers. The opening up of domestic demand through the expansion of passive buildings will encourage quality manufactures to expand and become better in competition. Berthold Kaufmann, an engineer at the Passive House Institute in Germany, said in 2014 that "If you ask me how many factories in China are producing windows for passive homes, the number is only five. However, if one starts, the others will follow. Already, some Chinese companies traveled to Germany to see passive homes and asked us for help."[37] The highly competitive nature of Chinese manufacturing means that they react to market changes very rapidly. The development of passive houses could lead to a green transformation of the entire industry.

Last but not least, the development of passive buildings will also provide experiences and expertise for the even bigger retrofitting industry in China. This is critical for reducing China's overall building energy consumption. The existing building may not be able to meet passive building standards, but expertise and building material developed through the passive building industry will significantly improve the retrofitting process and enhance the energy performance and comfort level of existing buildings.

Of course, the path of the passive house system is not going to be smooth. China is still in shortage of quality technological support, and much of the available building materials are insufficient and their endurance untested. The market has yet to be familiar with passive building concepts. The cost of passive buildings is still high, thus discouraging developers from adopting the approach. However, none of these problems is insurmountable if the government continues to promote and educate potential users about the benefits of such buildings. I argue elsewhere that one of the major barriers against GB development in China is the speculative real estate market which distorts incentive structures for developers, architects, and home buyers, and creates a context in which housing is viewed primarily as a capital asset rather than as a place to live. It also rewards faster rather than quality construction.[38] Since 2014, China's real estate market has slowed down significantly due to massive overbuilding in the many parts of the country.[39] This means that the competitive environment has changed, so developers are more interested in building higher quality houses to attract buyers.

8.4 Conclusion

Green building is a critical way for China to reduce its carbon emissions and reduce air pollution. The chapter reviews the Chinese efforts to build a GB program by focusing on the three GB standards: LEED, Green Star, and Passive Buildings. LEED was the earliest standard and not only brought to China cutting-edge, energy-efficient technology in building, but also introduced a much higher comfort level that resulted in increasing rather than decreasing energy consumption in LEED buildings. The high-tech bias embedded in the LEED system, combined with the developers' desire for showy technology, together leads to an enduring luxury bias in many GBs in China. China's Green Star attempts to correct this bias, but its top–down implementation and lack of financial incentive has generated little enthusiasm in the market. The state mandate of GBs in publicly funded projects helps create faster growth in those GBs meeting the minimal requirement, but China is still in need of a driver for higher level GBs. Passive buildings, originating in Germany, have begun to show promise in the Chinese market in the last few years. By combining extreme energy savings with proven record of comfortable living, this approach to GB fulfills the desire of the government to increase energy efficiency and meet public demands for better quality of life, thus providing a path to draw all stakeholders into the GB development. Chinese studies of several passive buildings recently completed in China show that such buildings are feasible in China's diverse climate and with local suppliers and workers. The expansion of passive buildings will not only reduce carbon emissions of Chinese buildings: it also removes the need for an entire heating supply and delivery system, thus reducing air pollution in winter. More importantly, it will transform the world's largest building material supply industry and lead to a green upgrade.

Notes

1. See World Resource Institute interpretation of the Sino-US Agreement: "The China–US Climate Agreement: by the numbers," *World Resource Institute* (2014), accessed 16 August 2016, http://www.wri.org/blog/2014/11/numbers-china-us-climate-agreement.
2. These include Beijing, Nanchang in Jiangxi province, Guangzhou and Shenzhen in Guangdong province, Fuzhou in Fujian, and Chengdu in Sichuan province.
3. Zhenqiang Xu (徐振强), "To make building green, policy incentives are necessary. --Summary of the green building policy in 25 Provinces and municipality" (建筑要想绿,政策得激励:25省市"绿政"大起底), *Xinhua*, accessed 16 August 2016, http://news.xinhuanet.com/info/2016-02/23/c_135122658.htm?from=timeline&isappinstalled=0.
4. Xufei Ren, *Building Globalization: transnational architecture production in urban China* (University of Chicago Press, 2011). See also: "An investment framework for clean energy and development—A platform for convergence of public and private investments," *The World Bank* (2007),

http://siteresources.worldbank.org/EXTSDNETWORK/Resources/AnInvestmentFrameworkforCleanEnergyandDevelopment.pdf?resourceurlname=AnInvestmentFrameworkforCleanEnergyandDevelopment.pdf.

5. Yu Zhou, "State Power and environmental initiatives in China: analyzing China's green building program through an ecological modernization perspective," *Geoforum* (2015): 61: 1–12. See also, Yu Zhou, and Yifan Cai, 打造中国绿色建筑推广的合力 (Creating "crowd-sourcing" for China's Green Building promotion program) 现代城市研究 (*Modern Urban Research*, Vol. 6), (2014): 89–96 (in Chinese).
6. Yanan Li, Li Yang He Baojie, Zhao Doudou, "Green Building in China: Need Great promotion," in *Sustainable Cities and Society* (2014): 11: 1–6. See also K. Mo, "From grey to green: Making China's rapid urbanization sustainable," speech presented at The Climate Conference/COP 15 in Copenhagen, Denmark, http://www.bcg.com.cn/en/newsandpublications/publications/reports/report20090907001.html.
7. Zhang Xiaoling, Peng Mengyue, Ma Yishuo, Niu Ben, Luo Song, (张小玲, 彭梦月, 马伊硕, 牛犇, 罗松), "Feasibility Study on Promoting Passive Residential Housing in China" (被动式居住建筑在中国推广的可行性研究) (2013), report for Energy Foundation, accessed 15 August 2016, http://www.efchina.org/Attachments/Report/reports-20131220-zh/%E8%A2%AB%E5%8A%A8%E5%BC%8F%E5%B1%85%E4%BD%8F%E5%BB%BA%E7%AD%91%E5%9C%A8%E4%B8%AD%E5%9B%BD%E6%8E%A8%E5%B9%BF%E7%9A%84%E5%8F%AF%E8%A1%8C%E6%80%A7%E7%A0%94%E7%A9%B6.pdf/view.
8. Yanan Li, Li Yang, He Baojie, Zhao Doudou, "Green Building in China: Need Great promotion," *Sustainable Cities and Society* (2014): 11: 1–6.
9. C. Zhou, X. Dai, R. Wang, J. Huang, "Indicators for evaluating sustainable communities," *ShengtaiXuebao/ActaEcologicaSinica*, (2011): 31(16): 4750–4759.
10. 绿色建筑行动方案发展改革委住房城乡建设部, 国务院办公厅关于转发发展改革委住房城乡建设部(2013), http://www.gov.cn/zwgk/2013-01/06/content_2305793.htm. See link for details.
11. Press release of the Green building action plan, http://news.dichan.sina.com.cn/2013/02/27/658127.html.
12. Yu Zhou, "State Power and environmental initiatives in China: analyzing China's green building program through an ecological modernization perspective," *Geoforum* (2015): 61: 1–12. See also, Yu Zhou & YifanCai, 打造中国绿色建筑推广的合力 (Creating "crowd-sourcing" for China's Green Building promotion program) 现代城市研究 (*Modern Urban Research*, Vol. 6), (2014): 89–96 (in Chinese).
13. Zhenqiang Xu (徐振强), "To make building green, Policy incentives are necessary. --Summary of the green building policy in 25 Provinces and

municipality" (建筑要想绿,政策得激励:25省市"绿政"大起底), *Xinhua*, accessed 16 August 2016, http://news.xinhuanet.com/info/2016-02/23/c_135122658.htm?from=timeline&isappinstalled=0.

14. Yu Zhou, "State Power and environmental initiatives in China: analyzing China's green building program through an ecological modernization perspective," *Geoforum* (2015): 61: 1–12.
15. Zhang Chuan, Song Lin, Sun Xiaoyue (张川,宋凌, 孙潇月), 年度绿色建筑评价标识统计报告 ("Annual Statistical report of 2014 Green building labels") (2014), accessed 16 August 2016, http://www.cngb.org.cn/cms/view/detailed.action?sid=aabec13351eda2360151f205532f001d.
16. Larisa Dobriansky, "Beijing 2008 Olympics US–China collaboration on greening the Olympic village," *EM: Air and Waste Management Association's Magazine for Environmental Managers*, (2008): 28–31.
17. See introduction: "Linked Hybrid," *Steven Holl Architects*, http://www.stevenholl.com/projects/beijing-linked-hybrid?.
18. Based on description: "Sliced Porosity Block—Raffles City Chengdu," *Steve Holl Architects*, http://www.stevenholl.com/project-detail.php?type=housing&id=98.
19. For more detailed comparison of this building: Yu Zhou, "State Power and environmental initiatives in China: analyzing China's green building program through an ecological modernization perspective," *Geoforum* (2015): 61: 1–12.
20. Green buildings built by Landsea are found to have large scale water leak in its exterior. This is because the developer deploys a piping system that is integrated into walls and floor to achieve heating and cooling. The system is supposed to be more efficient than conventional heating and cooling method but it is more fragile and difficult to repair. It is also not compatible with user habits as it requires constantly closed windows. 南京一"高科技住宅"墙壁开裂开发商承认房子娇气, *CNR Network*, last modified 17 March 2016, http://china.cnr.cn/xwwgf/20160317/t20160317_521635147.shtml. Other quality problems of Landsea buildings are also discussed in this report: 朗诗地产被指"伪绿色"沪宁沿线业主维权不断, *Sina Houses*, last modified 29 March 2015, accessed 13 August 2016, http://qhd.house.sina.com.cn/news/2015-03-29/10005987765119940360442.shtml.
21. "Development of Geothermal heat pump market in China," *National Renewable Energy Laboratory* (2006), http://www.nrel.gov/docs/fy06osti/39443.pdf. Also see: Keyan Zheng, Yiping Mo, Ling Chen, "Twenty Years of Geothermal Heat Pumps in China," Proceedings World Geothermal Congress 2015, Melbourne, Australia, accessed on 8 August 2016, https://pangea.stanford.edu/ERE/db/WGC/papers/WGC/2015/29025.pdf.

22. "China Low-E Glass Industry Report," ResearchInChina, (2009): Sect. 2.3.1, accessed 15 August 2016, http://www.researchinchina.com/FreeReport/PdfFile/633934440588302500.pdf.
23. Baoxing Qiu, "Action Plan on China's Green Building," speech presented by Vice Minister of Mohurd, 28 March 2011, http://wenku.baidu.com/view/2b40b9ea856a561252d36f6f.html. BaoxingQIU, speech at China Green Building Conference, 29 March 2013, accessed 21 May 2013, http://www.gbmap.org/article1.php?id=355.
24. Stanley CT Yip, Junqiang Liang, Hongjun Li, Yong Li,"Study on the Economics of Green buildings in China: A cost-benefit Analysis,"動感(生態城市與綠色建筑 (*Eco-city and Green building*, Vol. 4) (2011):4: 28–33 (in Chinese). Daming Sun and Wenxi Shao, 当前中国绿色建筑增量成本统计报告 (Statistical report of the Increased Costs of Current Chinese green building), Zhongguo Building Research Institute, Shanghai Branch, http://wenku.baidu.com/view/672cb11c650e52ea5518986b.html.
25. Yu Zhou, "State Power and environmental initiatives in China: analyzing China's green building program through an ecological modernization perspective," *Geoforum* (2015): 61: 1–12.
26. Albert Orrling, "The Economic Efficiency Of Market-Based Green Building Policy Instruments In China: A case study of the Chenghuaxinyuan Housing Scheme in Shanghai, Master thesis in Environmental Management and Policy," *The International Institute for Industrial Environmental Economics (IIIEE) Master Thesis* (2013). http://lup.lub.lu.se/luur/download?func=downloadFile&recordOId=4178207&fileOId=4178215.
27. Zhang Chuan, Song Lin个, Sun Xiaoyue (张川,宋凌, 孙潇月), 年度绿色建筑评价标识统计报告 (Annual Statistical report of 2014 Green building labels) (2014), accessed 16 August 2016, http://www.cngb.org.cn/cms/view/detailed.action?sid=aabec13351eda2360151f205532f001d.
28. National Development and Reform Commission (NDRC), Energy Research Institute (2012). Research of Green Building Action Plan, Beijing. Report in The China Sustainable Energy Program, Energy Foundation. Grant number G-1102-13760.
29. See analysis of China's distributive solar policy: "Rooftop Solar Gets Traction in China," *Chadbourne & Parke LLP*, accessed August 2016, http://www.chadbourne.com/rooftop_solar_china_june2014_projectfinance.
30. "The world's first Passive House, Darmstadt-Kranichstein, Germany," *Passidpedia, the Passive House Resource*, accessed August 2016, http://passipedia.org/examples/residential_buildings/multi-family_buildings/

central_europe/the_world_s_first_passive_house_darmstadt-kranichstein_germany.

31. Sven Schimschar, Kornelis Blok, Thomas Boermans, Andreas Hermelink, "Germany's path towards nearly zero-energy buildings—Enabling the greenhouse gas mitigation potential in the building stock," *Energy Policy*, (2011): 39(6): 3346–3360.
32. Landsea commissioned a residential hotel as a pilot project of passive house in Yangtze River Delta., "China embraces Passive House," Green Magazine, https://greenmagazine.com.au/china-embraces-the-passive-house/. The introduction of the project can also been seen in the architect page: "Passive Houses in southern China: Changxing Building," e-architect, last modified 24 August 2016, http://www.e-architect.co.uk/china/passive-house-bruck. In Chinese, the introduction of the project is at http://www.hughjs.com/show-836.html. Picture is available at Jan Siefke, *ArchDaily*, http://www.archdaily.com/569638/passive-house-bruck-peter-ruge-architekten-2.
33. Kong Wenliao, Gong Yanfeng, Yu Changyong, Wang Lihua, Wang Jiechun, 被动房冬季运行室温响应实测分析 (Test and analysis of the Passive House Room Temperature in real time) 建筑科学 (Building Science), (2016): 32(4): 71–76. Kong et al. (2016) tested the Bruck room temperature in winter and found that it is above 18 C indoor in 55% of the time without human occupation and 100% of time with human occupation, even without air exchange system in operation.
34. See report of these buildings: Coco Liu, "Energy efficiency: Chinese developers get active building passive energy homes," *E&E Publishing, LLC*, last modified 27 January 2015, http://www.eenews.net/stories/1060012314.
35. Zhang Xiaoling, Peng Mengyue, Ma Yishuo, Niu Ben, Luo Song (张小玲, 彭梦月, 马伊硕, 牛犇, 罗松), "Feasibility Study on Promoting Passive Residential Housing in China" (被动式居住建筑在中国推广的可行性研究), *Energy Foundation China*, accessed on 15 August 2016, http://www.efchina.org/Attachments/Report/reports-20131220-zh/%E8%A2%AB%E5%8A%A8%E5%BC%8F%E5%B1%85%E4%BD%8F%E5%BB%BA%E7%AD%91%E5%9C%A8%E4%B8%AD%E5%9B%BD%E6%8E%A8%E5%B9%BF%E7%9A%84%E5%8F%AF%E8%A1%8C%E6%80%A7%E7%A0%94%E7%A9%B6.pdf/view.
36. "DENA awards prize to top energy-efficient tower block in China," *DENA*, last modified 23 October 2013, http://www.dena.de/en/press-releases/pressemitteilungen/dena-awards-prize-to-top-energy-efficient-tower-block-in-china.html. See more detailed description of the process of construction: Coco Liu, "Energy efficiency: Chinese developers get active building passive energy homes," *E&E Publishing,*

LLC, last modified 27 January 2015, http://www.eenews.net/stories/1060012314.

37. Coco Liu, "Energy efficiency: Chinese developers get active building passive energy homes," *E&E Publishing, LLC*, last modified 27 January 2015, http://www.eenews.net/stories/1060012314.
38. Yu Zhou, "State Power and environmental initiatives in China: analyzing China's green building program through an ecological modernization perspective," *Geoforum* (2015): 61: 1–12.
39. Howard Yu, "This is why China's Housing market is such a mess," *Fortune*, last modified 10 February 2016, accessed 17 August 2016, http://fortune.com/2016/02/10/china-housing-market-mortgage-down-payment/.

Acknowledgements This research is supported by a grant of Lincoln Institute of Land Policy (CYZ012213) and by a research grant of the Peking University-Lincoln Institute of Urban Development and Land Policy. I would like to thank Jiajing Sun of Vassar College who helped with the data collection and analysis, Eroll Kuhn, Catherine Belleza, former and current Vassar College students, helped with editing, and Cai Yifan of Clark University who provided a valuable assistance in the fieldwork in China. I would also like express my appreciation to many people who have given me generous time and insights during my interviews.

References

An Investment Framework for Clean Energy and Development—A Platform for Convergence of Public and Private Investments. 2007. *The World Bank*. http://siteresources.worldbank.org/EXTSDNETWORK/Resources/AnInvestmentFrameworkforCleanEnergyandDevelopment.pdf?resourceurlname=AnInvestmentFrameworkforCleanEnergyandDevelopment.pdf.

China Embraces Passive House. *Green Magazine*. https://greenmagazine.com.au/china-embraces-the-passive-house/.

China Low-E glass Industry. 2009. *ResearchInChina*, Section 2.3.1, September. http://www.researchinchina.com/FreeReport/PdfFile/633934440588302500.pdf. Accessed 15 Aug 2016.

DENA Awards Prize to Top Energy-Efficient Tower Block in China. 2013. *DENA*. Last Modified 23 October 2013. http://www.dena.de/en/press-releases/pressemitteilungen/dena-awards-prize-to-top-energy-efficient-tower-block-in-china.html.

Development of Geothermal Heat Pump Market in China. 2006. *National Renewable Energy Laboratory*. http://www.nrel.gov/docs/fy06osti/39443.pdf.

Dobriansky, L. 2008. Beijing 2008 Olympics U.S. China Collaboration on Greening the Olympic Village. *EM: Air and Waste Management Association's Magazine for Environmental Managers*, pp. 28–31, August.

Green Building Action Plan (绿色建筑行动方案). 2013. *China State Council*, Document 1, January 1. http://www.gov.cn/zwgk/2013-01/06/content_2305793.htm. Accessed 28 May 2013.

Horizontal Skyscraper—Vanke Center. *Steve Holl Architects*. http://www.stevenholl.com/project-detail.php?type=mixeduse&id=60&page=0.

Kong, W., Y. Gong, C. Yu, L. Wang, J. Wang. 2016. 被动房冬季运行室温响应实测分析 [Test and Analysis of the Passive House Room Temperature in Real Time]. 建筑科学 [*Building Science*] 32 (4): 71–76.

Li, Y., Y. Li, B. He, and D. Zhao. 2014. Green Building in China: Need Great promotion. *Sustainable Cities and Society* 11: 1–6.

Linked Hybrid. *Steven Holl Architects*. http://www.stevenholl.com/projects/beijing-linked-hybrid?

Liu, C. 2015. Energy Efficiency: Chinese Developers Get Active Building Passive Energy Homes. *E&E Publishing, LLC*. Last Modified 27 January 2015. http://www.eenews.net/stories/1060012314.

Mo, K. 2009. From Grey to Green: How Energy-Efficient Buildings Can Help Make China's Rapid Urbanization Sustainable. Speech presented at The Climate Conference/COP 15, Copenhagen, Denmark, December. Accessed Aug 2016.

National Development and Reform Commission (NDRC), Energy Research Institute. 2012. Research of Green Building Action Plan, Beijing, Report in The China Sustainable Energy Program, Energy Foundation, Grant Number G-1102-13760.

Orrling, A. 2013. The Economic Efficiency of Market-Based Green Building Policy Instruments in China: Institute A Case Study of the Chenghuaxinyuan Housing Scheme in Shanghai, Master thesis in Environmental Management and Policy. The International for Industrial Environmental Economics (IIIEE) Master thesis. http://lup.lub.lu.se/luur/download?func=downloadFile&recordOId=4178207&fileOId=4178215.

Passive Houses in Southern China: Changxing Building. 2016. *E-Architect*. Last Modified 24 August 2016. http://www.e-architect.co.uk/china/passive-house-bruck.

Press Release of the Green Building Action Plan. http://news.dichan.sina.com.cn/2013/02/27/658127.html.

Qiu, B. 2011. Action Plan on China's Green Building. Speech presented by Vice Minister of MOHURD, March 28. http://wenku.baidu.com/view/2b40b9ea856a561252d36f6f.html.

Qiu, B. 2013. Speech at China Green Building Conference, March 29. http://www.gbmap.org/article1.php?id=355. Accessed 21 May 2013.

Rooftop Solar Gets Traction in China. 2016. *Chadbourne & Parke LLP*. http://www.chadbourne.com/rooftop_solar_china_june2014_projectfinance. Accessed Aug 2016.

Schimschar, S., K. Blok, T. Boermans, and A. Hermelink. 2011. Germany's Path Towards Nearly Zero-Energy Buildings—Enabling the Greenhouse Gas Mitigation Potential in the Building Stock. *Energy Policy* 39 (6): 3346–3360.

Sliced Porosity Block—Capitaland Raffles City Chengdu. *Steve Holl Architects*. http://www.stevenholl.com/project-detail.php?type=housing&id=98.

Sun, D., and W. Shao. 2008. 当前中国绿色建筑增量成本统计报告 [Statistical Report of the Increased Costs of Current Chinese Green Building]. Zhongguo Building Research Institute, Shanghai Branch. http://wenku.baidu.com/view/672cb11c650e52ea5518986b.html.

The China-US Climate Agreement: By the Numbers. 2014. *World Resource Institute*. http://www.wri.org/blog/2014/11/numbers-china-us-climate-agreement. Accessed 16 Aug 2016.

The World's First Passive House, Darmstadt-Kranichstein, Germany. 2016. *Passidpedia, the Passive House Resource*. http://passipedia.org/examples/residential_buildings/multi-family_buildings/central_europe/the_world_s_first_passive_house_darmstadt-kranichstein_germany. Accessed Aug 2016.

Xu, Z. (徐振强). 2016. 建筑要想绿,政策得激励:25省市"绿政"大起底 [To Make Building Green, Policy Incentives are Necessary. –Summary of the Green Building Policy in 25 Provinces and Municipality]. *Xinhua*. http://news.xinhuanet.com/info/2016-02/23/c_135122658.htm?from=timeline&isappinstalled=0. Accessed 16 Aug 2016.

Yip, C.T. Stanley, J. Liang, H. Li, and Y. Li. 2011. Study on the Economics of Green Buildings in China: A Cost-Benefit Analysis. 動感(生態城市與綠色建筑 [*Eco-city and Green building*] 4: 28–33.

Yu, H. 2016. *This is Why China's Housing Market is Such a Mess*. Fortune. Last Modified 10 February 2016. http://fortune.com/2016/02/10/china-housing-market-mortgage-down-payment/. Accessed 17 Aug 2016.

Zhang, C., L. Song, and X. Sun (张川, 宋凌, 孙潇月). 2014. 年度绿色建筑评价标识统计报告 [Annual Statistical Report of 2014 Green Building Labels]. http://www.cngb.org.cn/cms/view/detailed.action?sid=aabec13351eda236 0151f205532f001d. Accessed 16 Aug 2016.

Zhang, X., M. Peng, Y. Ma, B. Niu, and S. Luo (张小, 彭梦, 马伊, 牛, 罗松). 2013. Feasibility Study on Promoting Passive Residential Housing in China [被动式居住建筑在中国推广的可行性研究]. Report for Energy Foundation.

http://www.efchina.org/Attachments/Report/reports-20131220-zh/%E8%A2%AB%E5%8A%A8%E5%BC%8F%E5%B1%85%E4%BD%8F%E5%BB%BA%E7%AD%91%E5%9C%A8%E4%B8%AD%E5%9B%BD%E6%8E%A8%E5%B9%BF%E7%9A%84%E5%8F%AF%E8%A1%8C%E6%80%A7%E7%A0%94%E7%A9%B6.pdf/view. Accessed 15 Aug 2016.

Zheng, K., Y. Mo, and L. Chen. 2015. Twenty Years of Geothermal Heat Pumps in China. *Proceedings World Geothermal Congress 2015*, Melbourne Australia. https://pangea.stanford.edu/ERE/db/WGC/papers/WGC/2015/29025.pdf. Accessed 8 Aug 2016.

Zhou, C., X. Dai, R. Wang, and J. Huang. 2011. Indicators for Evaluating Sustainable Communities: A Review. *ShengtaiXuebao/ActaEcologicaSinica* 31 (16): 4750–4759.

Zhou, Y., and Y. Cai. 2014. 打造中国绿色建筑推广的合力 [Creating "Crowd-Sourcing" for China's Green Building Promotion Program]. 现代城市研究 [*Modern Urban Research*] 6: 89–96.

Zhou, Y. 2015. State Power and Environmental Initiatives in China: Analyzing China's Green Building Program Through an Ecological Modernization Perspective. *Geoforum* 61: 1–12.

南京一"高科技住宅"墙壁开裂开发商承认房子娇气. 2016. *CNR Network,* March 17. http://china.cnr.cn/xwwgf/20160317/t20160317_521635147.shtml.

朗诗地产被指"伪绿色"沪宁沿线业主维权不断. 2015. *Sina Houses,* March 29. http://qhd.house.sina.com.cn/news/2015-03-29/10005987765119940360442.shtml. Accessed 13 Aug 2016.

绿色建筑行动方案发展改革委住房城乡建设部， 国务院办公厅关于转发发展改革委住房城乡建设部. 2013. http://www.gov.cn/zwgk/2013-01/06/content_2305793.htm.

Author Biography

Dr. Yu Zhou Professor of Geography, Vassar College. She received Bachelor and Master's degree from the Department of Regional and Environmental Sciences (formerly Geography) in Peking University, China, and received Ph.D. in geography from the University of Minnesota in 1995. Her current research is on high technology industry and on green building and policy in China.

CHAPTER 9

Energy Efficiency and High-Performance Buildings

Ryan Colker

In the United States, the buildings and the functions conducted inside them (excluding industrial processes) are responsible for about 40% of primary energy use and over 75% of electricity use[1] (see Fig. 9.1). Within urban areas, the building-attributable energy use is often significantly higher. New York City, for instance, found that buildings accounted for 75% of energy consumption and 75% of greenhouse gas emissions within the city.[2]

Periodically, the US Department of Energy (DOE), Energy Information Administration, conducts a national survey of buildings to determine the characteristics of the building stock—the Commercial Buildings Energy Consumption Survey (CBECS).[3] Despite a significant increase in the number of buildings from 2003 to 2012, the overall energy use attributable to buildings increased only slightly[4] (see Figs. 9.2, 9.3).

Pressure is mounting from numerous sources to reduce this energy use. At an individual building or portfolio level, building owners are seeing

The original version of this chapter was revised: For detailed information please see Erratum. The erratum to this chapter is available at https://doi.org/10.1057/978-1-137-57446-6_11

R. Colker (✉)
National Institute of Building Sciences, Washington, DC, USA
e-mail: rcolker@nibs.org

N.E. Coulson et al. (eds.), *Energy Efficiency and the Future of Real Estate*, DOI 10.1057/978-1-137-57446-6_9

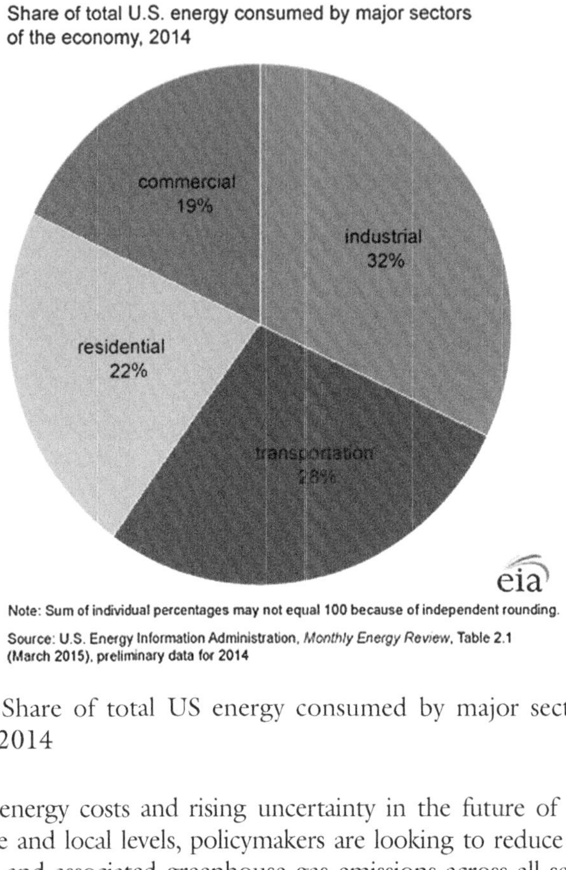

Fig. 9.1 Share of total US energy consumed by major sectors of the economy, 2014

increasing energy costs and rising uncertainty in the future of such costs. At the state and local levels, policymakers are looking to reduce the overall energy use and associated greenhouse gas emissions across all sectors in an attempt to improve their resilience, address public health issues, demonstrate leadership in protecting limited resources, and address climate change. At the federal level, policymakers are looking to increase energy productivity,[5] reduce reliance on foreign sources of energy, address obligations associated with climate change agreements, increase national and community resilience, and protect human health. Governments are also looking to demonstrate fiscal responsibility by addressing energy use within their own portfolios.

However, energy use is not the only consideration in the design, construction, regulation, and operation of buildings. Architects, engineers, facility managers, code officials, and building owners must address numerous other building attributes. These attributes are commonly addressed within the concept of a high-performance building[6] or through whole building

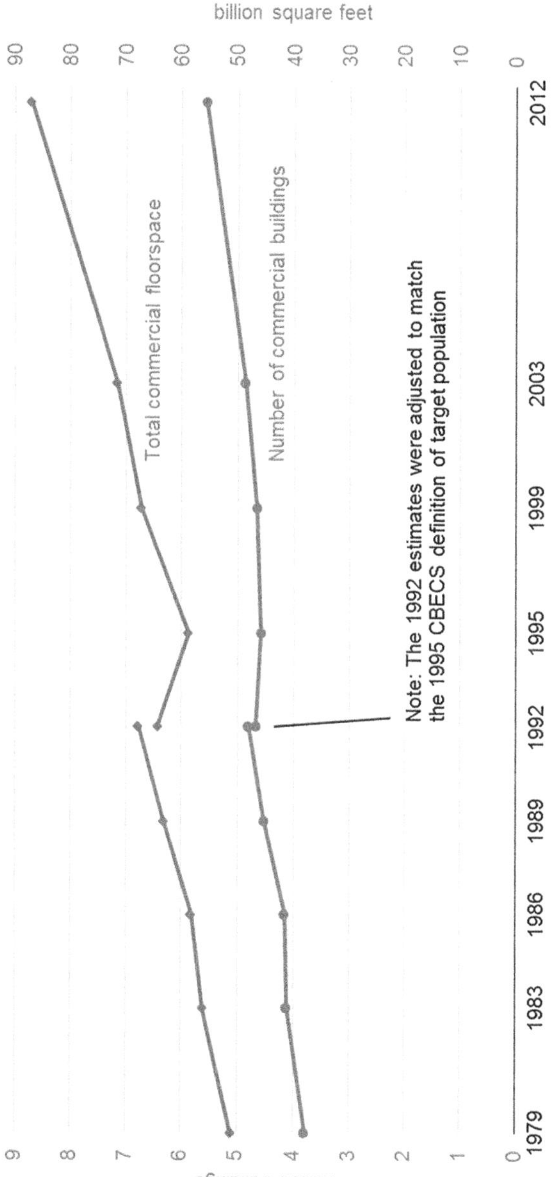

Fig. 9.2 Growth in commercial buildings

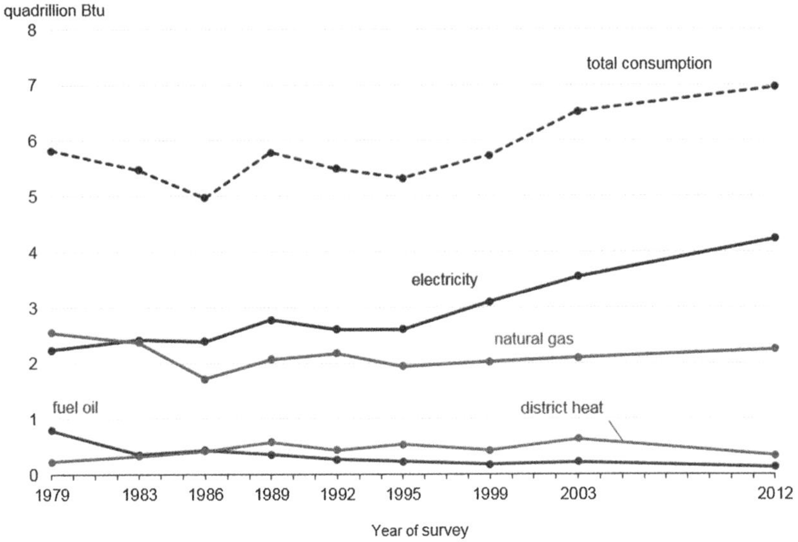

Fig. 9.3 Total commercial building energy consumption

design.[7] Both high-performance and whole building designs require the integration and optimization of high-performance attributes, including safety and security, accessibility, historic preservation, productivity, functionality, cost effectiveness, aesthetics, and sustainability (which generally includes energy and water efficiency). Green building attributes are a subset of the high-performance building attributes and they should be addressed in the context of the overall performance goals.[8] Achieving incredibly efficient and high-performance buildings requires the utilization of collaborative and integrative approaches to design, construction, and operations.

This chapter will cover the energy performance of buildings: past, present, and evolving attempts to reduce energy use; opportunities to address issues related to energy efficiency, including water efficiency and greenhouse gas emissions; the role of renewable energy; and how overall building industry changes will impact building energy use.

9.1 Energy Use Within Buildings

In the US, there were 5.6 million commercial buildings in 2012, comprising 87 billion square feet of floorspace. These commercial buildings consume about 16 quadrillion BTUs (or quads of energy).[9] To put thus in context, the entire economy of Canada used 14.3 quads of energy in 2010.[10] Residential buildings consume an additional 22 quads.[11] Globally, buildings are responsible for 32% of global energy consumption.[12]

While large buildings generally capture the public's attention, the majority of these buildings (90%) and half of the overall square footage (49%) are small buildings under 50,000 sq ft.[13] Fig. 9.4 shows that about half of buildings are 5000 sq ft in size or smaller, and nearly three-fourths are 10,000 sq ft or smaller. The median building size is 5000 sq ft (i.e., half the buildings are larger than this and half are smaller), while the average size is 15,700 sq ft.[14] Reducing the energy necessary to provide the same or an improved level of building services is frequently identified as the concept of energy efficiency. The effective implementation of energy-efficiency strategies requires understanding the overall energy use of buildings and the various different characteristics that drive such a use.

The overall efficiency of the building stock is improving—despite a 14% increase in total buildings and a 22% increase in total floorspace since 2003—energy use was up just 7% during the same period, according to the 2012 CBECS.[15] In addition, Fig. 9.5 shows the decrease in total energy used per square foot in commercial buildings from 1979–2012. Many measures have contributed to these improvements,

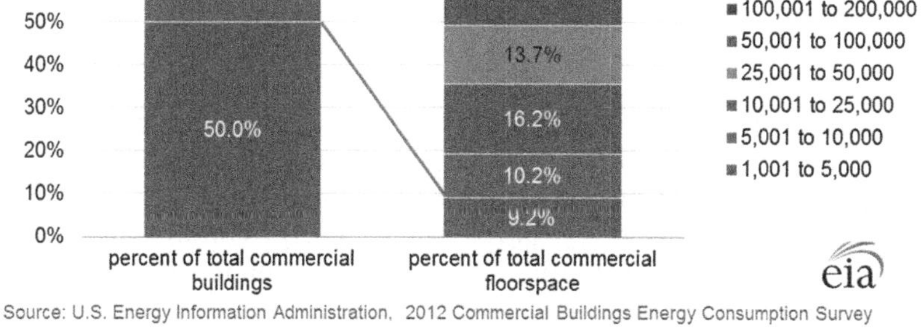

Fig. 9.4 Breakdown of commercial building stock by number and floorspace

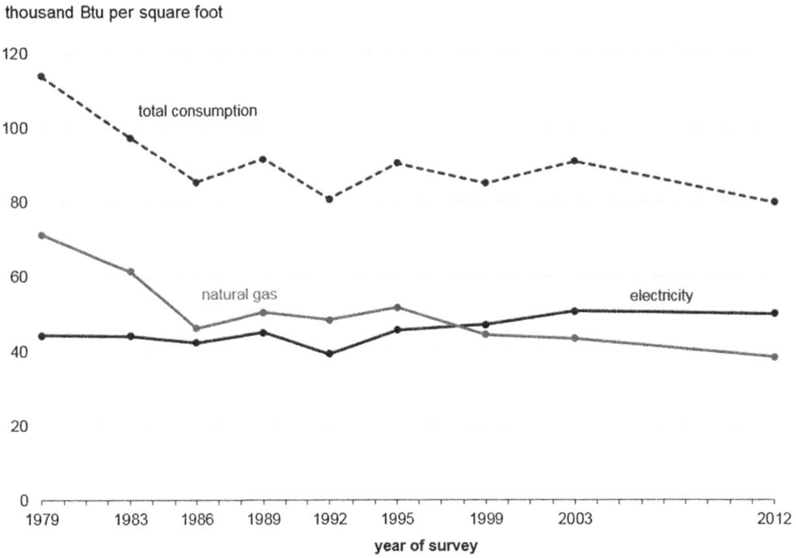

Fig. 9.5 Total energy used per square foot in buildings

including new energy code provisions and the expansion of green building rating systems.

Beyond the important information provided by CBECS, other characteristics and trends within the building stock must be understood to effectively address improvements in energy efficiency. Despite the significant growth in green buildings over the past 10 years or so, such buildings still remain a small segment of the overall building stock. Figure 9.6 shows that zero energy buildings (ZEBs) have also seen a significant growth from 2012–2015.

While the improvements in efficiency and the growth of green buildings and ZEBs are encouraging, many within the building industry see continued opportunity for improvement. In fact, as discussed below, many communities, portfolio owners, professional organizations, and other groups have set specific targets for improvement.

Broadly speaking, Fig. 9.7 shows that the energy consumed in buildings is used to provide heating, cooling, and lighting. The improved efficiency of key energy-consuming equipment has contributed to the decreased demand. From 2003–2012, space heating and lighting

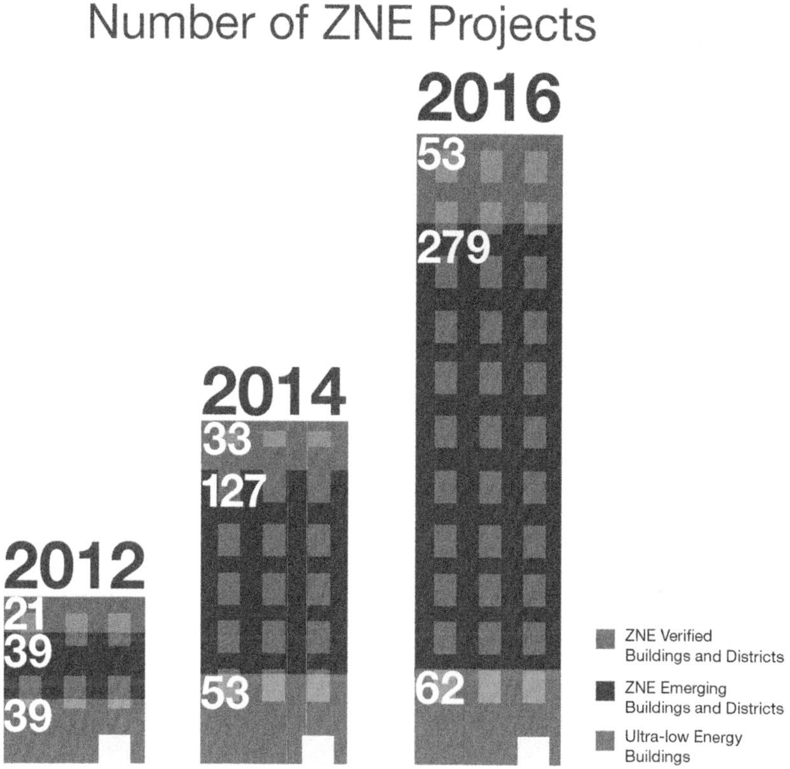

Fig. 9.6 Growth in commercial zero energy buildings. New Buildings Institute, "Names + Numbers: 2015 Interim Getting to Zero Status Update." http://newbuildings.org/resource/names-numbers-2015-interim-getting-zero-status-update/

energy use are each down by 11% points in their share of energy use in buildings.[16]

As the energy use attributed to specific building services decreases through efficiency improvements, the proportion of energy use designated as "other" is anticipated to grow. This "other" category generally includes plug loads—the items typically brought into buildings following construction and are not under the control of the design and construction team. Further discussion on addressing these "other" energy uses is included below.

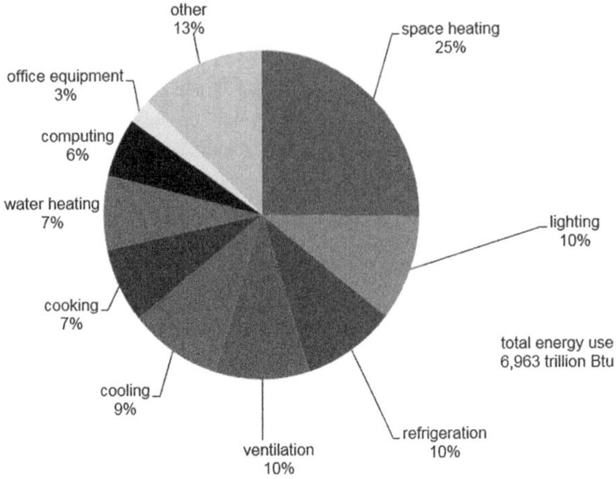

Fig. 9.7 Commercial building energy end uses

While the overall characteristics of the building stock are important for the development of policy and technology solutions to reduce energy use, the energy use associated with an individual building varies. To effectively reduce this use, building owners and operators must understand the energy use of their buildings and develop strategies to address these uses. Government and other stakeholders have also implemented strategies to help facilitate efficiency improvements.

9.2 The Energy-Efficiency Opportunity

Several studies have been undertaken to help identify the opportunities and impacts of energy-efficiency opportunities. The results of a study by Deutsche Bank found that implementing measures to improve efficiency 30% in residential, commercial, and institutional buildings built before 1980 will result in $279 billion of economic benefit, more than 3.3 million new direct and indirect cumulative job years, and 3000 trillion BTUs of energy savings.[17] At a community level, each additional $1 spent on energy efficiency avoids more than $2 in energy-related investments.[18]

Given the significant number of small commercial buildings, Fig. 9.8 shows that energy-efficiency opportunities within the small buildings

	Total	Commercial Buildings	Small Commercial Buildings[1]
Investment ($billion)	$279	$72	$35.64
Energy Savings (trillion BTUs)	3033	848	419.76
Energy Savings (10 years, $ billion)[2]	1000	$279.6	$138.4
Cumulative Job Years (thousand FTEs)	3305	857	424.2
GHG Reductions (million metric tons CO_2/year)	616	175	86.6

Sources:
Fulton Mark, et al., *United States Building Energy Efficiency Retrofits, Market Sizing and Financing Models*, DB Climate Change Advisors, Deutsche Bank Group, March 2012, pp. 3, 7
U.S. Energy Information Administration, "2012 CBECS Preliminary Results," June 2014, http://www.eia.gov/consumption/commercial/reports.cfm

Notes:
1. Small commercial building share estimated at 49.5% of commercial building share, per 2012 CBECS preliminary results.
2. Commercial energy savings in dollars derived from the ratio of commercial Btu savings to total BTU savings.

Fig. 9.8 Summary of energy-efficiency impact by market size, climate, and employment categories

sector can result in over $35.6 billion in economic benefit and 425,000 job years of full-time employment based on further analysis of the Deutsche Bank findings conducted by the National Institute of Building Sciences Council on Finance, Insurance, and Real Estate (CFIRE).[19] While these benefits are significant, several challenges must be overcome to realize them.

Despite the significant economic opportunities accompanying investment in energy-efficiency measures, many building owners are not implementing them. Other factors are at work.

9.3 Current Approaches to Energy Efficiency

Reducing building energy use requires a combination of policy and technical strategies implemented by various stakeholders within the design, construction, and operation process.

9.3.1 Building Energy Codes

Building energy codes have been identified as the most effective method to improving building energy efficiency to date. The International Energy Administration (IEA) identified building codes as the top priority for tackling climate change.[20] In general, building energy codes establish minimum requirements for the design and construction of buildings. In the US, energy codes are developed through a private sector-driven process that produce "model codes." These model codes often serve as the basis for regulation at the state or local level.[21] Codes have the benefit of establishing requirements for all new constructions—thus locking in design and construction strategies for the life of the buildings. The codes often also apply to renovations and retrofits that meet a particular threshold.

Codes typically focus on the design and construction process which establishes an important foundation for the long-term energy performance of the building. Because of this focus on design and construction, once these stages are complete, a certificate of occupancy is issued and most code-related enforcement stops. However, the scope of codes has been expanding to include some provisions that apply past the certificate of occupancy such as commissioning.[22]

Model energy codes in the US are developed by ASHRAE and the International Code Council (ICC). While their development processes are slightly different, they are developed through the participation of public and private stakeholders. As baseline or minimum codes and standards, they require a demonstration of cost effectiveness.[23]

Federal statutes require states to certify that they have adopted an energy code at least as stringent as the latest model codes once they are found to save energy by DOE.[24] Despite this mandate, energy code adoptions have varied significantly across the country. Figures 9.9 and 9.10 show the variation in commercial and residential building energy code adoption across the US as of July 2016.

Commercial buildings are generally subject to the provisions of *ANSI/ASHRAE/IES Standard 90.1: Energy Efficient Design of Buildings except Low-Rise Residential.* While the ICC-developed International Energy Conservation Code (IECC) also contains commercial specific provisions, it incorporates Standard 90.1 as an acceptable compliance path. Standard 90.1 has been developed since the 1970s (then just called Standard 90) in response to the energy crisis. The standard has provided significant improvements in energy efficiency; Fig. 9.11 shows the decline in the Energy Use Index as stricter energy codes were implemented.

The IECC contains both residential and commercial building requirements. It was first developed as the Model Code for Energy Conservation (MCEC) in 1977, but became the IECC in 1998 following the consolidation of several regionally-based code bodies into the ICC. The IECC has also seen significant advancements in its anticipated efficiency.

Both Standard 90.1 and the IECC are developed on a 3-year cycle. Once published by ASHRAE and ICC, jurisdictions initiate a process for adoption. The adoption process varies widely from state to state and even locality to locality.[25] Some states adopt codes that apply across the state with enforcement falling to local governments.[26] Other states may leave the decision to adopt codes to the local government—often, this leaves significant portions of the state without a code.

While the adoption of an energy code is necessary to achieve energy efficiency in new and renovated buildings, it is not sufficient. The enforcement of codes is essential to realizing the savings anticipated by

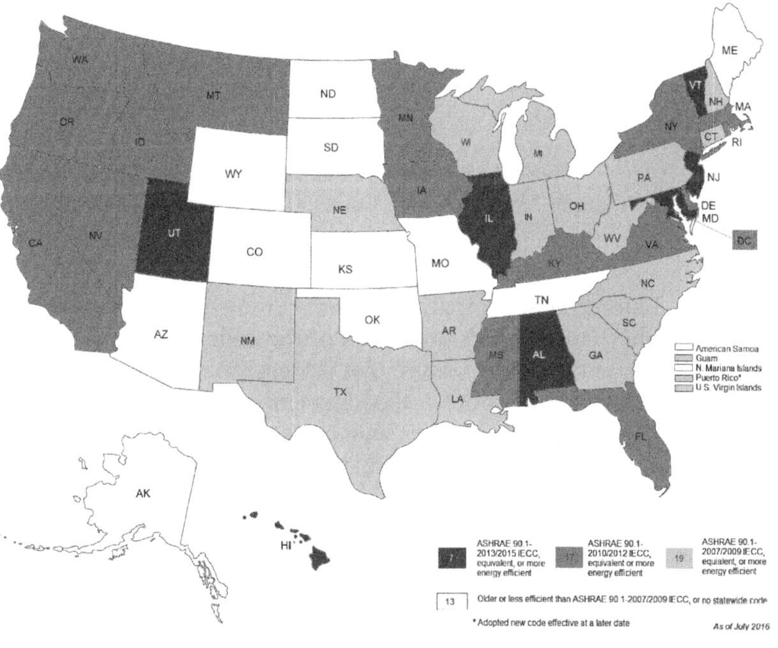

Fig. 9.9 Status of commercial building energy code adoptions. See DOE Building Energy Codes Program, "Status of State Energy Code Adoption," https://www.energycodes.gov/adoption/states

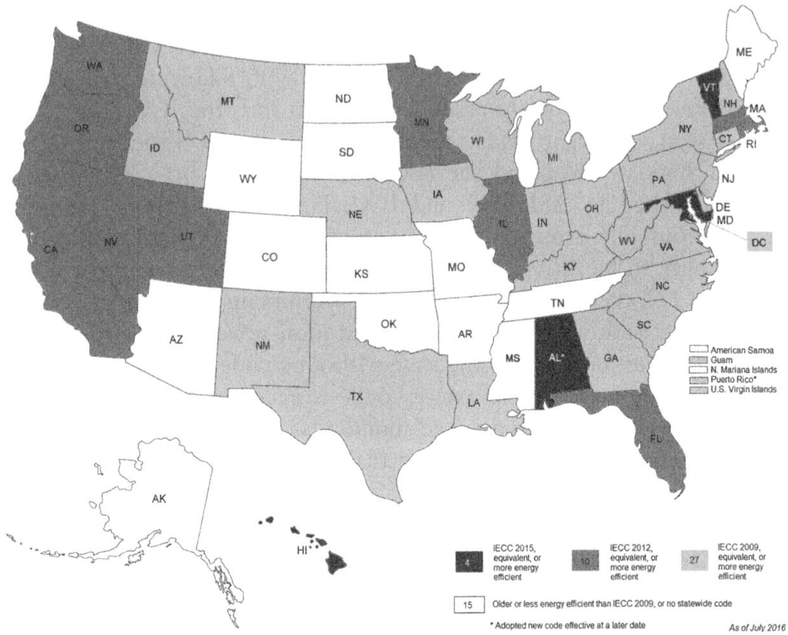

Fig. 9.10 Status of residential energy code adoptions. See DOE Building Energy Codes Program, "Status of State Energy Code Adoption," https://www.energycodes.gov/adoption/states

the code. Enforcement typically entails reviewing proposed designs to assure that they comply with provisions of the code (called plan review) and inspecting in the field to assure that what is installed and built match the design and code provisions (called inspection). To demonstrate compliance with the code, a designer and owner select a compliance path identified within the code. The paths typically available are outlined in the text box.

Compliance Paths Within Energy Codes

Energy codes typically have two main paths for compliance—prescriptive and performance. A third new compliance path—an outcome or target path—is emerging as a potential solution to some of the shortcomings of the current codes. The outcome-based compliance path and its benefits are discussed further in the body of the chapter.

Prescriptive: Prescriptive codes provide minimum characteristics for many building components (e.g., R-values for wall and ceiling insulation, U-values for windows, and SEER or EER for unitary air conditioners). Prescriptive codes represent a checklist of requirements and minimally acceptable specifications, making them relatively easy for building teams to comply with and code officials to enforce.

Performance: Performance-based codes set a desired level of energy performance, often based on the anticipated results of parallel prescriptive codes. This gives building teams flexibility in selecting how to meet the intent of the prescriptive code without necessarily complying with every prescription. Designers typically demonstrate compliance through energy modeling of the building, incorporating their selected building specifications, and then doing the same modeling but substituting the minimum prescriptive requirements from the code.

Outcome: Outcome-based codes establish a target energy use level and provide for regular measurement and reporting of energy use to assure that the completed building performs at the established level. Such a code can have significant flexibility to reflect variations across building types and can even cover existing and historic buildings. Most importantly, it can address all energy used in a building and provide a metric to determine the overall energy efficiency of the building's design, construction, and operations.

Adapted from "Developing Effective Codes and Standards for Net-Zero Energy Buildings" by Colker, R.M., D. Hewitt and J. Henderson. *Building Design + Construction White Paper on Zero and Near-Zero Energy Buildings + Homes*, March 2011. http://www.bdcnetwork.com/sites/default/files/5.%20Developing%20Effective%20Codes%20and%20Standards%20for%20Net-Zero%20Energy%20Buildings.pdf.

The actual level of compliance with code provisions is unclear. DOE recently funded studies to understand the compliance rates in commercial buildings and the measures that can enhance compliance. A similar initiative is

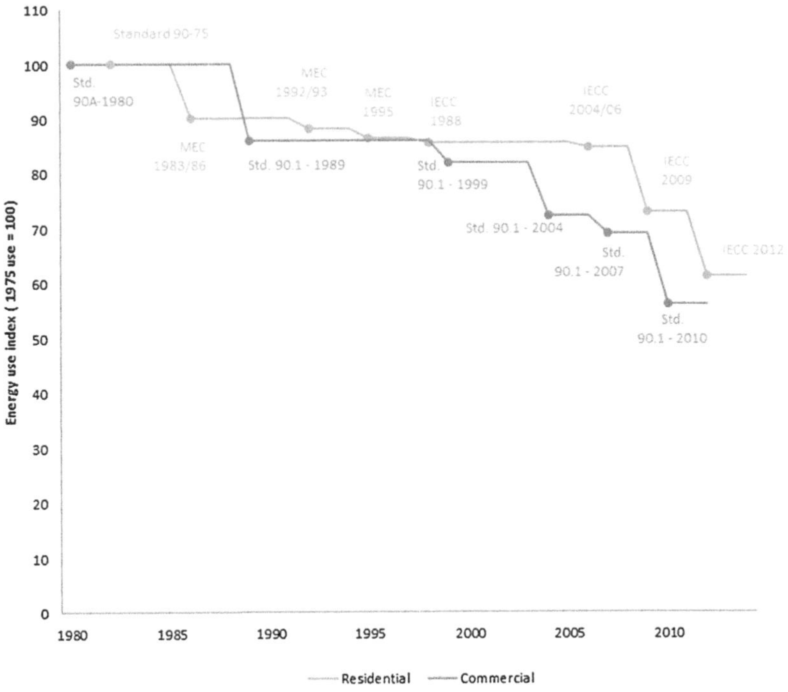

Fig. 9.11 Relative energy use under model building energy codes 1980–2015. From American Council for an Energy Efficient Economy (ACEEE) based on analysis from Pacific Northwest National Laboratory (PNNL)

underway within the residential sector.[27] Preliminary results within the residential sector have shown high compliance rates for some code provisions.

While Standard 90.1 and the IECC are considered minimum or baseline codes, communities and others within the industry have requested development of guidance in a code format that can be readily applied in instances where results above the baseline are desired. In many cases, green building rating programs were used to fill this void, but they were not necessarily a good solution as they are formulated as voluntary programs based on non-mandatory provisions. ASHRAE, cooperating with the US Green Building Council (USGBC) and the Illuminating Engineering Society (IES), published *ANSI/ASHRAE/USGBC/IES Standard 189.1: Standard for the Design of High-Performance*

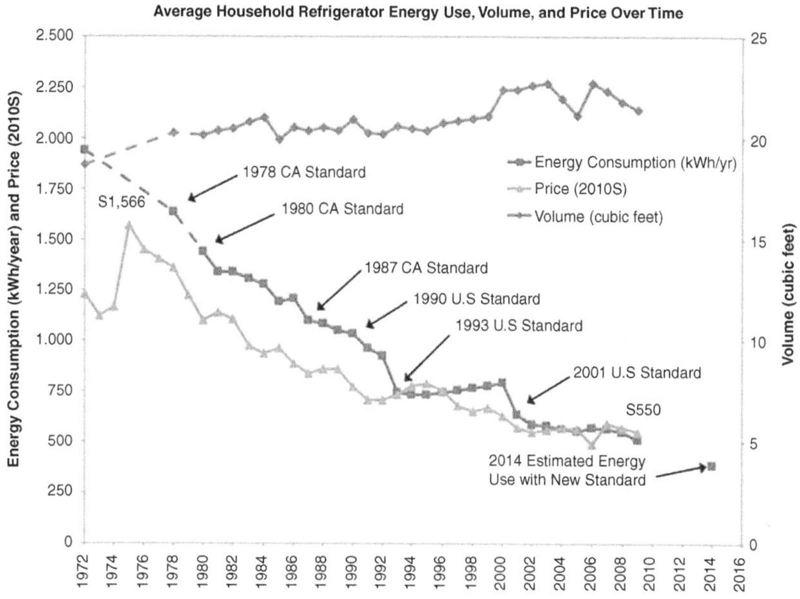

Fig. 9.12 Average household refrigerator energy use, volume, and price over time. http://aceee.org/blog/2014/09/how-your-refrigerator-has-kept-its-co

Green Buildings in 2011. ICC first published the International Green Construction Code (IgCC) in 2012. Some communities and states have also developed their own stretch or reach codes.

Currently, ASHRAE and ICC are working to consolidate the content of Standard 189.1 and the IgCC into a single document where the technical provisions will be developed through ASHRAE's process and the administrative procedures will be developed through ICC. This consolidation should result in greater uptake of stretch codes and limit potential confusion.

Communities will use stretch codes in a variety of ways depending on the specific goals of the community. The stretch code may be applied on a mandatory basis to a specific subset of buildings, including municipal facilities, buildings over a specific size, or within a special zoning area. On a voluntary basis, stretch codes may be recognized as a means to obtain particular incentives, including expedited permitting, density bonuses, and tax abatements. An individual building owner can use the stretch code to establish requirements for facilities within their portfolio.

It is important to note that both Standard 189.1 and the IgCC go beyond energy requirements and cover many of the areas contained within the green building rating programs.

Stretch codes serve a valuable role for the design and construction community and for regulators. Stretch codes often foreshadow content to be included in future editions of the baseline codes. This serves to help manufacturers and other members of the industry prepare for future code requirements.

9.3.2 *Appliance and Equipment Standards*

Appliance and equipment standards have been developed to assure that specific energy using components achieves a minimum level of energy performance. California enacted the first appliance standards in the US in 1974. The national Energy Policy and Conservation Act (EPCA) quickly followed in 1975 establishing a federal program consisting of test procedures, labeling, and energy targets for consumer products. Amendments to EPCA in 1979 directed DOE to establish energy conservation standards for consumer products.

The Energy Policy Act of 1992 (EPAct) added standards for some fluorescent and incandescent reflector lamps, plumbing products, electric motors, commercial water heaters, and heating, ventilation, and air-conditioning (HVAC) systems. In 2005, the Energy Policy Act (EPAct 2005) set new standards for 16 products and directed DOE to set standards via rulemaking for another five. In 2007, Congress passed the Energy Independence and Security Act (EISA 2007), enacting new or updated standards for 13 products.[28]

DOE appliance and equipment standards cover more than 60 products that account for about 90% of residential energy use, 60% of commercial building energy use, and 30% of industrial energy use. Based on standards implemented since 1987, consumers saved $63 billion in 2015 and reduced or avoided 2.6 billion tons of carbon dioxide (CO_2) emissions. Since 2009, DOE has issued 40 new or updated appliance standards for more than 45 products. These standards are projected to save consumers over $540 billion through 2030. The energy savings from these standards—43.8 quads by 2030—are more than the energy used by all US buildings over 1 year.[29]

As indicated above, the energy savings associated with appliance and equipment standards are significant. The American Council for an Energy Efficient Economy (ACEEE) produced an informative history of refrigerator standards and the significant energy savings that they have achieved, while cost has decreased and volume has increased.[30] A summary of these trends is included in Fig. 9.12.

In addition to minimum performance standards, labeling requirements have provided consumers with important information to allow an educated selection of products based on anticipated energy use. Energy Guide labels are required by the Federal Trade Commission for certain appliances and equipment, including boilers, central air conditioners, clothes washers, dishwashers, freezers, furnaces, heat pumps, pool heaters, refrigerators, televisions, water heaters, and window air conditioners.[31]

As discussed below, the ENERGY STAR program recognizes appliances, equipment and other building components that use less energy than the mainstream models.

9.3.3 Utility and Government Incentives

While codes set mandatory minimum requirements, many communities and other interested stakeholders provide incentives for building owners to go beyond the minimum requirements. As indicated above, sometimes, these incentives point to stretch codes, but there may be other bases for incentives.

The types of incentives and the building systems or activities that they cover can vary widely. In order to help designers, owners, and others to keep track of the availability of such incentives, DOE and the North Carolina Clean Energy Technology Center have created the "Database of State Incentives for Renewables and Efficiency" or DSIRE.[32] DSIRE includes information on nearly 3000 different programs focused on encouraging energy efficiency. Programs include those offered by federal, state and local governments and utilities.

9.3.3.1 Federal Incentives

At a federal level, incentive programs take a few forms. Tax incentives are the most common, but agencies such as DOE also offer technical assistance. First introduced in 2005, the Energy-Efficient Commercial Building Tax Deduction (often called 179D based on the section of the tax code) provides commercial building owners (and designers or contractors for non-profit owned buildings) a $1.80 per square foot tax deduction for improvements made to lighting, HVAC, and building enclosures. Unfortunately, the deduction has not received long-term approval from Congress causing some uncertainty for projects and limiting the development of large initiatives around the deduction.[33]

Tax credits 27C and 45L provide incentives to homeowners and homebuilders, respectively, to reduce energy use.

Federal agencies also provide tools and resources to assist private sector building owners in making investment decisions around energy efficiency. The most widely known is the ENERGY STAR program—a joint initiative of the DOE and Environmental Protection Agency. The program consists of two parts: a products' program and a buildings' program. Both efforts contribute to improved energy performance of buildings.

The products' program evaluates the energy performance of many different products found in homes and businesses. Based on these evaluations, an ENERGY STAR designation and label is placed on the top energy performers.[34] These labels provide an easy means for implementation and can be incorporated into incentive programs.

The ENERGY STAR for buildings' program recognizes buildings that perform in the top 25% of buildings based on their location and building type. The designation is based on data obtained through CBECS, so an adjustment in the scoring thresholds is underway based on the new data obtained through the 2012 survey. Several studies have demonstrated the value of recognition by ENERGY STAR as a top performer (see Fig. 9.13). In addition to the recognition program, ENERGY STAR provides Portfolio Manager as a free tool for building owners and operators to benchmark and track their energy and water use. A recent study found that commercial buildings that regularly benchmarked their energy performance in Portfolio Manager cuts their energy bills by 7% over 3 years (2.4% per year on average).[35]

In addition to the ENERGY STAR program, DOE's Building Technology Office has launched the Better Buildings Program to help facilitate energy-efficiency improvements with a goal of making buildings 20% more efficient in a decade.[36] The program focuses on four main strategies:

- developing innovative, replicable solutions with market leaders;
- making energy-efficiency investment easier;
- developing a skilled clean energy workforce;
- leading by example in federal government.

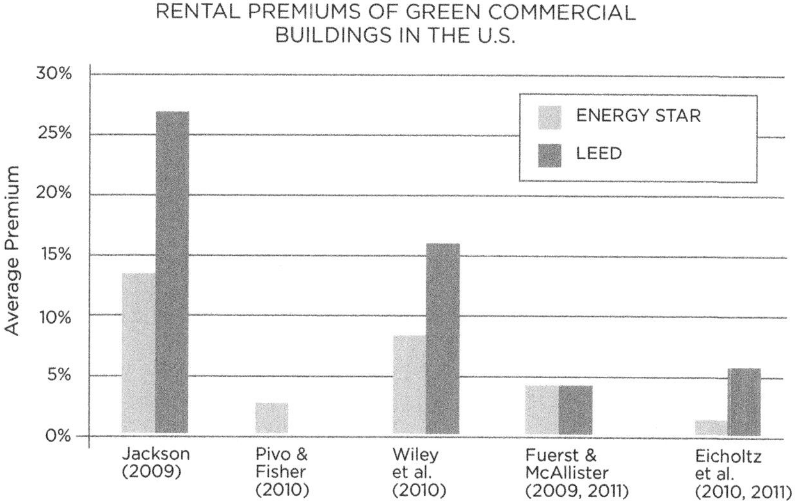

Fig. 9.13 Summary of studies on rental premiums for ENERGY STAR and LEED buildings. Institute for Market Transformation. 2015. *High-Performance Buildings and Property Value*. http://www.imt.org/resources/detail/high-performance-buildings-and-property-value

From a solution center offering links to the best practices[37] to accelerators looking to tackle key barriers or opportunities to advance energy efficiency, the Better Buildings program is providing valuable tools to assist building owners and other stakeholders to reduce building-related energy use.

9.3.3.2 State and Local Incentives

Many states and localities have implemented programs aimed at encouraging reductions in energy use. These programs can be part of a broad community-wide goal like 80 by 50 or Architecture 2030, which are discussed in further depth below. Other programs are property specific and are tied to real estate in a unique way.

Following a hiccup in implementation within the residential market, Property Assessed Clean Energy or PACE programs have expanded to provide financing for the implementation of energy-saving measures.[38]

PACE programs utilize government provided or enhanced financing to fund energy efficiency or renewable energy upgrades. Figure 9.14

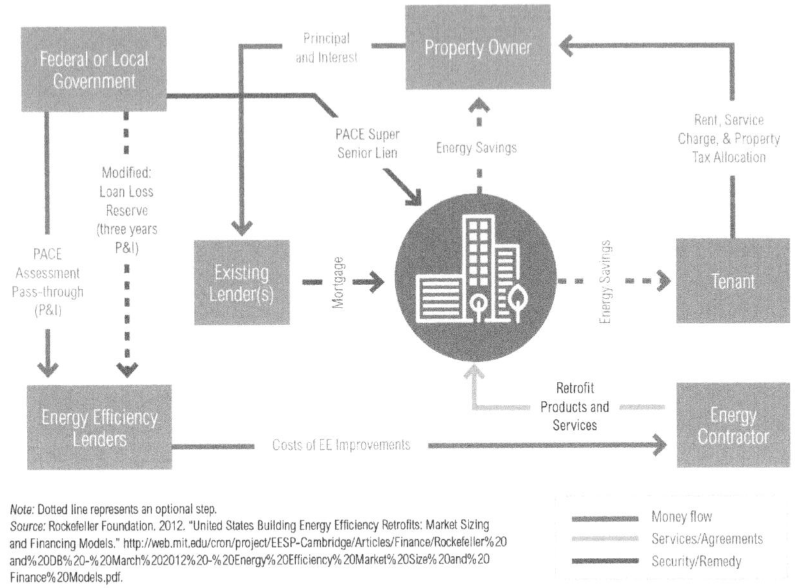

Fig. 9.14 Overview of typical PACE model. World Resources Institute. 2016. *Accelerating Building Efficiency: Eight Actions for Urban Leaders*. http://publications.wri.org/buildingefficiency/

shows a diagram of the typical PACE program. Repayment is tied to the property taxes for a period of up to 20 years. By linking repayment to property taxes, the obligation remains with the enhanced property upon sale. This helps to overcome several challenges associated with energy-efficiency investments—assuring that the value associated with the investment is recognized upon sale, avoiding the potentially high up-front costs for a benefit that may be realized by a future property owner, and allowing the costs of improvements to be passed on to tenants, thus avoiding split incentive issues. The PACE program also typically provides some level of technical oversight to assure that implemented measures can truly provide the energy-efficiency results anticipated.

Related to PACE are on-bill financing programs, where repayment of investments is made through utility bills rather than tax assessments.

In addition to financing opportunities, several states and localities are looking to encourage action on reducing energy use through market-based initiatives driven by the availability of information. They have implemented benchmarking and transparency laws requiring a certain set of buildings to benchmark their energy use annually (typically using ENERGY STAR Portfolio Manager) and provide the results to a government agency or publicly. The current adoptions of such requirements in the US are shown in Fig. 9.15. Such requirements have been more widespread internationally, including in the European Union and Australia. Building Rating maintains information on the content and status of such initiatives.[39]

Just like in the ENERGY STAR program, benchmarking and transparency allow comparisons across peer buildings to allow tenants, investors, and lenders to make informed decisions on whether to invest in particular buildings based on their performance and to support operational improvements. Having benchmark data on all properties of a particular type within a jurisdiction has the added benefit of allowing the city or

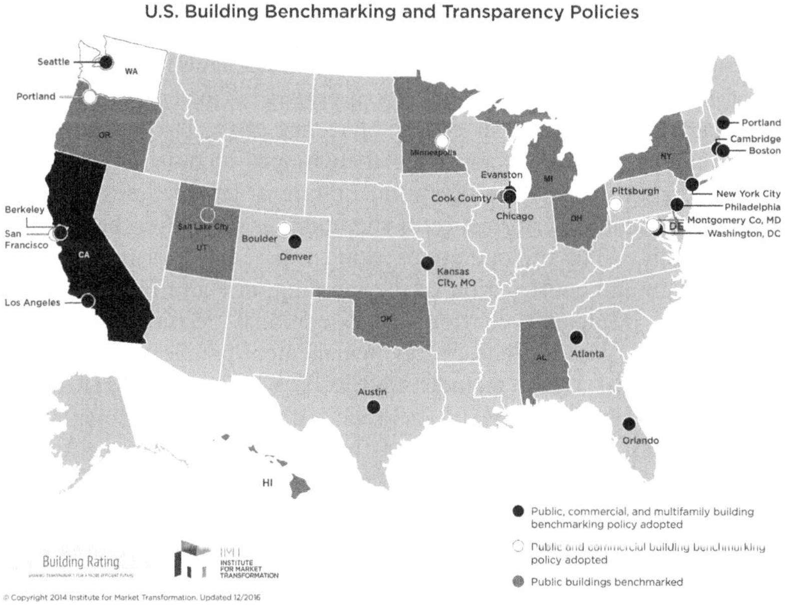

Fig. 9.15 US Building benchmarking and transparency policies. http://buildingrating.org/graphic/us-benchmarking-policy-landscape

state to tailor code changes, incentives, and other programs to address identified areas, where improvement would be most effective.

To date, most US benchmarking and transparency requirements have focused on the operational performance of facilities. However, operational performance is based on several factors, including the underlying design and construction of the building and the investments made in effective operations. As discussed in greater depth below, there is a growing interest in examining energy efficiency from a holistic, life-cycle perspective. Data and metrics representing the various stages in the building life cycle and how decisions made in each stage impact overall energy performance must be developed. Some initiatives to develop both asset and operational labels are discussed in the Building Energy Labeling text box.

Building Energy Labeling

Whether voluntary or part of a state or local regulation, building energy labels provide current and prospective building owners and operators with information on their current performance (operational label) and their potential performance based on the design and construction of the building (asset label). Combining information based on both labels can provide a clearer picture of a property's ability to meet energy efficiency goals. Definitions and examples of operational and asset labels are provided below.

Operational Label: An operational rating or label focuses on the actual, measured performance of the building. It is often based on utility bills. While the operations rating is based at least in part on the design and construction of the building, it is also highly influenced by occupant behavior and operational decisions such as maintenance practices and energy management practices. Examples of operational labels include ENERGY STAR and ASHRAE's BuildingEQ In Operations Label (See Fig. 9.16). Operational ratings are also provided as part of the DOE Home Energy Asset Score and Building Energy Asset Score.

Asset Label: An asset rating or label assesses the design and construction of the building including the building enclosure, mechanical and electrical systems, orientation and other aspects to determine the potential performance of the building. Determining this potential is often based on building energy modeling. The asset label is independent of occupant behavior and operational practices. Examples of asset labels include ASHRAE's BuildingEQ As Designed Label, DOE Building Energy Asset Score, DOE Home Energy Asset Score, and RESNET's Home Energy Rating System (HERS).

9.4 Voluntary Programs

Outside of government, private sector organizations have come together to help advance energy use reductions—from a regional level down to central business districts within a city. At a regional level, Regional

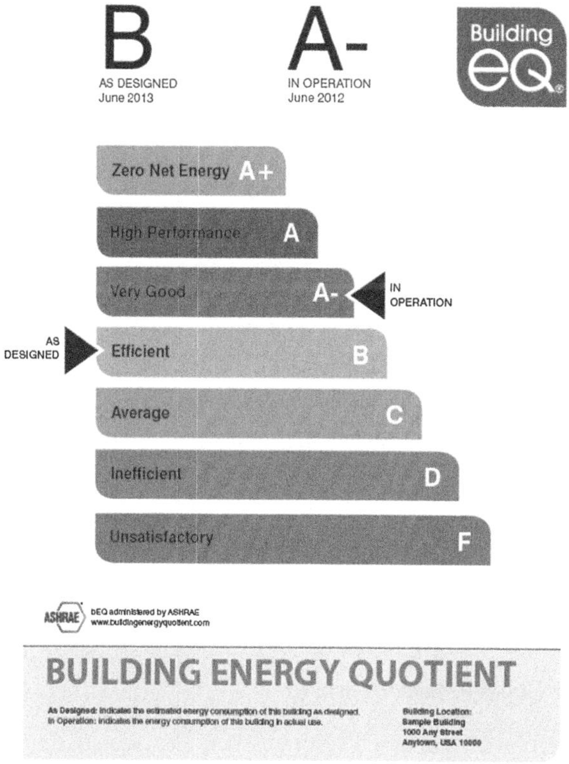

Fig. 9.16 ASHRAE BuildingEQ label with as designed and in operations designations

Energy Efficiency Organizations (REEOs) have formed (Fig. 9.17) to assist their respective states in energy code adoption and other means to reduce energy use.[40]

One REEO, the Northwest Energy Efficiency Alliance (NEEA) partnered with the Building Owners and Managers Association (BOMA) chapter in Seattle to launch the Kilowatt Crackdown in 2009. The Crackdown challenges building owners and managers to improve their energy performance and demonstrates progress through benchmarking in ENERGY STAR Portfolio Manager. Prizes are often awarded for most improved, most efficient, and many other categories. Since its initial launch in 2009, 14 communities now have similar competitions.[41]

In addition to the competitions, some communities have developed collaborative programs to accomplish specific energy use reduction goals. Several communities (13 as of summer 2016) have formed 2030 districts

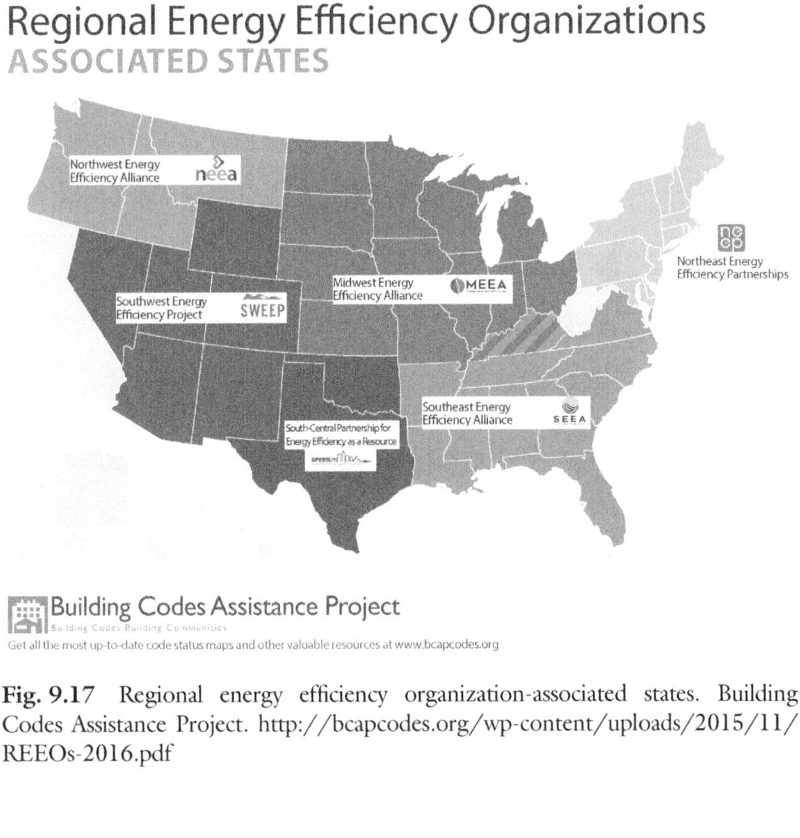

Fig. 9.17 Regional energy efficiency organization-associated states. Building Codes Assistance Project. http://bcapcodes.org/wp-content/uploads/2015/11/REEOs-2016.pdf

to achieve marked reductions in energy use by 2030.[42] The districts support peer exchanges, storing and sharing of data, and aggregation of member purchasing power to reduce costs.

9.5 Challenges to Implementing Energy Efficiency

Several historic functions of the building industry contribute to the slow implementation of energy-efficiency measures. The industry has been highly fragmented with multiple small actors from different disciplines contributing to the overall design, construction, and operation of a building with little coordination.

Despite being the period in the building life cycle where the bulk of energy is actually used, building operations is often an afterthought. Significant effort is spent on design and construction (including through the regulatory process), yet there is little interaction with the facility managers ultimately responsible for assuring that the building functions effectively. Furthermore, members of the design team do not receive important feedback on how their designs actually function in the real world. Bridging the gap between design and construction, and operations, will allow for a more holistic approach to understand where energy is actually being used and how building design can evolve to effectively reduce that use. Rethinking the current procurement process to allow increased collaboration by representatives from across the building life cycle (i.e., the establishment of feedback loops and concentration on actual, measured performance) can help overcome this challenge.

Just as individual disciplines engaged in the design, construction, and operations process operate in silos, so too does much of the equipment specified for buildings. Prescriptive standards for new construction and major renovations and many utility upgrade programs focus on component-level strategies to achieve savings. While such approaches are effective to some degree, they largely ignore the interactions and synergies realized at the system level. Furthermore, many components are reaching their technical and economical limits of energy efficiency—they are approaching a point of diminishing returns to energy use. Addressing energy use at a systems level will help drive the next level of energy use improvements. Performance- or outcome-based policies and practices and increased collaboration across the building life cycle will help make this approach a reality.[43]

Depending on the particular real estate market, leasing practices can lead to a challenge often referred to as split incentives. The building owner or manager may operate the building and make decisions on equipment, but pass the energy bills on to the tenants. The tenants would benefit from improvements in energy efficiency through reduced energy bills. However, the building owner has little to no incentive to invest in improvements in operations or equipment unless costs are the same—any savings would pass directly to the tenants.

The split incentive issue is being addressed through a few different strategies. Owners who invest in energy efficiency despite the fact that they do not pay the bills can receive other benefits including the rental premiums identified in the study of ENERGY STAR and LEED buildings discussed above. Improvements made in conjunction with PACE programs are tied to property taxes—an expense that can be passed on to tenants. A TENANT STAR program being developed by EPA will allow efficient tenant spaces to be recognized with a designation independent of the base building. This will help align the desire of the building owner and tenants towards energy efficiency. Finally, green leases have evolved as a means to address split incentives and better align the building owners and tenants around the efficient use of energy and achievement of other green objectives.[44] Utilizing green lease strategies, Jones Lang LaSalle's clients have realized a 3–13% reduction in short-term utility spending.[45]

Skepticism on the part of lenders and building owners that proposed energy savings will actually be realized further complicates the ability to realize efficiency improvements—despite numerous studies showing relatively short paybacks for some energy conservation measures.[46] Assuring that the measures put in place can persist requires a trained and knowledgeable operation workforce. An owner may be skeptical about the capabilities of her operation workforce to maintain any new technologies or practices implemented.

The final wild card in implementing energy-efficiency strategies is the building occupants. Whatever strategy a facility manager may employ, a crafty building occupant can defeat. Engaging and educating occupants on the strategies being employed and their role in assuring that performance goals are being achieved is essential. Energy managers are all too happy to share the stories of occupants who have employed innovative solutions to circumvent thermostats or occupancy sensors. Competitions between tenants can help engage building occupants.

As discussed above, the small commercial building stock offers a significant opportunity for energy-efficiency investments. However, CFIRE identified several challenges particular to small commercial buildings.[47] Factors limiting interest in energy-efficiency retrofits by owners, managers, and tenants of small commercial buildings include skepticism that the energy savings will actually materialize; a lack of understanding of energy performance analysis and technology; a lack of operational understanding and expertise to manage energy upgrades; and lower credit quality, with more restricted access to cash or debt.

In addition to challenges on the demand side of the equation, access to capital to undertake these investments can be equally challenging. Small commercial properties are frequently difficult to underwrite due to complex or atypical configurations, uses, and market characteristics. Energy-efficiency loans are a hybrid loan product, combining the characteristics of construction and permanent loans, thereby making it more difficult for lenders to evaluate and price risk. Fixed upfront transactions (such as legal, energy audits, financing fees, and appraisals) and ongoing loan management costs represent a larger component of the loan/investment amount, thereby rendering these transactions less attractive to investors and lenders.

Again, while the big picture of efficiency opportunities is informative, the decision to undertake efficiency measures comes down to individual building owners. Often, building owners require a trigger or incentive to undertake such measures. Triggers and incentives are covered below.

9.6 Current Approaches to Reduce Energy Use

Energy audits assist building owners in identifying the performance of current energy using systems and the opportunities to improve their performance. Unlike commissioning, the audits result in a report of potential energy-efficiency measures (EEMs) that an owner may or may not elect to implement.

ASHRAE has identified three levels of audits with increasing levels of information and cost[48]:

- Level 1: Site Assessment or Preliminary Audit. This simple audit is intended to identify high-level opportunities for energy improvement, understand the general building configuration, and define the current energy systems. It provides the building owner with an understanding of how their building performs relative to their peers and establishes a baseline for evaluating improvements.

- Level 2: Energy Survey and Engineering Analysis. This audit provides a more in-depth examination of energy using systems, including the building envelope, lighting, HVAC, hot water, and plug loads. The auditor provides a report outlining potential EEMs, including low- and no-cost measures, operational changes, modifications of controls, and potential capital upgrades. The report also includes likely costs and performance metrics to help the owner to evaluate implementation options.
- Level 3: Detailed Analysis of Capital Intensive Modifications. Often called an investment grade audit, the level 3 audit focuses on measures that may require significant capital and/or personnel resources. It requires significant data collection and analysis—typically through data loggers and an energy model. The model can then be used to evaluate potential measures and their resultant energy savings.

Many utilities or other incentive programs offer grants and rebates to conduct energy audits. For owner-focused guidance on the conduct of energy audits, DOE has prepared *A Guide to Energy Audits*.[49]

Energy modeling is the utilization of computer algorithms paired with information on the building systems, geometry, operations schedules, and other related factors to predict the energy performance of a building. The model can be highly informative during the design phase in supporting decisions and understanding how various choices in design can impact overall energy use. Of course, the quality and usability of the model are based on the assumptions made and the expertise of the modeler. Rule sets to provide consistency across models and to support their use in code compliance and incentive programs have been developed by COMNET.[50]

To date, energy models have largely been effective in making informed design decisions based on their relative impact on overall building performance. The American Institute of Architects (AIA) has published a guide to help architects to expand the utilization of energy modeling.[51] While used to demonstrate compliance through the performance path within codes or to demonstrate above-code levels of energy efficiency in green building projects, energy models have not realized their full potential. As identified in a study by the New Buildings Institute on LEED projects (Fig. 9.18), the predicted performance

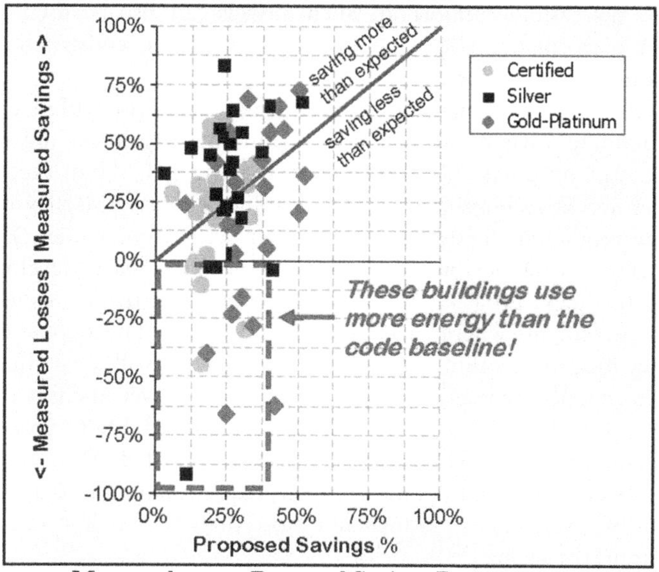

Measured versus Proposed Savings Percentages

Fig. 9.18 Measured versus expected savings' percentages. Turner, C., M. Frankel, "Energy Performance of LEED for New Construction Buildings," New Buildings Institute, March 4, 2008, http://newbuildings.org/wp-content/uploads/2015/11/Energy_Performance_of_LEED-NC_Buildings-Final_3-4-08b1.pdf

determined by the model had little correlation to the actual energy use of the building in operation.

As building owners and communities increase interest in actual, measured performance of buildings and blur the lines between design, construction, and operations, energy models will become increasingly valuable tools to help assure that what is designed actually performs to the anticipated levels during operations. Several engineering firms have begun calibrating building energy models post occupancy to better understand what is driving actual energy use and to support more accurate energy models in the future.

As interest in addressing energy performance across the building lifecycle expands—particularly through outcome-based policies, the ability of energy models to accurately predict performance in operations becomes increasingly important. Such models can also be used to help sort out performance responsibilities among design, construction, and operations team members.[52]

Despite the expanding interest in reducing energy use within a facility, some building owners—particularly within municipalities, universities, schools, and hospitals (affectionately called the MUSH market)—may not have access to internal capital to conduct energy-efficiency retrofits or install renewable energy systems. Energy service companies (ESCOs) and energy saving performance contracts (ESPCs) have developed to help fill this gap. Typically, the ESCO and building owner would enter into an agreement, where the ESCO would finance and deploy energy-efficiency measures within the facility and the owner will repay the ESCO from the energy savings achieved. The federal government has made extensive use of this mechanism. Since a formalized ESPC process was implemented in 1998, 344 projects have been awarded. More than $4.0 billion has been invested in improvements resulting in more than 4.3 trillion Btu life-cycle energy savings and more than $9.7 billion in cumulative energy cost savings.[53]

While the use of ESPCs has delivered significant energy savings, they are not without criticism. Based on their structures, ESCOs typically propose a package of energy-saving measures that represent a fairly short payback period and fairly certain energy savings. This limits the opportunity for future investment in additional energy-saving measures that may have a longer payback.

9.6.1 Life-Cycle-Focused Efforts

Industry leaders are looking to develop processes and practices that overcome the disconnect among design, construction, and operations and facilitate processes that look across systems and the building's life cycle to deliver actual, measured energy performance. These approaches include commissioning, outcome-based codes and policies, performance-based contracting, design–build–operate–maintain contracts or public–private partnerships, personnel certification, and life-cycle-focused energy policies.

9.6.1.1 Commissioning

Commissioning (Cx) is a quality assurance process focused on assuring that an Owner's Project Requirements (OPR) are achieved and documented throughout the planning, delivery, and verification, as well as managing risks to functions performed in, or by, facilities.[54] ASHRAE Standard 202-2013, The Commissioning Process for Buildings and Systems, and ASHRAE Guideline 0, The Commissioning Process, outline the overall process employed for effective commissioning of buildings. Many organizations have developed Cx guidance for particular building systems based on the process defined by ASHRAE.

Commissioning ensures building quality using design review, and in-field or on-site verification. Commissioning also helps to maximize energy efficiency, environmental health, and occupant safety. The process improves indoor air quality by making sure that the building components are working correctly and that the plans are implemented efficiently and effectively. Commissioning delivers preventive and predictive maintenance plans, tailored operating manuals, and training procedures for all users to follow.

The goals of commissioning are to:

1. Deliver buildings and construction projects that meet the owner's project requirements;
2. Prevent or eliminate problems inexpensively through proactive quality techniques;
3. Verify systems are installed and working correctly and benchmark correct operation;
4. Lower overall first costs and life-cycle costs for the owner;
5. Provide documentation and records on the design, construction, and testing to facilitate operation and maintenance of the facility;
6. Implement trend logs as well as automated and semi-automated Cx tools to enable O&M staff ongoing Cx; and
7. Maintain facility performance for the building's entire life cycle.

Commissioning assists in the delivery of a project that provides an efficient, safe, and healthy facility; optimizes energy use; reduces operating costs; ensures adequate O&M staff orientation and training; and improves installed building systems documentation. A study by Lawrence Berkeley National Laboratory found that across 643 buildings commissioned, owners realized a median energy savings of 16% for existing buildings and 13% for new buildings and a payback of 1.1 and 4.2 years, respectively. The study also found energy saving potential nationally that could be $30 billion by the year 2030, annual greenhouse gas emission reductions of about 340 megatons of CO_2 each year, and the potential job creation could be a sales volume of $4 billion per year and support for approximately 24,000 jobs.[55]

Commissioning requirements are beginning to find their way into energy codes. However, the tendency for codes to stop at the Certificate of Occupancy has limited the ability of codes to require completion of the commissioning process.

9.6.1.2 Outcome-Based Policies

Despite the perception that the applicability of codes ends at the Certificate of Occupancy, there have been attempts to address the disconnect between the design and construction activities covered by the energy code and the ultimate intent of the energy code to reduce energy use in building operations. As identified above, outcome-based code provisions focus on establishing a target for a building's energy use and then determining compliance based on whether the target was actually achieved operationally.

Within its 2012 energy code, the city of Seattle, Washington implemented a Target Performance Path.[56] The path allows design teams and owners to demonstrate compliance with the code by providing utility records that show the building has operated at or below the energy target.

The 2015 IgCC contains an optional outcome-based compliance path.[57] In this path, energy use targets are identified for different building types and climate zones. Upon completion of the project, the owner has 3 years to provide 12 months of consecutive energy use data that meet or beat the energy target.

Outcome-based code compliance paths are intended to provide design teams, owners, and operators with the flexibility to determine the most cost effective means to meet a required energy use level. It also provides communities with some degree of assurance that their energy use reduction goals are actually being achieved. The goal of outcome-based code requirements is to actually achieve expected energy results rather than relying on prescriptive measures or predicted models that may not yield actual energy savings.

While communities are looking at policy-based strategies to address building energy use, many leading building owners are also looking for procurement methods that provide greater certainty in life-cycle energy use.

9.6.1.3 Performance-Based Contracting

In performance-based contracting, the project owner provides the design and construction team with a desired level of energy performance once the building is in operations. This is often incorporated into the design contract with a clearly defined penalty or benefit for non-achievement of the target. In addition, the contract will specify the parameters by which achievement of the target will be measured. Such an approach requires the full engagement of the entire design and construction team, establishment of owner's performance requirements, and ongoing performance evaluation.[58] DOE has gathered resources to assist owners interested in utilizing an energy-performance-based acquisition process, including sample requests for proposals (RFPs) and case studies.[59] The General Services Administration's Federal Center South Building 1202 undertook such an approach, which is discussed further within the text box.

Federal Center South Building 1202: A Case Study Performance-Based Contracting

The Federal Center South 1202 building in Seattle, Washington is the result of both the 2009 American Recovery and Reinvestment Act (ARRA) and the US General Services Administration's (GSA) Design Excellence program. With aggressive reuse and energy-performance requirements, the new 1202 building transforms a 4.6 acre brownfield site into a highly flexible and sustainable 209,000 SF regional headquarters for the US Army Corps of Engineers (USACE) Northwest District.

Sellen Construction and ZGF Architects worked to design a new LEED Gold certified headquarters that would, at a minimum, obtain an energy use intensity (EUI) of 27.6 KBtu/sf/year or less; use 100% filtered outside air; achieve a minimum Energy Star Score of 97, and obtain energy performance 30% better than ASRAE 90.1 2007. The design solution includes optimized building orientation and integrates active and passive systems, materials, and strategies that place the 1202 building within the top 1% of energy-efficient office buildings in the US without sacrificing comfort, amenities, or innovative design.

The competition and design-build contract requires that the project actually perform at its energy performance as modeled.

The design team recognized that the actual consumption was dependent to a large degree on the appropriate use and operation of the building. A plug load study was conducted post-competition of the current US Army Corps of Engineers headquarters building to better understand how the future tenants work and use equipment. Operational assumptions were then developed and built into the energy model to allow the energy target to be measured and analyzed during the first year of occupancy. Tenant plug load assumptions are also informing the current design of manual building receptacle controls and modes of operation, which will be programmed for specific times of day and year.

The formal measurement and verification process updated the energy model's assumptions to reflect actual operation. This process includes notification of variations, engineering analysis that indicates the resulting energy impacts, and adoption of revised energy targets that correlate to an updated and accurate operation profile. Meters and sub-meters are an important part of this strategy for energy target management.

Very specific roles and responsibilities for the design team, building owner, and tenant are being established to ensure optimal operation of the new workplace. The goal is to create a shared responsibility and accountability for EUI targets. The design and construction team is responsible for building systems energy consumption and adaptability to minor tenant variations. The owner and tenant are responsible for providing information about the anticipated and actual operation of the building and equipment fit out. Additionally, all are working together to identify and implement manageable behavioral shifts for the users that will result in lower energy consumption.

The design-build team has 0.5% of the original contract value at risk pending verification of the building's energy performance after 1 year of occupancy. This risk is shared between design-builder/contractor, architect, major subcontractors, and design consultants who have primary responsibility for the building's energy performance. At the end of the first year verification period, any remaining construction contingency will be shared between the construction and the design team.

Adapted from "Federal Center South Building 1202 Case Study," Whole Building Design Guide. http://wbdg.org/references/cs_fcsb1202.php

To date, most performance-based contracting requirements have limited demonstration of performance to a relatively short period of time. The Federal Center South project shown in Fig. 9.19 had a 1-year period of performance. A Washington State Government project has a 5-year performance guarantee for energy, operation, and maintenance performance.[60]

9.6.2 Design–Build–Operate–Maintain Contracting or Public–Private Partnerships

Design–build–operate–maintain contracts (DBOM) or public–private partnerships (P3s) support the long-term performance of a project and delivering that performance in the most cost-effective manner across the life cycle of the building. The design, construction, and operation (and sometimes financing) of the project are the responsibility of a single entity, whose long-term profit on the project is tied to their ability to deliver on pre-defined levels of performance. Such an approach provides building owners with a level of certainty on operating costs while supporting greater collaboration across project teams and the establishment of important feedback loops to help bridge the gap between design and construction and operations.

While this type of P3 is limited within the US, it is seeing extensive use in Europe, Canada, and elsewhere.[61] Projects typically funded using P3s include schools, hospitals, prisons, and other social infrastructure. For a discussion on how P3s can support achievement of high-performance buildings in the US, see a report from the National Institute of Building Sciences and the Royal Institution of Chartered Surveyors.[62] The Governor George Deukmejian Courthouse in Long Beach, California was developed using a P3 (Figs. 9.20 and 9.21).

Fig. 9.19 Federal Center South Building 1202 interior and exterior views

Fig. 9.20 Governor George Deukmejian Courthouse

Governor George Deukmejian Courthouse

The old Long Beach Courthouse was functionally and physically deficient, ranking among the worst in California in terms of security and overcrowding. The building was outdated, overcrowded, not able to meet the State's current needs—and therefore incapable of meeting the region's growing demand for court services. The Judicial Council of California undertook a process to replace it with The Governor George Deukmejian Courthouse, on a six-acre site one block northwest of the previous courthouse. The five-story building houses 31 courtrooms, as well as court administration offices, Los Angeles County judicial agency lease space, and retail leasable space.

A main goal of this project was to use a delivery and operations method that would allow the Judicial Branch to deliver the building without creating debt while committing to regular maintenance, repair and replacement. The facility is the first social performance-based infrastructure (PBI) project in the United States. Under a turnkey public-private partnership (P3), the cost and risk of the courthouse, including development, design, construction,

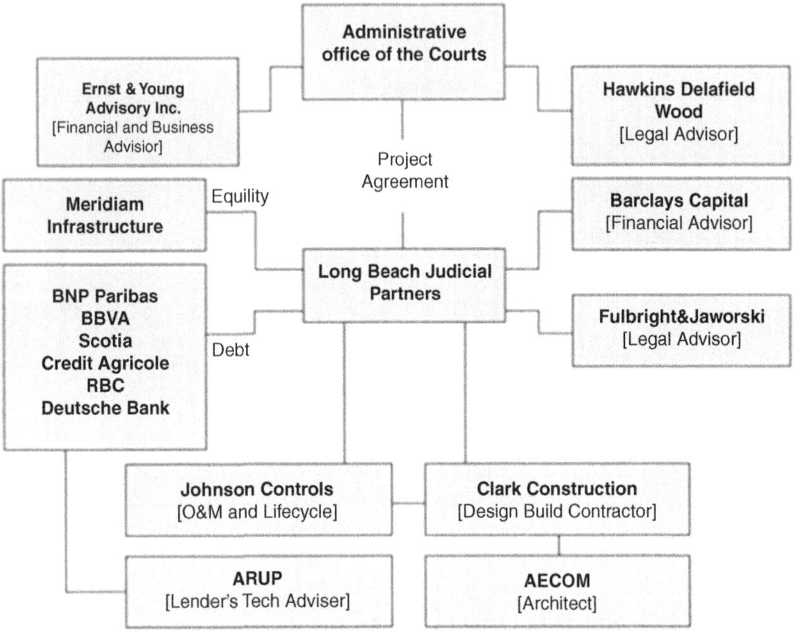

Fig. 9.21 Governor George Deukmejian Courthouse, Long Beach, CA.

operations, and maintenance, were transferred from the public sector to a private-sector team.

In contrast to traditional Design-Bid-Build delivery, the transactional requirements of the PBI turnkey approach drive the need for a fully integrated design process involving the architect, engineers, contractor, and facility manager. With the risk of long term operations and life-cycle costs built into the transaction structure, choices in mechanical systems and finish materials were driven not by initial cost but by total cost over the entire concession period. A good example of the types of choices made was the selection of terrazzo flooring versus carpeting in heavily trafficked corridors. Although a much higher first cost, this material is much more durable and enables the end user to avoid the higher cost of frequent carpet replacement. Another example is the construction of enclosed penthouses on the roof that provide additional protection for the mechanical systems against the marine environment of Long Beach. With guidance from the facility manager, the design team selected hard, durable but easily cleanable wall finishes to reduce potential for vandalism and for ease of daily servicing.

The PBI contract allowed the courthouse to be constructed without any public debt funding and provides for the ongoing maintenance and performance of the facility. Under the PBI agreement, the Judicial Council will own the building and the Superior Court of Los Angeles County will occupy the space. The Judicial Council will pay an annual availability payment for 35 years. Under the terms of the agreement, the Judicial Council can deduct a specific amount from the availability payment if components of the building do not meet specified performance levels. For example, there is a $5,000 deduction for every 2 h that certain elevators are inoperable.

Because the designer, builder, operator, and financial partners must collaborate on project development and implementation, the project itself is developed with a strong focus on long-term costs and operations. This collaboration is not possible under traditional project delivery, where each firm may interact only with the owner, not with each other and where operations and maintenance is separated from design and construction. An added benefit is that in PBI delivery a single firm is accountable for operation and maintenance throughout the 35-year contract term, providing the state with a single point of contact and responsibility, as opposed to the four firms that would be responsible for each of design, construction, operation, and maintenance in a traditional project.

Adapted from "Governor George Deukmejian Courthouse Case Study," Whole Building Design Guide. http://wbdg.org/references/cs_longbeach.php.

9.6.3 Life-Cycle-Focused Energy Policies

Benchmarking and transparency policies are often a community's first approach to addressing building energy use following issuance of a Certificate of Occupancy. While this provides valuable information and can influence market-based improvements, some communities have also implemented requirements triggering energy-efficiency improvements. Such requirements include periodic commissioning or conduct of audits, or required upgrades on a specific timeline or at a particular trigger.

New York City has been particularly progressive in implementing such requirements through Local Laws 87 and 88. Local Law 87 requires all buildings over 5000 sq ft to conduct an energy audit and perform retro-commissioning every 10 years and submit an Energy-Efficiency Report to the Department of Buildings.[63] The city found that lighting accounts for 18% of building-related energy use, so the city council implemented Local Law 88 to address this large energy use. Local Law 88 requires commercial and residential buildings over 50,000 sq ft to upgrade lighting to meet the New York City Energy Conservation Code.[64] The law also requires the installation of sub-meters for non-residential tenant spaces over 10,000 sq ft. Data from the submeters must be provided to tenants on a monthly basis. Lighting upgrades and sub-metering must be completed by January 1, 2025.

9.6.4 *Personnel Certification*

The technologies and practices employed in buildings to realize energy-efficiency improvements are only as effective as the personnel charged with maintaining them. Personnel certification is one means to advance the professionalism of energy-efficiency-related personnel. The US federal government has established mechanisms to support certification for personnel operating federal buildings and to assist other building owners in specifying certified personnel.

The Federal Buildings Personnel Training Act (FBPTA) was passed in December 2010. The Act requires the General Services Administration (GSA) to identify the core competencies required for the effective operations of federal facilities. Based on these core competencies, GSA is to identify certifications, certificates, licenses, and other methods that demonstrate mastery of these competencies. GSA personnel, building personnel in other federal agencies, and contractors performing tasks on federal buildings are then required to demonstrate achievement of the specified core competencies. GSA has developed the Facility Management Institute (FMI) to serve as a resource for implementation of the FBPTA.[65] FMI provides information useful to private sector entities looking to advance the operations of their facilities by assuring their staff possesses the identified core competencies.

Private sector and non-federal government building owners recognize the potential savings associated with having competent personnel operate facilities, but they have not had the means to identify credible certifications that can deliver on those competencies. To assist in such identification, DOE has developed the Better Building Workforce Guidelines.[66] Through these guidelines for four energy-related jobs—building energy auditor, building commissioning professional, energy manager, and building operation professional—DOE has established baseline criteria for certifications, including requirements for the organizations providing the certifications.

Certifications that meet the DOE criteria can receive recognition through the Better Buildings program. This recognition allows building owners, procurement professionals, and building codes to readily specify programs that have met an identified level of quality without needing to research multiple potential certifications.

9.7 Emerging Issues

In addition to specific building-level efforts to address energy efficiency, there are some larger issues and initiatives within the industry that will likely impact the achievement of energy use reductions. These include changes within the building process, an increased focus on the concept of resilience, the declining cost of renewable energy systems, the evolving utility landscape, the link between energy and water, and the relationship between energy use and greenhouse gas emissions.

9.7.1 An Evolving Building Process

For a variety of reasons, the procurement, design, construction, and operations process is evolving to be more collaborative and performance driven. Buildings are becoming increasingly complex as designers look to utilize the latest technology to deliver buildings that achieve the high-performance building requirements set by owners and government. An increased focus on performance requirements necessitates buy-in and collaboration across multiple disciplines involved in the design and construction process. Recognizing the need for greater collaboration, many owners have moved away from the traditional design-bid-build process, where the design team and the contractor are selected at different points in the process and have limited ability to interact.

Design–Build and early contractor involvement have emerged as means to create alignment between the design team and the contractor. This allows design decisions to be made with input on constructability and cost from contractors. A single contract establishes project goals and requirements thus reducing potential for misunderstanding and establishing a single point of contact for the owner. Figure 9.22 shows the increasing use of Design–Build relative to DBB for non-residential construction from 2005 to 2013.

Integrated Project Delivery (IPD) and other integrative project methods expand on the design-build approach to bring additional project stakeholders into the process—particularly key subcontractors and building operators.[67] Such integrative approaches establish performance requirements shared by all members of the project team—typically with shared risk and rewards for achieving the desired performance

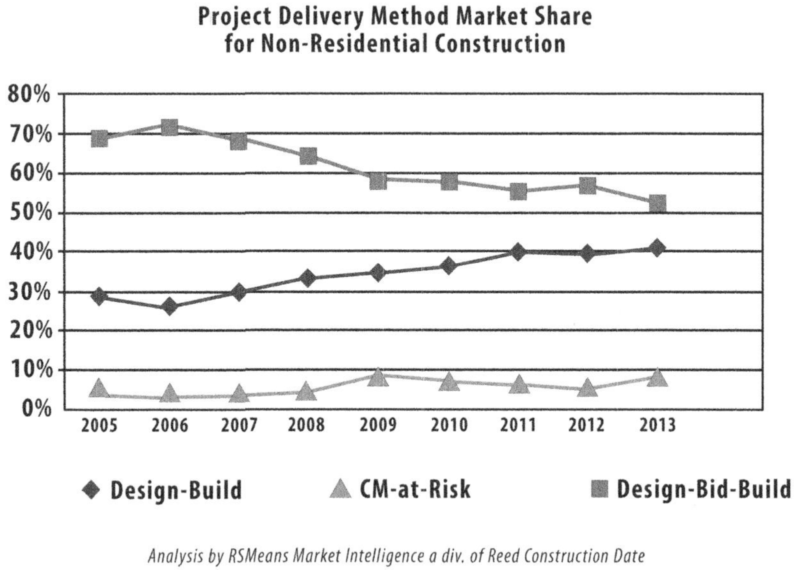

Fig. 9.22 Project delivery method market share for non-residential construction. See http://www.dbia.org/about/Pages/What-is-Design-Build.aspx

requirements. In IPD, the project goals, risks, and rewards are formalized in a common contract between key project participants (at a minimum, the owner, architect, and contractor, but ideally to include key subcontractors). The performance-based contracting and design–build–operate–maintain approaches discussed above rely on collaboration and integrative processes to achieve the intended results.

Tools such as building information modeling (BIM) facilitate collaborative approaches by providing members of the design, construction, operations, and regulatory process with a single repository of digital information intended to remain with the building throughout its life cycle. To date, the value of BIM has largely been demonstrated by its ability to reduce change orders and avoid conflicts between building systems. Additional uses, including within computerized maintenance management systems (CMMS) and building code enforcement, are continuing to evolve, but represent significant sources of additional value.[68]

Standards and guidance are being developed to support the effective exchange of data across various software programs and in formats useful for the numerous disciplines within the industry. The National BIM Standard-United States and the National BIM Guide for Owners provide means for assuring that a building information model can deliver the greatest value.[69]

Specific tools within BIM to support energy efficiency are developing. To date, the energy modeling process discussed above and BIM has been largely disconnected without a defined process to allow interaction between the design model and the energy model. New plug-ins to common BIM tools that allow near-real time analysis of how design decisions impact energy use will make energy use more visible to designers and owners. This represents a promising advancement in both energy modeling and BIM.

9.7.2 Resilience

The concept of resilience has garnered increased interest by both policy makers and building owners. As the frequency and intensity of natural disasters increase, policy makers and business owners are concerned about the impact such disruptions will have on the social, economical, and environmental fabric of the community.[70] As identified by the National Academy of Sciences, resilience is "the ability to prepare and plan for, absorb, recover from, or more successfully adapt to actual or potential events."[71] Leading organizations from across the planning, design, construction, operation, and regulation of buildings have come together to sign an Industry Statement on Resilience to help facilitate research, advocacy, education, and planning in this emerging area.[72]

The resilience of a community and its building stock is related to the resilience of its energy supply and the services that rely on such a supply. Many of the strategies being developed in support of energy efficiency also provide benefits for resilience. The expansion of onsite renewable energy generation, when coupled with energy storage and microgrids[73] (also called distributed generation), allows a building or several buildings on the microgrid to remain functional if there is a disruption in the larger electric grid. As discussed below, energy storage and microgrids can offer efficiency opportunities.

In addition to distributed energy generation, passive survivability has emerged as a resilience strategy. Passive survivability is the ability to maintain habitability when electrical and mechanical methods are not available.[74] Strategies for passive survivability often include ventilation strategies, super insulation, operable windows, thermal mass, and other techniques. These techniques can provide energy-efficiency benefits outside of hazard conditions. Identifying and implementing multi-benefit strategies like these can increase the achievement of high-performance buildings.

9.7.3 Zero Energy Buildings and Renewable Energy

As identified above, the number of zero energy buildings has expanded significantly. The Department of Energy undertook an effort to build consensus around a definition for zero energy buildings (also called net zero energy or zero net energy buildings).[75] DOE defined a zero energy building as "An energy-efficient building where, on a source energy basis, the actual annual delivered energy is less than or equal to the on-site renewable exported energy." The definition recognizes the importance of a life-cycle focus and the role of effective operations in achieving a zero energy building.

Many jurisdictions have adopted goals to achieve zero energy buildings (both in new construction and existing buildings and in commercial and residential buildings). While the requirements to achieve zero energy buildings and the desired timeline vary from jurisdiction to jurisdiction, these initiatives will certainly drive increased focus on delivering highly efficient buildings.

Many communities and professional organizations have adopted the 2030 Challenge, which calls for all new buildings, developments, and major renovations be designed to be carbon neutral by 2030.[76] The state of California has set goals to achieve zero net energy by 2020 for all new residential buildings and by 2030 for all new commercial and 50% of existing commercial buildings.[77] The World Green Building Council has called for all buildings globally to be net zero by 2050 with all new construction and major renovations net zero by 2030.[78] The American Institute of Architects has established the 2030 Commitment for member firms to commit to meeting the 2030 Challenge Goals and track individual and discipline progress towards meeting those goals.[79]

Inherent in the ability to achieve zero energy is the focus on lowering the actual energy required through energy efficiency and then offsetting the remainder through on-site renewable energy. However, the steady decrease in the cost of solar photovoltaics (PV) is changing the discussion. From the economic perspective of the owner, energy efficiency and renewable energy generation may be interchangeable if costs are equal. However, from the perspective of government, societies, and utilities, reduced overall energy demand provides greater resilience and reliability and reduced greenhouse gas emissions.

9.7.4 *The Smart Grid, the Internet of Things, and Demand Response*

Just as technology across multiple sectors of the economy expands to provide enhanced connectivity and two-way communication across systems, utilities and buildings are seeing similar expansions. The "smart grid" transitions the current electricity grid based on incremental improvements since the 1890s into a twenty first century technology that allows increased communication between the energy consumer and the utility.[80] This transition supports increased reliability, more efficient transmission of energy, better integration of renewable energy, and the ability to manage loads through demand response.

Demand response allows a utility to send a request to customers to reduce their current energy use in order to help the grid operator manage the available energy and the reliability of the grid.[81] The demand response efforts can be triggered by time-based rates or through direct load control of specific building components, such as air conditioners and water heaters. At an individual building level, the availability of on-site renewable generation, energy storage, or microgrids can assist the facility in taking advantage of incentives triggered by demand response programs.

Like the smart grid at a utility scale, the Internet of Things (IoT) supports communication across devices within a facility.[82] Through this communication, the building systems can determine the most effective strategies to reduce energy use. For example, an onsite PV system may be able to determine the current solar intensity and communicate that to the HVAC system, daylighting sensors, and shading devices to determine the ideal combination of measures to find the optimal use of air conditioning, daylighting, and shading. These systems could also take into account the current electricity rate as provided through the smart grid. The IoT will also allow ongoing monitoring of building systems to assure that they continue to operate efficiently and even allow adjustments to be made by off-site personnel.[83]

Increased connectivity across building systems and with the electricity grid will allow the optimization of such systems to cost effectively realize energy-efficiency goals.

9.7.5 DC Microgrids

In an effort to improve both resilience and energy efficiency, interest in direct current (DC) microgrids is expanding. Many of the energy using components within a building are native DC, but rely on the conversion of the alternating current (AC) provided by the electric grid. This conversion results in energy losses. Furthermore, the electricity generated by renewable energy is generated in the form of DC but ultimately converted to AC for utilization on-site or for feeding into the grid. By providing a dedicated DC microgrid at the building level or across several buildings, energy wasted from conversions between AC and DC power can be avoided.

The EMerge Alliance was formed in 2008 to facilitate the development of standards to support the use of low voltage DC power within commercial buildings.[84] In addition to the energy savings, the DC power system will allow easy reconfiguration and addition of lights, sensors, and other components.

One study estimates that more than 8% of the total national electricity load, or about 400 million kilowatt hours per year in losses can be avoided.[85] This does not include the potential cooling energy saved by reducing the conversion devices. In addition, linking DC-based renewable energy with DC-based energy storage will be simplified.

9.7.6 Energy Storage

Related to the ability to achieve zero energy buildings (particularly zero carbon buildings), supporting resilience of both the individual facility and the electric grid, and effectively implementing demand response, is the ability to store energy when generation is advantageous and access it when costs are high or energy cannot be economically generated. The intermittent nature of many renewable energy sources requires a means to capture and store energy for use when such sources are not available. Battery technology is advancing significantly to help to address this issue.

With respect to resilience, as the amount of the traditional electricity generation on the grid decreases in favor of less carbon-intensive sources, concern raises as to the ability to maintain the necessary quantity of electricity available to meet demand. Energy storage can help provide electricity when it is needed. Furthermore, if storage is deployed within individual buildings or within a micro-grid across several buildings, the buildings could remain functional using a combination of on-site generation and energy storage should an event limit access to grid-level energy.

When responding to a call to reduce energy demand from the grid, energy stored on-site can be deployed to avoid penalties or gain favorable incentives. The amount of energy storage required is based on the energy profile of the building, so effective deployment of energy-efficiency strategies can reduce the future costs associated with energy storage.

9.7.7 The Energy/Water Nexus

Energy and water are linked. It takes significant quantities of water to produce energy. Over 45% of water withdrawn (primarily from surface water sources) is for the production of electricity.[86] The treatment and movement of water also are energy intensive. According to the California Energy Commission, water-related energy use in California consumes 20% of the state's electricity and 30% of the state's non-power plant natural gas.[87]

Concerns about more frequent and intense droughts and the rising costs of water are driving increased interest in water efficiency. While not as developed as efforts to achieve energy efficiency, the water-efficiency market is beginning to mature. Benchmarking, audits, and incentive programs aimed at reducing water use are growing.

9.7.8 Energy Use and Greenhouse Gas Emissions

It is difficult to talk about the benefits of implementing energy-efficiency measures without discussing the link between energy use and greenhouse gas emissions. As governments at all levels seek to reduce the release of carbon dioxide and other gasses that contribute to climate change, the building industry is squarely in their sights. Many programs, such as Architecture 2030 and 80 by 50, are actually aimed at reducing greenhouse gas emissions by reducing energy use.

With 40% of the total primary energy use and over 70% of the electricity use, the building sector contributes a significant portion of greenhouse gas emissions. In fact, the greenhouse gas emissions of the US building stock are approximately 2300 metric tons CO_2—equivalent to the entire emissions of Russia and Canada combined. These emissions account for 40% of the US emissions and 7.4% of global CO_2 emissions.[88]

As shown in Fig. 9.23, the World Resources Institute and Intergovernmental Panel on Climate Change (IPCC) have identified the building industry as the sector with the greatest opportunity to reduce greenhouse gas emissions—particularly in a low carbon price scenario.

If implemented globally, building-related energy-efficiency measures could reduce CO_2 emissions by as much as 5.8 billion tons by 2050—an 83% reduction from the business-as-usual scenario.[89]

Many communities have established goals to reduce greenhouse gas emissions across all elements of their economy by 80% by 2050. Buildings are naturally a significant area of focus given their contribution. Cities, such as New York, Philadelphia, Seattle, Boston, Washington, DC, Minneapolis, and Portland (OR), have committed to the effort. Figure 9.24 shows NYC's pathway to achieving its 80 × 50 goal.

9.7.9 Embodied Energy

While much of the effort to reduce energy use within the built environment has focused on building operations, there is growing interest in understanding and addressing the energy it takes to produce

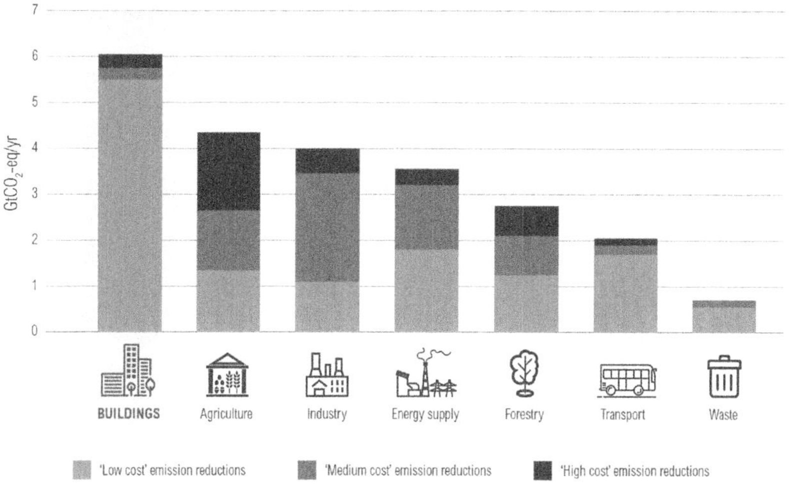

Note: 'Low cost' emission reductions = carbon price <20 US$/t$CO_2$-eq. 'Medium cost' emission reductions = carbon price <50 US$/t$CO^2$-eq.
'High cost' emission reductions = carbon price <100 US$/t$CO_2$-eq.
Source: IPCC. 2007. IPCC Fourth Assessment Report: Climate Change 2007: Synthesis Report. "4.3 Mitigation options."
https://www.ipcc.ch/publications_and_data/ar4/syr/en/mains4-3.html

Fig. 9.23 Economic carbon mitigation potential by sector. World Resources Institute. 2016. *Accelerating Building Efficiency: Eight Actions for Urban Leaders.* http://www.wri.org/publication/accelerating-building-efficiency-actions-city-leaders

and assemble the components that go into a building. Several efforts are underway to help designers make informed decisions based on the materials they select. As companies look to reduce their greenhouse gas emissions, they will look to designers to reduce the embodied energy within their designs.

9.8 Capturing the Value of Energy Efficiency

Many of the challenges associated with realizing potential energy efficiency in a facility are tied to the ability to capture the value that such an investment provides. As much as leaders within the industry would like the industry to move away from a first cost focus, many building owners still have a relatively short investment window. Unless the owner will realize additional value for investing in life-cycle performance, they are unlikely to make such an investment.

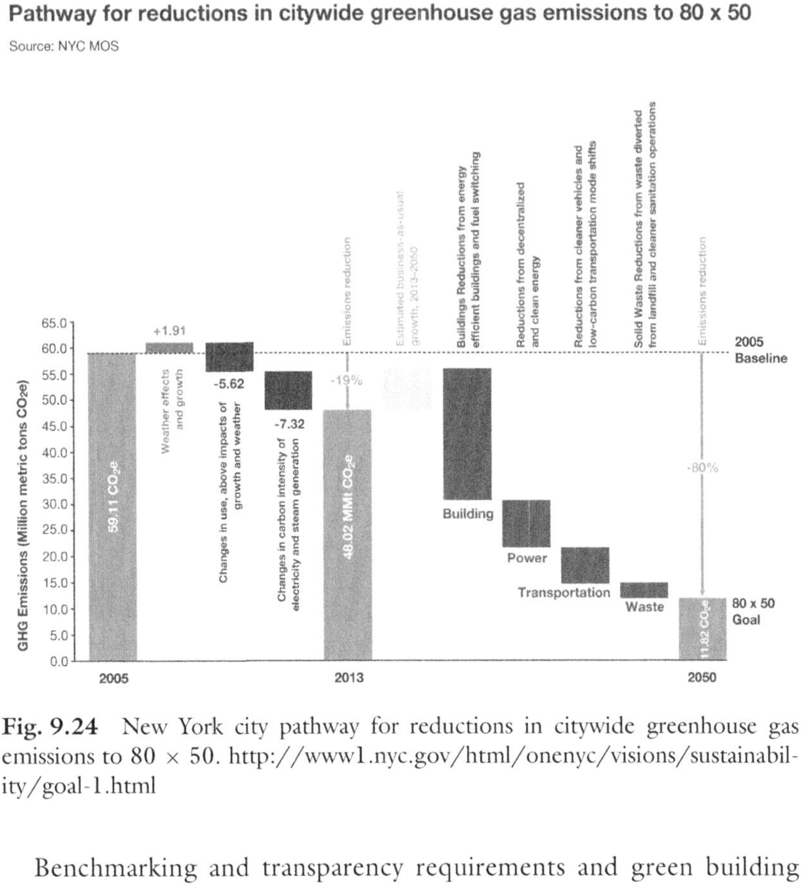

Fig. 9.24 New York city pathway for reductions in citywide greenhouse gas emissions to 80 × 50. http://www1.nyc.gov/html/onenyc/visions/sustainability/goal-1.html

Benchmarking and transparency requirements and green building rating programs are intended to help reveal this value, but additional efforts within the traditionally conservative finance and insurance industry are required. Within the appraisal and underwriting process, guidance is being developed to help to assure that energy efficiency and other sustainability features are being recognized within the valuation process. The Appraisal Institute and Institute for Market Transformation (IMT) have issued guidance for building owners and the appraisal community.[90] The Appraisal Foundation's Appraisal Practices Board is in the process of developing a Valuation Advisory for green and high-performance properties.[91] IMT monitors progress on advancing property valuations that reflect energy efficiency and green building attributes.[92]

9.9 Conclusion

A $279 billion opportunity to provide over 3000 trillion BTUs in energy savings, energy efficiency within the building sector supports achievement of numerous goals within government, by building owners, and by society as a whole. Building energy codes have provided a strong foundation, but additional efforts to reduce actual energy use across the building life-cycle are developing. Through coordinated policies and a collaborative process across design, construction, and operations, the challenges surrounding split incentives and the need for resilience will be overcome.

Notes

1. Building Energy Data Book, Tables 1.1.3 and 1.1.9. http://buildingsdatabook.eren.doe.gov/ChapterIntro1.aspx.
2. Howard, B., L. Parshall, J. Thompson, S. Hammer, J. Dickinson, V. Modi, "Spatial distribution of urban building energy consumption by end use." *Energy and Buildings*. Vol. 45, February. 2012, p. 141–151.
3. See CBECS for the latest data. In general, CBECS is conducted every 3–4 years, but due to statistical issues and lack of funding, no surveys were conducted between 2003 and 2012. While CBECS provides valuable data for the industry and policymakers, there has been a growing call for closer to real-time assessments of the building stock. This issue is discussed further below. See Frankel, M., J. Edelson and R. Colker. *Getting to Outcome-Based Building Performance: Report from a Seattle Summit on Performance Outcomes*. New Buildings Institute and National Institute of Building Sciences. 2015. http://newbuildings.org/wp-content/uploads/2015/11/Performance_Outcomes_Summit_Report_5-151.pdf.
4. Energy Information Administration. 2015. "A Look at the U.S. Commercial Building Stock: Results from EIA's 2012 Commercial Buildings Energy Consumption Survey (CBECS). http://www.eia.gov/consumption/commercial/reports/2012/buildstock/?src=%E2%80%B9%20Consumption%20%20%20Commercial%20Buildings%20Energy%20Consumption%20Survey%20(CBECS)-b2.

5. Energy productivity is the amount of energy required to produce a specified output. See Energy 2030. http://energy2030.org/.
6. A high-performance building as defined by the U.S. Congress as "a building that integrates and optimizes on a life-cycle basis all major high-performance attributes, including energy conservation, environment, safety, security, durability, accessibility, cost-benefit, productivity, sustainability, functionality, and operational considerations." Energy Independence and Security Act of 2007 §401 (PL 110–140).
7. The concept of whole building design is covered extensively on the Whole Building Design Guide. See http://www.wbdg.org.
8. Green building attributes are discussed in Chap. 10, but generally include aspects of energy and water use, material selection, site selection, waste reduction and occupant health/indoor environmental quality.
9. CBECS Table 9.8. Total energy consumption by energy source, 1979 to 2013. Consumption was converted to source energy by multiplying electricity consumption by 3.15. http://www.eia.gov/consumption/commercial/reports/2012/energyusage/xls/Table8_by%20source%20by%20year.xlsx.
10. Buildings Energy Data Book 2011. http://buildingsdatabook.eren.doe.gov/TableView.aspx?table=1.1.13.
11. Buildings Energy Data Book 2011. http://buildingsdatabook.eren.doe.gov/TableView.aspx?table=2.1.1.
12. International Energy Agency. 2013. *World Energy Outlook*. http://www.worldenergyoutlook.org/weo2013.
13. Energy Information Administration. 2015. "A Look at the U.S. Commercial Building Stock: Results from EIA's 2012 Commercial Buildings Energy Consumption Survey (CBECS). http://www.eia.gov/consumption/commercial/reports/2012/buildstock/?src=%E2%80%B9%20Consumption%20%20%20Commercial%20Buildings%20Energy%20Consumption%20Survey%20(CBECS)-b2.
14. Energy Information Administration. 2015. "A Look at the U.S. Commercial Building Stock: Results from EIA's 2012 Commercial Buildings Energy Consumption Survey (CBECS). http://www.eia.gov/consumption/commercial/reports/2012/buildstock/?src=%E2%80%B9%20Consumption%20%20%20Commercial%20Buildings%20Energy%20Consumption%20Survey%20(CBECS)-b2.
15. Energy Information Administration. 2016. "2012 Commercial Building Energy Conservation Survey: Energy Usage Summary." http://www.eia.gov/consumption/commercial/reports/2012/energyusage/.
16. Energy Information Administration. 2016. "2012 Commercial Building Energy Conservation Survey: Energy Usage Summary." http://www.eia.gov/consumption/commercial/reports/2012/energyusage/.

17. Fulton Mark et al. United States Building Energy Efficiency Retrofits, Market Sizing and Financing Models, DB Climate Change Advisors, Deutsche Bank Group, March 2012. https://www.db.com/cr/en/docs/Building_Retrofit_Paper.pdf.
18. International Energy Agency. 2013. *World Energy Outlook*. http://www.worldenergyoutlook.org/weo2013.
19. National Institute of Building Sciences Council on Finance, Insurance and Real Estate. 2015. "Financing Small Commercial Building Energy Performance Upgrades: Challenges and Opportunities." https://www.nibs.org/resource/resmgr/CC/CFIRE_CommBldgFinance-Final.pdf. See also Navigant Research. 2016. "Energy Efficiency Retrofits for Small and Medium Commercial Buildings." https://www.navigantresearch.com/research/energy-efficiency-retrofits-for-small-and-medium-commercial-buildings.
20. The Guardian. "Make Building Standards Top Priority for Tackling Climate Change, Says IEA Chief." June 1, 2016. https://www.theguardian.com/environment/2016/jun/01/make-building-standards-top-priority-for-tackling-climate-change-says-iea-chief.
21. Almost all jurisdictions that adopt the model codes go through an amendment process. Some jurisdictions develop their own codes, but this is becoming rarer due to the costs associated with such a process,
22. The commissioning process formalizes review and integration of all project expectations during planning, design, construction, and occupancy phases by inspection and functional and performance testing, and oversight of operator training and record documentation. See "Building Commissioning" on the Whole Building Design Guide, http://www.wbdg.org/building-commissioning.
23. See "Codes and Standards Development" on the Whole Building Design Guide (WBDG) for a more in-depth discussion of the various development processes. http://wbdg.org/resources/codedevelopment.php.
24. See 42 U.S.C. 6833.
25. For more details on the code development and adoption process, see DOE's "Building Energy Codes 101" resources at https://www.energycodes.gov/training-courses/building-energy-codes-101.
26. In this scenario, localities may or may not be able to amend the code to make it more stringent.
27. See DOE Building Energy Codes Program, "Residential Energy Code Field Study," https://www.energycodes.gov/compliance/residential-energy-code-field-study.
28. DOE Appliance & Equipment Standards, "History and Impacts." http://energy.gov/eere/buildings/history-and-impacts.

29. DOE Appliance & Equipment Standards, "Appliance and Equipment Standards Fact Sheet." http://energy.gov/eere/buildings/downloads/appliance-and-equipment-standards-fact-sheet.
30. ACEEE, "How your refrigerator has kept its cool over 40 years of efficiency improvements." http://aceee.org/blog/2014/09/how-your-refrigerator-has-kept-its-co.
31. Federal Trade Commission, "EnergyGuide Labels." https://www.ftc.gov/news-events/media-resources/tools-consumers/energyguide-labels.
32. See http://www.dsireusa.org/.
33. In 2008 the deduction was extended through 2013. Congress passed a retroactive extension in December 2014 to cover 2014 projects and passed another extension in December 2015 to include 2015 and 2016.
34. See https://www.energystar.gov/productfinder/ for the products covered under the ENERGY STAR program.
35. ENERGY STAR. 2012. "DataTrends: Benchmarking and Energy Savings." https://www.energystar.gov/sites/default/files/buildings/tools/DataTrends_Savings_20121002.pdf.
36. See http://betterbuildingssolutioncenter.energy.gov/.
37. Ibid.
38. In 2010, the Federal Housing Finance Agency (FHFA) directed Fannie Mae and Freddie Mac not to purchase any mortgage where PACE financing with a priority lien was placed on the underlying property. Such financing moves ahead of the pre-existing first mortgage in lien priority, and thereby subordinates Fannie Mae and Freddie Mac security interests in the property. FHFA took this action based on its determination that PACE financing arrangements present a safety and soundness concern by transferring financial risks to the regulated entities and lacking in adequate consumer protections and standards for energy retrofitting. See http://www.fhfa.gov/Media/PublicAffairs/Pages/FHFA-Statement-on-Certain-Energy-Retrofit-Loan-Programs.aspx.
39. See http://www.buildingrating.org.
40. See http://bcapcodes.org/getting-started/regional-energy-efficiency-organizations/.
41. See https://www.boma.org/sustainability/info-resources/Documents/Kilowatt%20Crackdowns.pdf.
42. See http://www.2030districts.org/.
43. For a more thorough analysis of the opportunities through a systems-based approach to energy efficiency, see ASE Systems Efficiency Initiative. http://www.ase.org/systemsefficiency.
44. See http://www.greenleaselibrary.com/.
45. Jordan, M. "10 Reasons for a Green Lease." *JLL Green Blog*. April 22, 2013. http://www.jllblog.com/greenblog/2013/04/22/10-reasons-for-a-green-lease/.

46. See McKinsey & Company. *Unlocking Energy Efficiency in the U.S. Economy*. 2009. http://www.mckinsey.com/~/media/mckinsey/dotcom/client_service/epng/pdfs/unlocking%20energy%20efficiency/us_energy_efficiency_exc_summary.ashx.
47. Council on Finance, Insurance and Real Estate. 2015. *Financing Small Commercial Building Energy Performance Upgrades: Challenges and Opportunities*. National Institute of Building Sciences. https://www.nibs.org/resource/resmgr/CC/CFIRE_CommBldgFinance-Final.pdf.
48. ASHRAE. *Procedures for Commercial Building Energy Audits*. 2011. https://www.ashrae.org/resources–publications/bookstore/procedures-for-commercial-building-energy-audits.
49. DOE. *A Guide to Energy Audits*. 2011. http://www.pnnl.gov/main/publications/external/technical_reports/pnnl-20956.pdf.
50. See http://www.comnet.org/.
51. American Institute of Architects. *An Architect's Guide to Integrating Energy Modeling in the Design Process*. 2012. http://www.aia.org/aiaucmp/groups/aia/documents/pdf/aiab096060.pdf.
52. See Frankel, M., J. Edelson and R. Colker. *Getting to Outcome-Based Building Performance: Report from a Seattle Summit on Performance Outcomes*. New Buildings Institute and National Institute of Building Sciences. 2015. http://newbuildings.org/wp-content/uploads/2015/11/Performance_Outcomes_Summit_Report_5-151.pdf.
53. DOE, "Awarded DOE IDIQ Energy Savings Performance Contract Projects." http://energy.gov/eere/femp/awarded-doe-idiq-energy-savings-performance-contract-projects.
54. For a more in-depth discussion on commissioning, see http://wbdg.org/project/buildingcomm.php.
55. Evan Mills. 2009. "Building Commissioning: A Golden Opportunity for Reducing Energy Costs and Greenhouse-gas Emissions." Lawrence Berkeley National Lab. http://cx.lbl.gov/2009-assessment.html.
56. See "2012 Seattle Commercial Energy Code Involves Building Managers and Occupants," Building Connections. Seattle Department of Construction & Inspections. http://buildingconnections.seattle.gov/2013/10/01/2012-seattle-commercial-energy-code-involves-building-managers-and-occupants/.
57. International Code Council. *2015 International Green Construction Code*. http://www.iccsafe.org/codes-tech-support/codes/2015-i-codes/igcc/.
58. See Whole Building Design Guide, "Outcome-Based Pathways for Achieving Energy Performance Goals." National Institute of Building Sciences. http://wbdg.org/resources/outcomebasedpathways.php.
59. See https://buildingdata.energy.gov/cbrd/energy_based_acquisition/.
60. See http://www.des.wa.gov/about/pi/1063Block/Pages/ProjectSummary.aspx.

61. RICS Research Report, Private Finance Initiative and Public Private Partnership, http://www.rics.org/us/knowledge/research/research-reports/the-future-of-private-finance-initiative-and-public-private-partnership-/.
62. See http://www.nibs.org/resource/resmgr/Docs/NIBS-RICS_P3_Summary.pdf.
63. See http://www.nyc.gov/html/gbee/html/plan/ll87.shtml.
64. See http://www.nyc.gov/html/gbee/html/plan/ll88.shtml.
65. See http://fmi.gov.
66. See https://www4.eere.energy.gov/workforce/projects/workforceguidelines.
67. See American Institute of Architects. *Integrated Project Delivery: A Guide.* 2007. http://www.aia.org/groups/aia/documents/pdf/aiab083423.pdf and http://www.aia.org/about/initiatives/AIAS076981.
68. For more information on BIM, see http://wbdg.org/bim/bim.php.
69. See https://www.nationalbimstandard.org/ and https://www.nibs.org/?nbgo.
70. NOAA National Centers for Environmental Information (NCEI) U.S. Billion-Dollar Weather and Climate Disasters (2017). https://www.ncdc.noaa.gov/billions/.
71. The National Academies. *Disaster Resilience: A National Imperative.* 2012. http://www.nap.edu/catalog/13457/disaster-resilience-a-national-imperative.
72. Industry Statement on Resilience. http://www.nibs.org/resource/resmgr/Docs/Statement_2016-0425.pdf.
73. Microgrids are "electricity distribution systems containing loads and distributed energy resources, (such as distributed generators, storage devices, or controllable loads) that can be operated in a controlled, coordinated way either while connected to the main power network or while islanded." Lawrence Berkeley National Laboratory. "About Microgrids." https://building-microgrid.lbl.gov/about-microgrids.
74. "Passive Survivability." NJ Green Building Manual. 28 April. 2011. http://greenmanual.rutgers.edu/newcommercial/strategies/survivability.pdf.
75. Department of Energy, *A Common Definition for Zero Energy Buildings.* September 2015. http://energy.gov/sites/prod/files/2015/09/f26/bto_common_definition_zero_energy_buildings_093015.pdf.
76. See http://architecture2030.org/2030_challenges/2030-challenge/.
77. California Energy Commission. *2013 Integrated Energy Policy Report.* http://www.energy.ca.gov/2013publications/CEC-100-2013-001/CEC-100-2013-001-CMF.pdf.

78. World Green Building Council. "WorldGBC launches groundbreaking project to ensure all buildings are "net zero" by 2050." June 28, 2016. http://www.worldgbc.org/activities/news/global-news/worldgbc-launches-groundbreaking-project-ensure-all-buildings-are-net-zero-2050/.
79. See http://www.aia.org/practicing/2030Commitment/.
80. See https://www.smartgrid.gov/.
81. See http://energy.gov/oe/services/technology-development/smart-grid/demand-response.
82. See IEEE. *Towards A Definition of the Internet of Things (IoT)*. 2015. http://iot.ieee.org/images/files/pdf/IEEE_IoT_Towards_Definition_Internet_of_Things_Revision1_27MAY15.pdf.
83. While this offers significant benefit to building owners and operators who may not have expertise onsite to manage building energy use, it also poses a potential cybersecurity risk. See http://wbdg.org/resources/cybersecurity.php for information on the risks associated with industrial control systems.
84. See http://emergealliance.org/Home.aspx.
85. Savage, P., Nordhaus, R., Jamieson, S., "DC Microgrids: Benefits and Barriers," *From Silos to Systems: Issues in Clean Energy and Climate Change*, REIL, Editor, Yale Publications, 2010. http://environment.yale.edu/publication-series/5981.html.
86. Maupin, M.A., Kenny, J.F., Hutson, S.S., Lovelace, J.K., Barber, N.L., and Linsey, K.S., 2014, Estimated use of water in the United States in 2010: U.S. Geological Survey Circular 1405, 56 p., http://pubs.usgs.gov/circ/1405/.
87. California Department of Water Resources. *Managing an Uncertain Future: Climate Adaptation Strategies for California's Water.* October 2008. http://www.water.ca.gov/climatechange/docs/ClimateChangeWhitePaper.pdf.
88. Building Energy Data Book, Table 1.4.1. http://buildingsdatabook.eren.doe.gov/TableView.aspx?table=1.4.1.
89. International Energy Administration. 2015. "Energy Technology Perspective 2015—Mobalising Innovation to Accelerate Climate Action." http://www.iea.org/etp/etp2015. World Resources Institute. 2016. *Accelerating Building Efficiency: Eight Actions for Urban Leaders.* http://www.wri.org/publication/accelerating-building-efficiency-actions-city-leaders.
90. Institute for Market Transformation and Appraisal Institute. *Green Building and Property Value: A Primer for Building Owners and Developers.* 2013. https://www.appraisalinstitute.org/assets/1/7/Green-Building-and-Property-Value.pdf. Institute for Market Transformation and Appraisal

Institute. *Recognition of Energy Costs and Energy Performance in Real Property Valuation: Considerations and Resources for Appraisers.* 2012. http://www.imt.org/uploads/resources/files/Energy_Reporting_in_Appraisal.pdf.

91. See https://appraisalfoundation.sharefile.com/share?cmd=d&id=s6a7295fad9f43f59#/view/s6a7295fad9f43f59.
92. See http://www.imt.org/finance-and-real-estate/green-building-and-value.

Author Biography

Mr. Ryan Colker Presidential Advisor, National Institute of Building Sciences. NIBS is a non-profit, non-governmental organization bringing together representatives of government, the professions, industry, labor and consumer interests to focus on the identification and resolution of problems and potential problems that hamper the construction of safe, affordable structures for housing, commerce, and industry throughout the United States.

CHAPTER 10

Future Research Directions of Energy Efficiency

N. Edward Coulson, Clifford A. Lipscomb and Yongsheng Wang

10.1 Introduction

This book has addressed a wide range of issues related to energy efficiency and real estate, from building certification to the use of green building materials. While some of the research presented here has been conceptual and others more empirical, one commonality is in how meaningful metrics are derived or used to measure behavior changes. Green certification, for example, can be viewed as a signal of one's desire to

The original version of this chapter was revised: For detailed information please see Erratum. The erratum to this chapter is available at https://doi.org/10.1057/978-1-137-57446-6_11

N.E. Coulson
University of California, Irvine, CA, USA
e-mail: n.edward.coulson@gmail.com

C.A. Lipscomb (✉)
Greenfield Advisors, Cartersville, GA, USA

Y. Wang
Washington and Jefferson College, Washington, PA, USA

N.E. Coulson et al. (eds.), *Energy Efficiency and the Future of Real Estate*, DOI 10.1057/978-1-137-57446-6_10

obtain additional green rent premiums balanced against the additional costs of achieving the certification. What this emphasizes is the translation of the conceptual into the empirical (something that can be measured or quantified in some meaningful way). This is important, because the information value of variables that researchers use to quantify the effects of green building activities and green rent premiums needs to be greater than zero. Research conducted by Hubbard (2010) suggests that "[m]ost of the variables in a business case had an information value of zero .... Something like one-to-four variables were both uncertain enough and had enough bearing on the outcome of the decision to merit deliberate measurement efforts." This is one of the fundamental issues to energy-efficient real estate—how to measure different aspects of risk related to energy efficiency. Chegut et al. in Chap. 4 said that risk for the bottom line is always a factor in the adoption of innovative technologies.

In this concluding chapter, we discuss other related issues that we expect to see as the energy-efficiency research agenda matures and contemplates the contributions from other fields.

10.2 Triple Bottom Line, or Quadruple Bottom Line?

In Chap. 2, Devine discusses certification as a signal that is incorporated into property markets with an application to apartments. She also discusses how green certification enhances corporate image and helps to attract and retain talented employees. Finally, she discussed the operational benefits of green construction. The concurrent management of these factors is often referred to as viewing an organization's "triple bottom line" of social, economical, and environmental factors and the metrics used to determine the degree of sustainability being achieved by the organization. Much of the empirical research surveyed by Devine, and augmented in Chap. 7 by Yoshida et al., has commonly used certification labels as metrics for the impact of sustainable building characteristics on this triplex. However, as the results of Yoshida et al. show, certification is but a means to an end, and we can in fact discover changes in the actual environmental bottom line of green building certifications. Their additional finding that the economic bottom line is directly discernible from the environmental bottom line, additionally suggests that with time certification may cease to be necessary as a metric. This future outcome would have widespread implications on the green building industry, including the organizations that proffer various degrees of environmental certification.

Recent research, however, has added a fourth item to the items under consideration—and that fourth item goes by various names. Some authors use the term "purpose", others use "culture", and even others use "educational", "experiential", or "engagement/empowerment." Regardless of the term that is used, the end goal is to capture those things that are tangential to economical, environmental, and social factors. One possible research agenda for the future is the capture of even more data on this fourth line, given our newly-discovered ability to capture and analyze data from social media and Web searches. Research has shown that these online resources can be used to analyze real estate markets (Das et al. 2015; Beracha and Wintoki 2013). However, such resources are ideal for the investigation of otherwise nebulous concepts, such as sentiment, attention, experience, and so on that are important for the evaluation of efforts in green and sustainable building.

10.3 Risk

Another relatively under-researched dimension of green real estate is the risk that is attendant upon such efforts. Some of this risk had been due to asymmetric information, and Devine and other authors in this volume have noted the partial reduction in this risk via the signaling that arises through certification. However, as shown in Chap. 6 by Wang and Stanley for the case of office building in the U.S., while there are still rental premia after controlling for policy effects, they are subject to perhaps rapidly diminishing returns. Chapter 7 by Yoshida et al. has similar findings for the case of the Japanese office building market through direct observation on utility costs. It is difficult to monetize social payoffs and record it in the firm's financial statement. It could be an implied, but not quantifiable, factor reflected in goodwill. Thus, it is beneficial to have non-social benefits (e.g., utility cost reduction and other observable operational/productivity-related benefits) over a long-term business operation period of the building. A before-and-after cost comparison can be recorded on the financial statement. These observable benefits directly decrease the risk of building operation and may increase productivity and decrease production risk of businesses as indicated in Simons et al. (2014).

As Chegut and her coauthors have noted, regardless of the reduction in risk with respect to direct and possibly "soft" benefits of current green technology, the risks to green *innovation* remain. All innovations are subject to uncertain payoffs, of course, but when the upside of the uncertain outcomes has a social payoff, the case for public subsidization of research becomes more favorable. Far more research is needed on the interplay between social and economical motivations for green building research.

In order to price risk related to the investment and operation of green building, it is important to clearly define and identify these risks first. There is extra cost associated with the construction of green building, including the hiring of a certified architect for the design, using approved materials, and designating staff to manage the entire certification process. What are the risks/consequences if the building did not get the green certification or the level of management planned? How do we select the right features applicable in the local environment and not just for the points for certification process? A comprehensive risk plan could help to avoid adding features with extreme low utilization rates (e.g., an extra shower facility designed for employees who ride their bikes to the office) when most employees utilize other forms of transportation due to a long-distance commute.

10.4 Politics

And then, there is the topic of the interaction between the green technologies and the political world. On the one hand, the demonstrated revenue-enhancing effects of green buildings for the economic bottom line might remove any tradeoffs between it and politics. Regardless of the truth of that statement, the relationship between political beliefs and green adoption should be at the forefront of the collective research agenda. Some progress has been made in this area (e.g., Kahn 2007) and Harrison adds to this literature in Chap. 5. He says that political attitudes might play a role in the adoption of green technology, but it might also be the case that there is a complex interaction between the availability of the traditional fuels and preference formation, which suggests that changes in the political landscape pose even greater risks in both the innovation and the adoption of sustainable real estate technology. As noted in Chap. 8 by Zhou, a similar dynamic can potentially play out in China, where an even greater share of the innovation budget is guided by centralized forces.

10.5 Engineering

The growth of the green building market has greatly promoted the development of innovative building material and design. Builders not only pay attention to the environmental impact and cost during construction, but also those of building materials during the selection process, as discussed in Chap. 9 by Colker. The recent 2015 International Green Construction Code (IgCC) contains an optional outcome-based compliance path that gives flexibility to builders and designers to focus on the final outcome rather than a list of rigid mandatory features. The consideration of environmental impact from building material could curb the "disposable" culture which only focuses on construction convenience. The high degree of reuse and recycle not only creates environmental benefits, but also makes economic sense.

In addition to material considerations, green building has also pushed the innovation of structural and interior design considerations. It seems that an increasing number of high-rise buildings are considering the possibility of bringing in natural light and air. This kind of healthy work environment is preferred by employees as surveyed by Simons et al. (2014). A happy and healthy workforce is a workforce with higher productivity. With the frequent changes of businesses and requests from tenants, the flexibility of interior design could lower the total cost of temporary adjustment in the working place and fit the business needs better. This kind of flexibility in using the existing material also makes environmental sense.

However, there are significant efforts needed to train facility managers and tenants on operating the designed features correctly, especially for features that are foreign to the general public. Most of the calculations of the green benefit are under the assumption of normal or "correct" operation. Meanwhile, engineers continue to expend effort to speed up the development of more robust and user-friendly building designs.

References

Beracha, E., and M.B. Wintoki. 2013. Forecasting Residential Real Estate Price Changes From Online Search Activity. *Journal of Real Estate Research* 35 (3): 283–312.

Das, P., A. Ziobrowski, and N.E. Coulson. 2015. Online Information Search, Market Fundamentals and Apartment Real Estate. *The Journal of Real Estate Finance and Economics* 51 (4): 480–502.

Hubbard, Douglas W. 2010. *How to Measure Anything: Finding the Value of "Intangibles" in Business*, 2nd ed., 35–36. Hoboken: Wiley.

Kahn, Matthew E. 2007. Do Greens Drive Hummers or Hybrids? Environmental Ideology as a Determinant of Consumer Choice. *Journal of Environmental Economics and Management* 54 (2): 129–145.

Simons, Robert A., Spenser Robinson, and Eunkyu Lee. 2014. Green Office Buildings: A Qualitative Exploration of Green Office Building Attributes. *Journal of Sustainable Real Estate* 6 (1): 211–232.

Authors' Biography

Dr. N. Edward Coulson is Professor of Economics and Public Policy in the Merage School of Business at the University of California, Irvine. He is also co-editor of *Journal of Regional Science* and served as President of the American Real Estate and Urban Economics Association in 2016.

Dr. Clifford A. Lipscomb Vice Chair and Co-Managing Director, Greenfield Advisors. He is the Chairman of the American Real Estate Society's Practitioner Research Award committee, an Associate Editor of the Journal of Real Estate Literature, and a Visiting Scholar at the Federal Reserve Bank of Atlanta. His research interests include automated valuation models, survey research, and econometrics.

Dr. Yongsheng Wang Associate Professor of Economics, Director of Financial Economics, Washington and Jefferson College. He is also a visiting scholar at the graduate school of public and international affairs at the University of Pittsburgh. His research focuses on energy economics and real estate economics. His past research was funded by LUCE Foundation, Freeman Foundation, Heinz Endowments, and NIST (Department of Commerce).

Erratum to: Energy Efficiency and the Future of Real Estate

N. Edward Coulson

Erratum to:
N.E. Coulson et al. (eds.), *Energy Efficiency and the Future of Real Estate*, https://doi.org/10.1057/978-1-137-57446-6

The original version of the book was inadvertently published without incorporating the corrections in Chaps. 1, 2 and 4 and the page numbers for Chaps 5–10 have to be updated. The erratum book has been updated with the changes.

The updated online version for this book can be found at https://doi.org/10.1057/978-1-137-57446-6

N.E. Coulson et al. (eds.), *Energy Efficiency and the Future of Real Estate*,
DOI 10.1057/978-1-137-57446-6_11

Index

N.E. Coulson et al. (eds.), *Energy Efficiency and the Future of Real Estate*, DOI 10.1057/978-1-137-57446-6

The manufacturer's authorised representative in the EU is Springer Nature Customer Service Centre GmbH, Europaplatz 3, 69115 Heidelberg, Germany. If you have any concerns regarding our products, please contact ProductSafety@springernature.com

Printed and bound by CPI Group (UK) Ltd, Croydon, CR0 4YY
13/10/2026
02232377-0008